Mudra Vigyan

Mudra Vigyan

Philosophy and Practice of Yogic Gestures

From the teachings of

Swami Satyananda Saraswati
Swami Niranjanananda Saraswati

Yoga Publications Trust, Munger, Bihar, India

Printed by Yoga Publications Trust
  First edition 2013

ISBN: 978-93-81620-89-2

Assistant Editor: Swami Mudraroopa Saraswati

Publisher and distributor: Yoga Publications Trust, Ganga Darshan, Munger, Bihar, India.

Website: www.biharyoga.net
        www.rikhiapeeth.net

Printed at Thomson Press (India) Limited, New Delhi, 110001

Dedication

*In humility we offer this dedication to
Swami Sivananda Saraswati, who initiated
Swami Satyananda Saraswati into the secrets of yoga.*

Contents

Preface

Across the spectrum of creation, sentient beings use their bodies to express and communicate their state of consciousness. A little worm will curl up if it senses danger, a monkey will bare its teeth when it is feeling aggressive, and a dog will wag its tail to convey affection. The higher a creature is on the scale of evolution the more refined will be its bodily signals. Human beings, being on the top of the rung, use the most remarkable gestures to project their thoughts, feelings and states of mind. If they are trying to recall a fact, they may join the tips of the index finger and the thumb at the eyebrow centre; if they are supplicating, they may bring the palms together at the chest; if they are trying to emphasize a point, they may raise a fist into the air, and so on. Then, even among human beings, those with the finest perception will use the most elegant gestures: poets, philosophers and scientists are often seen using their hands in distinctive ways.

Eons ago, this subtle aspect of human nature was explored by the yogis of India. They reached deep into the art of gesticulation, and developed it to the level where they could alter the states of body and mind by simply modifying the way they held their hands. Conversely, when they entered altered states of consciousness, their body would respond with corresponding gestures. These gestures were called *mudra*. As the insights and experiences developed, it was found that not just the hands, but the eyes, the tongue, the throat, the abdomen, the perineal region, in fact, the whole body could be held in a mudra to create a desired effect. Over the centuries, this knowledge of mudras was consolidated and it became a science unto itself. Mudras came to be used in yogic practices as well as in rituals of worship and dance.

Mudra Vigyan: Philosophy and Practice of Yogic Gestures brings the wisdom of these ancient practices into a contemporary context. Generally, mudras are introduced as an adjunct to asana, pranayama, bandha and meditation, and the efficacy of mudras as a complete system of sadhana is not delved into. This book offers the yoga practitioner an opportunity to understand and practise mudras as an independent yogic science.

The magic of mudras lies in the simplicity of the practices. Although there are mudras that incorporate advanced asanas, most can be performed irrespective of the condition of the body. Yet, they can have such profound impact on the psyche and energy circuits that utmost discernment is cautioned by all yogic texts. It must also be remembered that the subtlety of these effects can be appreciated only through maturity of perception. To be able to realize a mudra, one must develop pranic sensitivity, purification of the body and mind, and *drashta bhava*, the witnessing attitude. Therefore, it is advised that mudra sadhana is taken up only after practising asana, shatkarma and pranayama for an appropriate length of time.

Mudras are powerful transformative practices that can alter the mood, attitude and perception, and deepen the awareness and concentration. They also have a strong therapeutic effect, and particular mudras are prescribed to alleviate debilitating conditions of the body. At another level, mudras awaken and sublimate energy, and act as a bridge to higher states of mind and consciousness.

Mudras are used throughout the various stages of meditation to guide the awareness inwards. They are used to cultivate the first stage of meditation, where connection to the outer world is withdrawn and awareness of the inner world develops. The second stage of meditation, one-pointed awareness, is achieved through the regular practice of mudra. Over time, the mind is trained to remain one-pointed on the focal point of the mudra. When one-pointedness is maintained, through sustained effort, the experience transforms into meditation. This inner process does not occur unless there is constant and steady practice, so that one becomes established in the state of mudra. The purpose of this book is to guide one gradually into these deeper states.

Mudra Vigyan is divided into two parts. The first part discusses the philosophy and theory of mudra, and elucidates the origins of mudra, the context in which they are practised, the effects of mudra on the pranas, the brain, the endocrine system, the state of mind and the quality of meditation. In addition, the correlation between mudra and the oriental system of acupuncture is presented.

The second part of the book outlines a range of mudra techniques, including classical yoga mudras, therapeutic mudras, sadhana mudras and worship mudras. The approach to be adopted for each category of mudras is outlined at the beginning of a chapter, as well as within the description of individual techniques. The classical yoga mudras are delineated in step-by-step practice modules and their respective effects and benefits, precautions and contra-indications are provided. The effects of individual mudras from the point of view of acupuncture theory indicate their therapeutic aspect.

The book is an outcome of the inspiration of the gurus of the Bihar Yoga tradition: Swami Satyananda Saraswati and Swami Niranjanananda Saraswati. Realized masters and siddha yogis, they have revealed the various dimensions of mudras over the years during satsangs and discourses. These talks form the basis of this work. The structure and content was created under the guidance of Swami Niranjanananda, who also clarified various esoteric aspects of the subject.

The wealth of wisdom contained herein is likely to benefit every practitioner and aspirant, and deepen the awareness of their own selves. May the grace of the gurus continue to illumine all paths!

Mudra Vigyan: The Science of Mudra

1

Origins of Mudra

There is a state that manifests beyond the mind when the thoughts have been transcended. Thoughts are the form and substance of the mind. When there are no thoughts, there is no mind. In this state, a higher power manifests known as intuition, or *prajna*, which is beyond the realm of *antahkarana*, the instrument of the mind. Mind and intellect operate through words, logic and language, which are finite and limited, however the state of intuition transcends all these. Therefore, higher knowledge is revealed through intuition. When the sadhaka perceives intuitively, they are able to know something that is beyond the mind and the intellect, as prajna is the source of unlimited knowledge. At times, such knowledge may seem irrational to a mind that has not transcended the finite boundaries of analytical thought. However, the higher mind or supermind perceives the truth behind intuitive knowledge. When intuition begins to manifest in the sadhaka, mudras are revealed to further enhance and elevate the awareness.

Mudras, just like mantra and yantra, were realized by ancient yogis in states of deep meditation. While the yogis were in union with the higher mind, their bodies adopted particular poses that correlated to their states of consciousness. In everyday life, when pain is felt, the response to the pain signal that is generated by the lower mind leads to an involuntary, spontaneous movement

3

of the body away from the source of pain. It is an instinctive, reactive response. Similarly, when a connection or signal from the higher mind is experienced during deep meditation, a spontaneous, involuntary movement of the body also occurs, and this is mudra. It is an intuitive response, an expression of the inner experience being felt, a gesture. As with the discovery of mantras, the ancient yogis gave the knowledge of these realized postures to aspirants so they could access the higher realms of their own consciousness.

Mudras are often considered a part of other yogic practices. However, the science of mudra is vast and complete within itself, every mudra being an exact and significant yogic tool. There are countless mudras that bring about changes and improvements in the body, influence the glands and hormonal secretions, harmonize pranic imbalances and calm the agitations of the mind. In doing so, many physical and mental diseases are alleviated.

On a more subtle level, mudras can develop specific internal and external dispositions, thereby assisting the sadhaka to experience altered states of consciousness. Through the regular practice of mudra, the subtle powers that lie dormant within can be cultivated. The highest aim of mudra practice is to awaken the cosmic energy and help to unite the individual consciousness with the cosmic consciousness. Devotion, energy, light and knowledge can all be achieved by deepening the experience of mudras.

History

According to tantric texts, it is traditionally believed that Lord Shiva was the first exponent of mudras and he revealed this knowledge to his consort, Parvati. Addressing the goddess Parvati, Lord Shiva says (*Gheranda Samhita*, 3:4–5):

मुद्राणां पटलं देवि कथितं तव संनिधौ ।
येन विज्ञातमात्रेण सर्व सिद्धि: प्रजायते ॥

4

गोपनीयं प्रयत्नेन न देयं यस्यकस्यचित् ।
प्रीतिदं योगिनां चैव दुर्लभंमरुतामपि ॥

O Goddess! I have imparted the knowledge of mudras.
Mere knowledge of these provides *siddhis*, mastery. Their
knowledge provides bliss to yogis. Their knowledge is
not easily accessible even to gods. Keep this knowledge
always secret.

The declaration that this knowledge is not easily accessible
even to the gods reflects the significance of mudras. These
practices should be done with reverence. They should not
be undertaken aimlessly. Only competent and deserving
practitioners and disciples should try to master them.

Across the ages, different religions throughout the world
have used mudras during rituals of prayer and worship.
Mudras have been described in tantra shastra, upasana shastra
and nritya shastra. They have been prescribed for worship,
for example, while offering arati, abhisheka, prasad, flowers,
during dhyana and prayer and while doing nyasa. From
ancient times the science of mudra was considered to be a very
enigmatic subject, closely guarded by the ancient rishis, saints
and mystics. Due to such secrecy, many aspects of this ancient
science have been lost over time. However, it continues to be
practised by yogis and priests in India, as well as the lamas of
Tibet, and Buddhists monks in Japan during their meditations
and prayers. In fact, the use of mudras during worship can be
seen across Indonesia, Bhutan, Malaysia, Sri Lanka and Burma.

Thousands of paintings and statues all over the world
reflect the influence of the science of mudra. Many ancient
yogis and sages are depicted displaying characteristic
mudras. In the portraits, images and idols of saints,
sages, gods and goddesses, mudras such as jnana mudra,
chinmudra, shankha mudra and abhaya mudra are often
seen. *Abhaya mudra*, the gesture of bestowing fearlessness,
is seen in statues of Buddha. Our gurus, Swami Sivananda
and Swami Satyananda, can also be often seen in pictures

blessing the seeker in abhaya mudra. In such instances, the different attitudinal hand mudras denote a projection of mind and prana for the wellbeing of others.

Another source of development of mudras is ayurveda. The rishis of ancient India studied the science of the body in depth and their studies evolved into the Indian ayurvedic system of medicine. Ayurveda is based mainly on the understanding of five primary elements: ether (space), air, fire, water and earth. According to yogic philosophy and physiology, the microcosm of the human body is composed from the same five elements that constitute the universe, the macrocosm. These five elements come into existence through the interaction of *purusha*, consciousness, and *prakriti*, energy. The balance of the elements within the body is of crucial importance for the maintenance and health of both body and mind, which is seen as a prerequisite for spiritual development. Conversely, physical and mental ailments are the result of some sort of disturbance in the equilibrium of the five elemental forces in the body. In order to keep the elements in proper proportion, to restore proper balance and to bring them back to normalcy, various methods are used, including mudras.

Mudras have been described in various texts from antiquity to the present day, including the Vedas and the Upanishads, ayurvedic texts such as *Charaka Samhita* and *Sushruta Samhita*, tantric texts such as *Kularnava Tantra*, *Pancharatra Tantra*, hatha yoga texts such as *Hatha Yoga Pradipika*, *Gheranda Samhita*, and so on. However, such references were never detailed or clearly delineated. On the contrary, they were presented in a coded and incomplete manner, as these techniques were not intended to be learnt from a book. Practical instruction from a guru was always considered to be necessary before attempting them.

Etymological meaning

The word *mudra* is generally translated as 'gesture' or 'attitude' and can be described as psychic, emotional, devotional and aesthetic gesture or attitude. Mudras are psychophysiological expressions that connect the psyche and body. They are the keys which create that link. Mudras are not just one type of technique or practice, like asana, pranayama, bandha or kriya. They are a combination of subtle, physical movements or gestures that alter the mood, attitude and perception, and deepen the awareness and concentration.

In his dialogue with Parvati, Lord Shiva says that mudra is that which pleases the gods and melts the mind. According to *Kularnava Tantra*, the word 'mudra' comes from the root *mudh*, which means 'delight' or 'pleasure', and *dravay*, the causal form of *dru*, which means 'to draw forth'. Thus, in this context mudra is 'that which brings happiness'. In its ultimate form, mudra is a way of being and living that reflects the divine and the divine qualities. To achieve this state, there are practices in which a specific movement or gesture is performed in order to remove all the spikes, agitations and dissipations of prana and corresponding states of mind. In doing so, mudras bring a sense of ease and contentment to the body-mind unit, which is essential for spiritual evolution.

Significance

Mudras concern the mind. They represent a seal; sealing the mind with the soul or *atman*. They do not allow the mind to wander outside towards objects. They direct the externalizing mind towards atman in the chambers of the heart and fix it there. It is said that the practice of mudras and bandhas will bestow all that one wants.

In yoga and tantra, mudras are used to affect the energy flow within the body. Although mudras appear to be merely physical gestures or positions made with the hands, eyes or the whole body, yogis have experienced mudras as attitudes of energy flow intended to link the individual pranic force with the universal or cosmic force. Therefore, in spiritual terms, mudras are a means to unite oneself with the inner

7

being. They are attitudes of psychic power that attract the divine forces. They are very potent and can eliminate the negative influences the sadhaka may encounter during sadhana.

Mudra can also be interpreted to mean insignia or symbol. Just as crying is the symbol of unhappiness, and dancing, singing and laughing are symbols of happiness, the inner consciousness also has symbols, which are mudras. The purpose of mudras is to express the inner experience. By practising mudras, the individual dwells on and tries to experience the indescribable meaning contained within each mudra. In this way, it is possible to evoke the inner forces which otherwise lie hidden and dormant. This is why mudras are so powerful.

Yoga and tantra

Even though hatha yoga uses only a limited number of mudras, enumerated in texts like *Gheranda Samhita* or *Hatha Yoga Pradipika*, there are actually innumerable mudras. Almost every tantric text has its own list of mudras. Yoga is a part of tantra, and thus the yogic mudras are a part of tantra. However, tantra employs many more mudras. For example, the nyasa system of tantra from which yoga nidra is derived involves profuse use of mudras along with mantra. In this context, mudras and mantra are used to focus the awareness on a particular area of the body and to invoke the presence of *shakti*, energy, and *devata*, divinity, into that particular part. Such invocation utilizes various deities, each possessing different divine qualities, with specific mudras for each one. The esoteric tantric sadhanas use still other sets of mudras to induce a different level of awareness.

The *Hatha Yoga Pradipika* and other yogic texts consider mudra to be a *yoganga*, an independent branch of yoga, requiring a deeply subtle awareness. Mudras are introduced after some proficiency has been attained in asana, pranayama and bandha, and gross blockages have been removed. A mudra may involve the whole body in a combination of

8

asana, pranayama, bandha and visualization techniques, or may constitute a simple hand position. Some mudras are done separately after asana and pranayama, and others are performed with asana and pranayama to help awaken the chakras and arouse kundalini shakti. When practised in conjunction with asanas and pranayamas, the specific body position adopted in the mudra channels the energy produced by asana and pranayama into various *chakras*, or energy centres, arousing particular states of mind.

There are many mudras and they have come to mean different things according to their usage and each individual's level of understanding. Various traditions, schools of philosophy and sadhana use different groups of mudras to attain whatever goal they have set for themselves. There are mudras for meditation, mudras for worship, mudras of invocation, the classical yoga mudras, and so on. Classical yoga mudras are chiefly categorized into five groups: *hasta mudra*, or hand mudra; *shirsha mudra*, or head mudra; *kaya mudra*, postural mudra; *bandha mudra*, lock mudra; and *adhara mudra*, perineal mudra. Some of these mudras have become part of the current yogic parlance; however, there is a whole world of these subtle techniques that remains unexplored.

Like all yogic and tantric practices, the mudras have to be practised to be experienced. The subtle science of mudras cannot be understood intellectually. Here especially, an ounce of practice is better than tons of theory.

Expressions of emotion

An attitude is something that reflects the mind in the body, and body in mind. With observation, a lot can be learnt about someone's mental state by the way they walk, sit, act, and so on. A person who is frightened will walk quite differently to someone who is angry. Body language reflects the constant communication that occurs between the *annamaya kosha*, the physical body and the other koshas, via the network of nadis in the pranayama kosha. Even simple hand or facial gestures will have a corresponding gesture in the subtle body. Tantra has developed this knowledge into a system of mudras where specific gestures of the body relate to specific attitudes of mind. As mentioned, mudras may be a whole body position or a simple finger position, nevertheless, the effect is transmitted through all levels of the five koshas, and the appropriate signal is transferred from gross to subtle.

This flow of information through the *pranamaya kosha*, the energy body, is a two-way process. People experiencing altered states of consciousness have been known to perform mudras spontaneously, representing a transmission from subtle to gross. Conversely, the signal can be reversed and a message sent to the mind by adopting a physical attitude or mudra. The effects are extremely subtle. It requires great sensitivity to perceive a change of consciousness simply by joining the thumb and index finger together. However, with practice the mind becomes conditioned to this signal, and when this hand position is adopted, the signal for meditation is transmitted.

In India, mudras occupy an important place in the arts as well as the spiritual sciences. For instance, in *bharat natyam*, a classical Indian dance form, a large number of mudras are used to express different sentiments, *bhavas*, attitudes, moods, and they represent various responses to situations that are created in dance. Anger is depicted through the eyes, the position of the hands and the physical posture. This is just one example.

The reverse is also true; mudras can arouse specific emotions. It has been observed that if a particular mudra is practised for long periods of time, a feeling created by that mudra is experienced. The same kind of sensation depicted by the mudra is created in the body and mind. This also happens in daily life. For instance, an angry person raises the eyebrows, tenses the hands and clenches the fists. Even if one is not angry, this feeling will gradually manifest if these physical actions are adopted.

10

Whichever physical state is adopted creates a particular kind of sensation in the nervous system and brings about a change in the activity of the brainwaves. This change influences the state of consciousness, and for some time that particular feeling is experienced inside on the mental plane. When the pranic level is increased and the conscious mind withdraws, mudras occur spontaneously. The hands, feet, eyes, arms and legs move slowly into definite positions like those of Indian dancers. At such times, the mudras invoke specific qualities of Shakti or Devi and the practitioner becomes overwhelmed by that power.

2

Mudra and Prana

The mudras described in the yogic scriptures are expressions of particular states of consciousness and energy. Yogis have always maintained that the different experiences of human consciousness can be easily monitored and controlled by altering and channelling energy, or *prana*. Prana influences the different realms of experience: physical, mental, emotional, psychic and spiritual. At the same time, prana itself is influenced by these different layers of body, mind and spirit. The inner environment of thoughts, emotions and attitudes, as well as the external environment, influence both the movement of prana and the biorhythms of the body.

Based on this interconnectedness, the practices of yoga, including mudra, consciously awaken, balance and redirect prana to influence the physical and subtle aspects of the body and mind.

Regulation and redirection of prana

The word *mudra* has been defined as a 'seal', 'shortcut' or 'circuit bypass' and one of its main function is to link various circuits within the network of *nadis*, or energy channels. Many mudras are performed in the extremities of the body, such as the head, hands and perineum. According to both yogic philosophy and traditional Chinese medicine, the body is said to constantly discharge energy through the extremities. In the 1970s, this belief was observed and verified by Kirlian photography research. Kirlian photography is a technique that shows the aura or energy field around the body. Research in this technique has shown that there is a greater flow of pranic energy at the extreme ends of the body such as the hands, feet and head.

The practice of mudra stops and rechannels the flow of pranic energy. Thus, prana flowing out of the body is redirected back into the body. This not only contains the prana shakti, it also reverses its flow. By changing the physical posture, the flow of prana can be diverted to another area of the body. A mudra may be performed in a variety of ways, such as joining the fingers together in a hand mudra, or pressing or closing a certain part of the body.

With hand mudras, there is a relationship between the hands, the prana and the mind. In *jnana mudra*, the mudra evoking wisdom, for example, the hands are placed palm downward on the knees with the index finger curled into the root of the thumb. This causes the energy that is continuously flowing out of the index finger to re-enter the body. *Chinmudra*, the mudra focusing on consciousness, is similar to jnana mudra, however, the palms face upwards. When these mudras are practised, the prana is pulled back into the body, and the mind becomes still and one-pointed, especially when sitting in padmasana or siddhasana.

The manipulation of prana through mudras takes place in much the same way that energy in the form of light or sound waves is diverted by a mirror or a cliff face. The effect of mudra can also be likened to shining a torch at night on a blank wall. The light will hit the wall and then spread out in all directions, as there is a block. The energetic body works in a similar way; the nadis and chakras are like torches that are constantly shining and radiating their energy into infinity. How far that energy radiates is not known. Maybe it gets lost or becomes invisible at some point. By closing gates within the body through the practice of mudra, the energy is redirected within.

13

For example, by closing the openings in the head, especially the eyes, with the fingers in shanmukhi mudra, the significant amount of prana being radiated through the eyes is reflected back. In the same way, the sexual energy emitted through vajra nadi is redirected to the brain through the practice of vajroli mudra. Another example is the advanced asanas in hatha yoga, in which the body automatically triggers a particular bandha or mudra, such as brahmacharyasana, where there is an automatic contraction of the perineal muscle, causing an automatic moola bandha and redirecting the flow into the body.

Mudras also help regulate the flow of prana through the body, thereby eliminating various psychophysiological disorders. Mudras activate glandular functioning and bring about control of the involuntary organs connected with the nerves of the body. Thus, particular mudras have the potential to rectify defects in the organs of the body. For example, in the practice of hridaya mudra, the fingers actually act as pressure points, stimulating the prana shakti in the heart and bringing about a calming effect. Many people have practised hridaya mudra for heart problems and felt that this practice has helped them. The practice of these mudras, apart from realigning the flow of prana in a particular organ, also activates the prana shakti.

The mudras that are classified as yoga mudras induce states of concentration and awareness as well as reverse the direction of prana shakti. With the regulation of prana shakti, the mental activity is reduced so that greater peace and concentration, and a broader awareness is experienced.

Hand mudras: aids to meditation

The position of the hands while practising a meditational technique is important. At first, it may seem to be an insignificant aspect of the practice, yet it remains true that if the hands are positioned wrongly it is difficult to practise meditation successfully.

The meditation mudras have a common aspect, which is to channel the flow of prana being emitted by the fingers and redirect it within the body. Hand mudras aim at providing greater concentration, awareness and internal physical relaxation. With the channelling of prana and the gentle opening up of the different muscles and cavities, the body is made more stable.

Mudras that join the thumb and index finger engage the motor cortex at a very subtle level. They generate a loop of energy that moves from the brain down to the hand and then back again. Conscious awareness of this process rapidly leads to internalization. Techniques included in this category are: jnana mudra, chinmudra, yoni mudra, bhairava mudra and hridaya mudra.

Generally, hand mudras should be practised in conjunction with meditative asanas. Even in meditative asanas such as vajrasana and veerasana, mudras can be practised. In the case of vajrasana the hands will be placed on the upper part of the thighs instead of the knees, and in veerasana the hands have to be placed either one on top of the other or on the feet.

Balancing the koshas

According to yoga, a human being is capable of experiencing five dimensions of existence, which are called the *pancha kosha* or five sheaths. These are the five spheres in which a human being lives at any given moment and range from gross to subtle. The pancha kosha are: i) annamaya kosha ii) pranamaya kosha iii) manomaya kosha iv) vijnanamaya kosha, and v) anandamaya kosha.

The first sheath or level of experience is the physical body, or *annamaya kosha*. The second sheath is *pranamaya kosha*, the energy field of an individual, described as the pranic, astral and etheric counterpart of the physical body. The third sheath is *manomaya kosha*, the mental dimension. This level of experience is the conscious mind, which holds the two grosser koshas, annamaya and pranamaya,

15

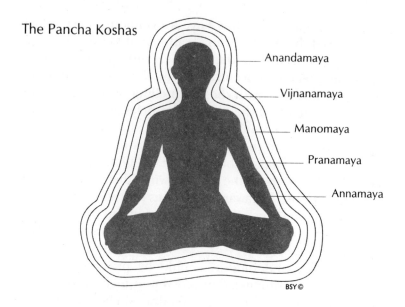

The Pancha Koshas

Anandamaya

Vijnanamaya

Manomaya

Pranamaya

Annamaya

BSY©

together as an integrated whole. It is the bridge between the outer and inner worlds, conveying the experiences and sensations of the external world to the intuitive body, and the influences of the causal and intuitive bodies to the gross body. The fourth sheath is *vijnanamaya kosha*, the psychic level of experience, which relates to the subconscious and unconscious mind. This sphere pervades manomaya kosha, yet is more subtle than it. Vijnanamaya kosha is the link between the individual and universal mind. Inner knowledge comes to the conscious mind from this level. The fifth sheath is *anandamaya kosha*, the level of bliss and beatitude. This is the causal or transcendental body, the abode of the most subtle prana.

The five sheaths are interlinked and what happens in one affects the others. When annamaya and pranamaya are cleansed, mental problems and barriers are also reduced, and the mind, body and energy work in unison. Consequently, the veiling of vijnanamaya kosha is thinned. When the psychic sheath is accessed, concentration becomes refined and the deeper mind comes to the surface, psychic experiences and extrasensory perceptions manifest and deep-rooted samskaras are purged. As vijnanamaya kosha is cleared, creativity becomes inspired and clarity comes intuitively and effortlessly. At this stage, the mind is actually and truly being emptied and prepared to experience anandamaya kosha.

All the sheaths are pervaded by prana, which nourishes and sustains them and maintains their appropriate relationship. The movement from one kosha to another is also achieved with the help of prana. Thus, with the activation of prana, one gains access to the physical, mental, psychic and spiritual dimensions. In the body, there is a continual discharge of pranic force due to tension in pranamaya kosha. This is caused by its function of coordinating the activities of annamaya, manomaya and vijnanamaya kosha. This continual discharge results in lethargy, fatigue, tiredness and other symptoms of energy depletion experienced either mentally or physically. For example, with excessive physical work, often the physical body is extremely tired, yet the mind is fully active and charged, or vice versa. This type of imbalance and pranic depletion takes place in every sphere of life.

Possibly, this is the reason why yogis considered the use of mudras to be a valid and important tool; there is a constant need to rebalance the flow of prana in the annamaya, manomaya and pranamaya systems. As mudras facilitate the link or connection between the physical body and the internal body, the manomaya kosha and vijnanamaya koshas are influenced. Thus, mudras can be described as psychophysiological locks or psychoenergic locks that redirect the flow of energy. The psyche is being reached by a physiological posture that creates an attitude or feeling; each mudra is an appropriate signal transferring energy and feelings from a gross to subtle level.

Mudras become a process through which one begins to experiment withand explore the relationships between the different koshas, especially annamaya, pranayama and manomaya kosha. They enable the practitioner to develop awareness of the flow of prana in the body and to establish pranic balance within the koshas. When harmony and integration of the various faculties of these koshas has taken place, then the psychic or spiritual aspects become known. Ultimately, mudras enable the redirection of subtle energy to the upper chakras, inducing higher states of consciousness.

Awakening of kundalini

The effect of mudras on the pranic circulatory system can be understood from another perspective. Ida, pingala and sushumna are the main nadis, or pranic streams, that flow along the spinal passage. Ida and pingala flow in a criss-cross

Location of the Chakras

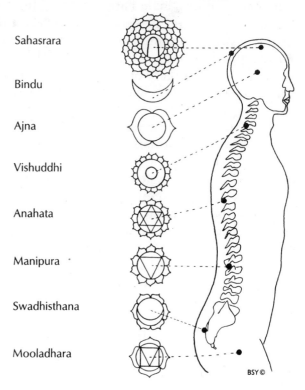

Sahasrara

Bindu

Ajna

Vishuddhi

Anahata

Manipura

Swadhisthana

Mooladhara

BSY©

18

pattern, going from side-to-side, while sushumna flows along the centre. There are six junction points where there is union of the three nadis, creating a *chakra*, or vortex of energy. These six points are the six chakras, from mooladhara up to ajna. From ajna, the three nadis become one, and they go up to sahasrara as one flow. Mudras activate these three nadis and ensure that the flow of prana takes place properly and without waste.

To guide the prana towards a specific chakra, a particular mudra is adopted. Different mudras stimulate different nadis and different chakras. For instance, in the practice of *shambhavi mudra*, gesture of eyebrow centre gazing, the movement of the eyeballs pulls and pushes, stretches and contracts the eye muscles and nerves. After some time a pull is felt, and that stimulates a particular visual nadi that supplies prana to the eyes. Also, by focusing the eyes together at *bhrumadhya*, the eyebrow centre, sushumna nadi is stimulated, and with concentration at bhrumadhya, ajna chakra is activated.

Similarly, *nasikagra mudra*, the gesture of nose tip gazing, focuses energy at the nose tip. This stimulates certain nerves that govern the sense of smell, thereby awakening mooladhara chakra, which is associated with this faculty. Practices such as vajroli mudra and ashwini mudra block the downward flow of energy. Their influence is felt on the brain as well and they help to awaken a sensation in chitta that encourages introversion. In vipareeta karani mudra, the half shoulder-stand posture is adopted, also known as *vipareeta karani asana*, which reverses the downward flow of energy. Thus, the energy that is normally lost in external affairs is drawn back up to the higher centres in the brain.

According to Swami Sivananda, mudras are certain postures of the body by which kundalini is successfully awakened. This is due to their ability to redirect prana, and thus mudras are incorporated extensively in kriya and kundalini yoga practices. It is stated in *Hatha Yoga Pradipika* (3:5):

तस्मात्सर्वप्रयत्नेन प्रबोधयितुमीश्वरीम् ।
ब्राह्मद्वारमुखे सुप्तां मुद्राभ्यासं समाचरेत् ॥

Therefore, the goddess sleeping at the entrance of Brahma's door should be constantly aroused with all effort by performing mudra thoroughly.

Kundalini is often depicted as a goddess. At the level of mooladhara it manifests as Kali and Dakini. In the tantra shastras, it says that the shakti in mooladhara is in the form of a sixteen-year-old girl in the first bloom of youth.

The various aspects of Shakti indicate different stages in the evolution of energy and consciousness, and as an aspirant awakens each chakra, he or she will manifest some of the attributes of the related devi. *Kankalamalini Tantra* describes the Shakti in front of Brahma's door as resplendent like millions of moons rising simultaneously, with four arms, three eyes and seated on a lion. As kundalini ascends through each chakra, her form changes until she unites with her lord, Shiva, in sahasrara. Then there is no individuality; energy and consciousness are one and they manifest in the form of pure light.

3

Mudra and Acupuncture

An understanding of the similarities between yoga and oriental acupuncture cultivates a broader appreciation of the science of mudra. Like yoga, the treasure of traditional Chinese medicine has been preserved and is widely used in both the East and the West in forms such as shiatsu and acupuncture.

Traditional Chinese medicine is based on the knowledge of *Qi*, pronounced 'chi', which refers to energy or life force. Qi is channelled around the body via meridians or energy channels. This view complements yogic thought, which uses the word *prana* for vital energy, and *nadi* for meridian. While not identical, the concepts of nadis in yoga and meridians in acupuncture are very similar. Both sciences acknowledge the existence of a complex system of subtle energy channels that run throughout the body. In both systems the energy channels are open, as opposed to a closed circuit; energy can enter or leave through the extremities: the hands, fingers, feet, toes and head. Based on this knowledge, mudras are performed to redirect energy or to form closed energy circuits that retain energy within the body. How this translates to the language of meridians is discussed individually for the major mudras in the practice section.

The flow of Qi

In traditional Chinese medicine, there is a fundamental understanding of the interconnectedness of the physical, pranic, emotional and mental bodies, as well as the subtle bodies. A smooth and abundant flow of energy is said to result in health and wellbeing on all levels, whereas a blockage or deficiency of energy is said to result in disease. Chinese medicine recognizes five substances that form the basis for the development and maintenance of the body: Qi, blood, essence, spirit and fluids. They have a dynamic relationship upon which the harmonious functioning of the whole system depends. They interact with each other, yet at the foundation of that interaction is Qi. Qi is considered the basis of all phenomena in the universe. Hence, in one way or another, everything that is done in acupuncture has to do with Qi, and treatment is concerned with exerting a beneficial influence on the flow of Qi.

The flow of Qi is continuous, although it is subject to change under the influence of different forces in nature. A properly balanced state of Qi means that changes are happening at the proper time and at a proper rate so that the whole system remains in harmony with both itself and the environment. If the changes are too slow, this will create deficiency in the systems; if they are happening too fast, an excess state will ensue. In both cases, there is an imbalance in the transformation and flow of Qi, which is the first step away from health.

In the theory of acupuncture it is believed that emotions have a strong influence on Qi. the effect of emotions on the harmony of the human body and mind is so powerful that they are regarded as one of the major pathological factors that bring about disease. The seven emotions have been grouped as: joy, anger, worry, sadness, pensiveness, fear, and shock such as terror. These are normal emotions that are experienced almost daily. They give rise to a disturbance of Qi and consequent disorders only if they are excessive, and if that kind of emotional excessiveness lasts for a prolonged period of time.

Yin and yang

All sentient and insentient beings, according to Chinese Taoist thought, live and die activated by the two principles of yin and yang. This concept is very simple and yet so profound that everything in creation can be reduced to it. In the symbol, yang is white and yin is black. In its purest form, yang is totally immaterial and corresponds to energy. In its densest form, yin is totally material and corresponds to matter. There is

The traditional Chinese symbol of the concept of energy, shows yin and yang in perpetual balance.

nothing that is totally yin or totally yang; everything has both principles inherent within it. However, the one that is most predominant determines whether it is classified as yin or yang. Each and every part of human anatomy and physiology can be classified as either predominantly yin or yang.

Yin and yang are interdependent; one cannot exist without the other. The small black circle within yang symbolizes that in the midst of yang, when it is at its peak, the seed of yin is born and vice versa. The demarcation line between yin and yang is not straight and fixed. This denotes that there is no absolute border between these two qualities; they are constantly intermingled, interwoven, in constant complementary motion. Thus, when one of them is out of balance, it automatically affects the other in an attempt to create a new balance.

Although far from identical, the concept of yin and yang has certain points in common with the yogic concept of ida and pingala, as can be seen in the following list of qualities:

Yin	Yang
Earth	Heaven
Female	Male
Cold	Heat
Wet	Dry

23

Dark	Light
Night	Day
Contraction	Expansion
Internal	External
Front	Back
Downward	Upward
Negative	Positive
Inhibition	Stimulation
Slow	Rapid

Meridians corresponding to organs

The names of the organs in traditional Chinese medicine correspond to the names of the organs in western medicine; however, the organs in Chinese medicine are described and defined in a much broader way. Furthermore, their functions are much more diverse and complex than those described by the western model. Thus, organs should be understood as concepts, or complexes of closely related functions. Twelve major organs have been described, paired in a yin-yang relationship.

In the classical texts of Chinese medicine that elaborate on the science of acupuncture, meridians are described as the flows of Qi. This implies that meridians have definite functions, yet no substantial structure. Their existence has been observed clinically, and even proved indirectly in the laboratory, but they cannot be found in the physical body. Internally, every meridian has a connection with its corresponding organ, where Qi transfers itself into a solid or hollow organ. There are different types of meridians. Of these, the most important ones, and most commonly used in acupuncture, are the twelve regular meridians corresponding to the twelve organs:

Yang meridian	Yin meridian
Gallbladder (GB)	Liver (Liv)
Small Intestine (SI)	Heart (H)
Stomach (St)	Spleen (Sp)

Lung (Lu)   Large Intestine (LI)
Urinary Bladder (UB)   Kidney (K)
Triple Heater (TH)   Pericardium (Pc)

There are eight extraordinary meridians, two of which
are more important than the others: the governing vessel
(GV) and the conception vessel (CV). Therefore, fourteen
main meridians are mainly used in practical clinical work.
Only these fourteen meridians have their own acupuncture
points.

Acupuncture points

There are areas in which Qi comes close to the surface of the
body and can be easily directed. Actually, an acupuncture
point is not a 'point' as such; rather, it should be understood
as a space in the body that is relatively close to the skin.
Today, about five hundred points are used in clinical
practice. Each acupuncture point has a Chinese name that is
often very descriptive and which depicts the main property
of the point. However, in order to systematize the points for
easier usage, the points have been numbered and the name
of the meridian abbreviated. For example, the point *Shang-
Yang*, 'Merchant of Yang' refers to the first point on the large
intestine meridian and is abbreviated as 'LI 1'. Some of these
meridians have their terminal or end points in the fingertips.
These are known as *sei* or well points.

Acupuncture points can be accessed in various ways.
The acupuncture-related techniques that complement
yoga and mudra are: i) acupressure, where various types of
pressure exerted by the hands stimulate acupuncture points,
ii) acumassage, where other parts of the body are used to
stimulate acupuncture points, iii) acu-yoga, where pressure
on acupuncture points is created by putting the body into
certain positions or postures, and (iv) meridian exercises,
practices that resemble yoga asanas that have the effect of
stretching the meridians and are combined with self-massage
using the hands.

The Fourteen Meridians

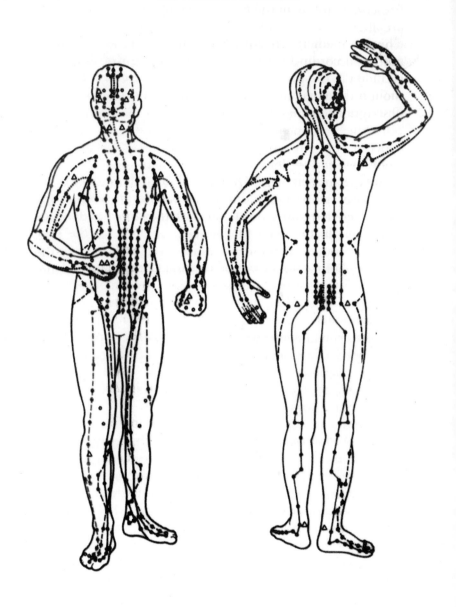

Research has shown that in the performance of mudra, certain acupressure points are affected, and the effects prescribed for a particular mudra in the yogic tradition are aligned with the prescribed results from the traditional Chinese medicine perspective. The effects of individual mudras according to the science of acupuncture, have been included in the practice chapters. Research shows that even though the yogic and Chinese systems are unique in their descriptions and methodology, the effects remain the same.

While acupuncture meridians are described in detail, nadis of yoga are not so well known today. Nevertheless, blockages in the flow of prana or Qi through the nadis or meridians will lead to imbalance and disorders. All techniques and methods used in yoga and acupuncture are directed towards purifying and restoring the normal flow through these energy channels. In the ayurvedic text, *Charaka Samhita,* there is reference to 'vital points in the body', called *marmas,* which correspond to the acupuncture points to some degree.

Five elements

The five elements in traditional Chinese medicine refer to the elements in a broad way. There are five basic processes,

----- Lung Meridian of Hand Tai-Yin

— Large Intestine Meridian of Hand Yang-Ming

- - - - Stomach Meridian of Foot Yang-Ming

— Spleen Meridian of Foot Tai-Yin

- - - - Heart Meridian of Hand Shao-Yin

······· Small Intestine Meridian of Hand Tai-Yang

— Bladder Meridian of Foot Tai-Yang

— Kidney Meridian of Foot Shao-Yin

······· Pericardium Meridian of Hand Jue-Yin

----- Three Heater Meridian of Hand Shao-Yang

---- Gall Bladder Meridian of Foot Shao-Yang

- - - - Liver Meridian of Foot Jue-Yin

········ Governor Vessel Meridian (Du-Mai)

········ Conception Vessel Meridian (Ren-Mai)

• Accupuncture point

• He-Sea Point (where energy accumulates)

Δ Connecting point

qualities or phases of change inherent in all things and these are represented by the five elements: wood, fire, earth, metal and water. Wood represents germination, spreading outward. Fire represents heat and growth, spreading upward. Earth represents nourishment and transformation. Metal represents the maturing process, concentrating. Water represents coolness, decay, transmutation, storage and a downward movement. In this sequence the elements represent a generative cycle, an endless process of creation and preservation in which every element supports the next one.

Another way in which these elements interact with each other is known as the control cycle, which is a counterbalance to the generative cycle tendencies. Here each element exhibits a controlling, suppressing tendency upon one of the other elements. Working together, both the generating and control cycle ensure maintenance of the equilibrium in the universe, in nature and in the body. Both of them operate simultaneously, creating a natural biofeedback mechanism that maintains homeostasis and harmony in the systems.

Similarly to yin and yang, everything in nature is composed of all five elements, with one element pre-dominating. Thus, each organ in the human body can be attributed as belonging to a certain element. The theory of the five elements is used to rectify invisible subtle levels of energy disturbances, where illnesses are only partially physical. Specific acupuncture points are stimulated to bring about a direct change in the pranic body. The overall effect is one of balancing the elements, by strengthening deficient elements and dispersing excessive ones.

Correlation between mudras and acupuncture
Acupuncture and yoga mudras have many features in common. Both systems emphasize and utilize the same or similar principles: the dual qualities within nature represented by yin-yang and ida-pingala; the existence of five elements that pervade the whole universe; the meridians

and nadis; Qi and prana; acupuncture points and marmas, chakras and kshetrams.

The process of understanding yogic mudras from an acupuncture perspective unveils subtle connections that exist between these two systems. These connections reflect the similarities in thinking, perceiving and living that exist in the traditions from which yogic mudras and acupuncture have emerged. In both vedic and Taoist traditions the philosophy of 'simple living and high thinking' is emphasized. Life is meant to be lived in accordance with the laws of nature, flowing smoothly through different stages and phases. To ensure this, certain techniques and methods were designed in both traditions that enabled one to pursue various aims in life, from physical and mental wellbeing to the ultimate aim of self-realization. Yoga mudras and acupuncture are two such techniques.

The essential aspect of both systems is the knowledge of the vital principle, prana or Qi, and the guiding of that vital force. The science of the vital force was researched and developed to the highest standards in both systems. Although the method differs, the essence of both systems remains the same. Confucius, the famous exponent of Taoism, has said that the purpose of the exercises in mysticism is 'to preserve the essence of life by seeking expression in outward form'. This reflects the original approach towards life used by the sages of ancient China, which was based on the proper use of the body and the mind, and did not rely on acupuncture and herbs. The very idea of 'seeking expression in outward form' in order to 'preserve the essence of life' sounds like the perfect definition of yogic mudra, which uses the physical body as a medium to preserve and increase the level of the essential life force. The physical body is shaped into a posture that reflects a particular state of mind, a particular inner attitude. When the vital force reaches a critical level, this inner attitude of an altered, higher state of consciousness becomes a reality. Mudra acts as a subtle means of

29

intrapersonal communication between all the levels of human experience, like a special language that unites the body and mind.

In fact, the correct way of using the body, as taught by the sages of ancient China, proves that the meridians and the flow of Qi is far more fundamental and universal than it is applied in acupuncture. At the same time, it is the basic difference between the yogic and acupuncture model.

It seems that the yogic model has a broader vision than traditional Chinese medicine, and it also appears to be more subtle, in that the vital energy of the nadis is more subtle than that of the acupuncture meridians. The aims of the two systems are also different. Yogic mudras strive to achieve a very high goal: to achieve states of pratyahara and dharana, and eventually dhyana or meditation, which then lead to realization or samadhi. Health benefits that come during this process are simply by-products, although good health is a prerequisite for higher spiritual achievements. On the other hand, acupuncture is primarily concerned with the health of the body and the mind to establish the state of optimal harmony within, and between oneself and nature, leaving higher spiritual goals to other techniques.

Though having different aims, the two systems share a fundamental theory of interconnectedness and belief in the vital principle of life. The study of the correspondence between the two lends a greater understanding to the effects of mudras, besides indicating a shared history in ancient times.

4

Mudra and the Brain

If the doors of perception were cleansed, everything would appear to man as it is – infinite.

—*William Blake*

There is more potential existing within this physical body than one can possibly imagine. Yoga believes that this physical body is but a microcosmos, a mini replica of the macrocosmos, the universe, and thus there are many ways that the human body can connect with the macrocosmos and its rhythms and vibrations. These rhythms and vibrations, continually flowing in the universe, are not perceptible to most, yet they can still be registered. Similarly, existing within the human brain are centres that may be ultrasonic or supersonic, as they are not of the nature of mind or thinking. These areas are not at all connected with daily life and experience. They are in the form of frequencies or rhythms similar to those of the universe, and the known or frequently used areas in the brain are not yet developed enough to register them.

There are also certain untapped secretions in the physical body. These potential processes are usually sealed and lying dormant. Furthermore, there are certain centres existing in the physical body that are not functioning, yet they possess the potential to function. The possibility of awakening all these latent potentials, and altering and expanding the

31

consciousness within this body and mind, is the subject of mudras.

A look at the brain

To understand what lifts a simple posture, movement or gesture into the realm of mudra requires an awareness of the psychophysiological interaction of the body and mind. The best way to understand this is to look at the brain.

The cortex is a relatively recent anatomical and physiological evolution of the brain. It can be described as the higher physical representation of the psyche. One can destroy a large part of the cortex and still receive sensations, however, the cortex gives depth, meaning and understanding to the signals that one is receiving. The cortex is the centre where the thought process takes place, thus when the cortex is engaged, one is no longer only in the realm of sensations; one is in the realm of higher functions. If the frontal cortex is destroyed, thoughts will come, but one will no longer be able to plan or grasp abstract concepts; there will be no depth to the thoughts. Thus, the cortex adds a huge dimension to the sensory inputs that are received from the world around.

In the process of human evolution, the higher functions of the cortex must be linked with the deep primitive structures of the brain. The focus of the primitive, sensory life needs to be lifted out of the base of the brain back into consciousness, back into the cortex. When the cortex links to the base of the brain, this process is called telencephalization, which means bringing what normally is instinctive into conscious control. The aim of mudras is to create fixed, repetitive postures, gestures and attitudes that can snap one out of these old, instinctive habitual patterns and bring one back into a more refined state of consciousness, thus unifying the internal layers of the personality.

In scientific terms, mudras provide a means to access and influence the unconscious reflexes and primal, instinctive patterns of habit that originate in the primitive areas of the brain around the brain stem. They establish a subtle, non-intellectual connection with these areas. Each mudra sets up a different link and has a correspondingly different effect on the body, mind and prana.

Modern neurophysiologists have been able to demonstrate the obvious relationship between the body and

Cross Section of the Brain

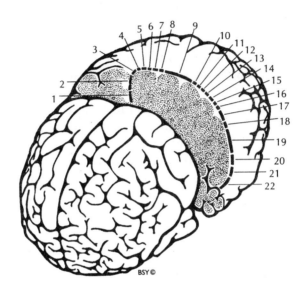

Cross-section of the brain revealing the motor cortex and indicating the areas of the body as mapped along the precentral gyrus. This is the motor homunculus – the symbolic man lying within the brain matter.

1. Toes	9. Hand	17. Eyelid & eyeball
2. Ankle	10. Little finger	18. Face
3. Knee	11. Ring finger	19. Lips
4. Hip	12. Middle finger	20. Jaw
5. Trunk	13. Index finger	21. Tongue
6. Shoulder	14. Thumb	22. Larynx
7. Elbow	15. Neck	
8. Wrist	16. Brow	

the brain that was discovered by ancient yogis thousands of years ago. Using stimulating electrodes to probe the brain's surface, neurosurgeons have shown that each part of the body is precisely mapped out along the surface of the central gyrus or fold of the sensory motor cortex of the brain. Based on this knowledge, neurosurgeons are able to rectify imbalances in the physical body by stimulating the brain. Yogis begin at the other end of the nerve pathway; they heighten the awareness of the body in order to stimulate the brain.

The entire body is represented in the motor cortex. The area from the shoulder to the ankle is given only about a quarter or a fifth of the space that is designated to the hand. The hands and the head alone take up about fifty percent of the cortex, and the rest is for all the other parts of the body. Researchers have named this neuronal map or hologram of the physical body existing within the cerebral white matter the homunculus or 'little man'. By physical standards, the motor homunculus is a little man of grotesque proportions, with enormously enlarged hands, fingers and facial features.

The mudras for the eyes, hands, tongue and genitals aim at controlling and bringing the awareness to large areas of the cortex and sensory motor area of the brain.

Communication between body and mind

The communication between the body and the mind goes mainly through the central nervous system, which is composed of the brain and the spinal cord. It is the biological medium through which the mind operates. Mudras influence the central nervous system through direct stimulation, and indirectly through the manipulation of prana, but in reality there is only one way in which the body, mind and brain are stimulated by mudra, and that is through manipulation of pranic flow.

Direct stimulation occurs mainly in head mudras, in which optic and other cranial nerves are directly stimulated through contraction of related muscles or through mental concentration. Neural impulses generated in this way travel straight to corresponding areas in the brain. In fact, when any mudra is performed, neural impulses are first generated in the brain itself. For example, in order to place the eyes in a mudra, the command is sent from the motor cortex section of the brain down through the neural pathways to the eyes. When the mudra is performed, impulses are sent back to the brain through sensory neural tracts and subcortical structures, all the way up to the cortex.

The effort, which is psychophysical in nature, to maintain the practice of mudra properly for some time triggers a new influx of impulses from the brain towards the periphery, and also from the periphery back to the brain. In this way a loop or circuit is created, through which nerve energy moves in a circular pattern, gradually building up the energetic charge throughout the neural circuit which has been formed by the mudra. Prana builds up as it circulates through the neural loop created by the mudra. When a sufficient quantum of prana is created, the neuronal circuits in the brain are modified and become silent. Unused areas of the brain are then set in motion and brought into the realm of consciousness, bringing about an integration of the brain and the mind. No matter what kind of brain stimulation takes place, in mudra there is always intense activity of certain brain areas.

With regular practice of mudra, progressively larger areas of the brain that are normally dormant are activated in a harmonious and controlled way. During this process many psychological, mental and emotional problems such as unconscious neuroses, complexes, fears, phobias, inhibitions, and so forth, are brought to the surface of the consciousness and dissolved. This releases the negative charge that was stored in corresponding brain areas and their power over the personality is lost. They can then be replaced with new, creative and positive habits and patterns of thinking and behaviour. In this way, deep transformation can take place.

Redirecting energy to the brain

The five groups of classical yoga mudras, comprising hand, head, perineal, lock and postural mudras, in particular, redirect energy back to the brain from the extremities. Between these five groups, a substantial area of the cerebral cortex is engaged. Furthermore, the comparatively large number of head and hand mudras reflects the fact that the operation and interpretation of information coming in from these two areas occupies approximately fifty percent of the cortex.

Perineal mudras are techniques that redirect prana from the lower centres to the brain. Mudras concerned with sublimating sexual energy are in this group. Techniques included in this category are: ashwini mudra, vajroli mudra and sahajoli mudra.

In vipareeta karani mudra, the gentle inverted pose of vipareeta karani asana is assumed, which reverses and redirects the downward and outward movement of energy to the brain. This revitalizes the body and expands the awareness. Physiologically, this asana allows a greater flow of blood to the cerebral capillaries and blood vessels which helps to activate the brain. For this reason the posture gives a fresh charge to the brain. The position is almost the same as that of sarvangasana, however, there is a slight difference in the position of the spinal column. In vipareeta karani asana, the trunk is raised from the ground to make a forty-five degree angle, whereas in sarvangasana the trunk is perpendicular to the ground. In sarvangasana, the chin is pressed into the chest so that jalandhara bandha happens automatically. During vipareeta karani there is no jalandhara bandha and the chin does not touch the chest. This is an important difference as it means that the flow of blood and prana to the brain in vipareeta karani are not restricted. It is the flow of prana that has relevance to the practice being called a mudra.

The lock mudras combine bandhas and kumbhaka. In this process of bringing the body into alignment and inhibiting organs, the entire brain is affected. When performing bandhas with kumbhaka, the body is squeezed like a bag of fluid. Stimulation of mooladhara chakra works in the area of the upper brainstem where the reticular activating system is located. By squeezing the perineum, an immediate reflex of energy comes up and illumines the whole brain. As so many different structures are inhibited simultaneously, the cortex is pushed very rapidly into a single, pulsating unit.

The brainwaves are also synchronized in meditation practice, but normally this is a slow process. With the lock mudras, the brain and the process of catabolism are slowed down immediately, like putting on the brakes quickly. This has a powerful effect on metabolism, which can be disturbed if the constitution or psyche is weak.

Endocrine systems and the brain

The nervous system continuously receives inputs from the external environment for the brain to assimilate. In response to the stimuli, the brain sends messages back through the nervous system to the body to effect change or movement. One aspect of this process is a two-way communication between the nervous system and the endocrine system.

Within the endocrine function there are two other systems that are of relevance. One is the dopamine system, which awakens the body. The other is the serotonin system which, when it is active, puts one to sleep, reduces pain and induces calmness. It chemically supports a shift of awareness, which otherwise requires deep relaxation.

Vipareeta karani mudra and yoga mudra, for instance, represent two ways of taking the awareness through the brain, from the limbic system to the cortex. However, the two positions have different effects. In vipareeta karani mudra, the dopamine system is being stimulated, which is activating, and in yoga mudra, the serotonin system is being stimulated, inducing a calming effect.

Generalized and specific systems of the brain

The brain consists of both a generalized system that continuously and automatically operates, and a specific system. The generalized system operates unconsciously. One can be sitting quietly and passive while the whole brain remains active, controlling the breathing, the heartbeat, digestion, and so on. without any conscious interaction from the person. However, if something touches the body, a specific system within the brain will immediately become active and a sensation will be felt consciously.

Mudras form a pathway into the generalized system from the specific system, bringing the unconscious areas of the brain into conscious control. When the hands are held in a mudra for a period of time, a signal goes to the brain via the specific system. After about one or two minutes, the brain becomes habituated and blocks out the signal. Even though the signal is still going to the brain, it is no longer felt and the generalized system of the brain is now operating. In this way, mudras allow one to enter and then to develop control over the generalized system of the brain. For this to occur, consciousness of the mudra needs to be maintained for a period of time, so that when the sensory information is dissolved into the general system, it can be followed consciously.

Brain hemispheres

In most mudras the body is held in a symmetrical shape. In this way, excitation of the brain, triggered by the mudra, is spread equally through both hemispheres of the brain. This brings about their controlled, coherent, synchronous and balanced function. After prolonged and regular practice, this phenomenon can result in harmonious cooperation and availability of both creative and analytical thinking. This manifests in the form of increased intelligence, understanding, perception, intuition and discrimination.

The head mudras work through the brain to influence the mind, to relax and internalize the mind, and to sharpen the awareness. For example, when practising *nasikagra drishti*, the gesture of nosetip gazing, nerves connected to the left and right hemispheres of the brain are activated. This harmonizes the brain hemispheres, inducing a more tranquil, peaceful, calm and quiet attitude. Or, as the practice of vipareeta karani mudra is perfected, the flow of prana in the ida and pingala nadis becomes balanced, manifesting as an equal flow of breath in the nostrils. The breath flowing through the left nostril activates the right brain hemisphere, and the breath flowing through the right nostril activates the left brain hemisphere. When there is an equal flow of breath through both nostrils, the hemispheres of the brain are harmonized and balanced.

Important glands within the brain
Ajna chakra is situated in the midbrain at the very top of the spine. It is the energy centre that monitors and commands each and every function in the physical body and has great control over the autonomic nervous system. When this centre is healthy, the balance between the emotions and the body is maintained.

Ajna chakra is related to the physical pineal gland, the pea-sized endocrine gland located in the centre of the head. The physiological functions of the pineal gland have baffled medical scientists for centuries. Even today it is not very well understood, though gradually it is divulging its secrets. It seems that the pineal gland acts as a biological clock that regulates one's activities according to external circumstances. It has been found that the eyes and the pineal gland are connected via the sympathetic nervous system, and that light entering the eyes directly influences some of the functions of the pineal gland. The pineal gland in turn regulates the whole sympathetic nervous system, which greatly controls human behaviour. Thus, cosmic rhythms such as night and day, and the cycles of the moon and the sun influence one's behaviour via the pineal gland. Melatonin and other hormones are produced in response to external stimuli;

these in turn produce changes in sexual behaviour, menstrual cycles, nervous energy and other biological rhythms. Thus, it seems that the pineal gland acts like a radio antenna, which picks up outside signals and regulates one's behaviour accordingly.

Besides being a link between the outer material environment and the individual, the pineal gland also acts as a gateway to the more subtle realms of the psyche. It is a physical transducer between the physical and psychic planes. Psychic changes can induce corresponding physical changes via the pineal gland. Conversely, physical, chemical or any other stimulation of the pineal gland can bring about repercussions in the psyche. Thus, it is a switch or a sluicegate which restricts or opens up psychic awareness. Direct stimulation of the pineal gland by various yogic practices can help to awaken ajna chakra.

The pineal gland is also the master gland which controls the behaviour of the pituitary gland, another important gland within the brain. The pituitary gland is associated with sahasrara and is a wild, complicated gland. It produces many hormones that must be properly regulated. If the wild behaviour of the pituitary gland is not regulated, then physical and emotional problems may develop. At the age of seven or eight, the pineal body starts its natural decay and the pituitary hormones begin to form and enter the bloodstream, and the dawning of sexual consciousness follows. The function of the pineal gland is to control the pituitary so that these hormones manifest at the right time.

In yoga, one strives to keep the pineal body healthy for as long as possible, and this is especially relevant for children. If the pineal gland continues to function, the onset of the pituitary hormone secretions, the sex hormones, becomes a slower process. Usually these particular secretions influence the personality structure in a dramatic way and bring about sudden changes in behaviour and temperament, often throwing the child off balance. If this process is more gradual, it can contribute to a positive development of

40

the personality. In this way, children gain the possibility of maintaining mental and emotional balance as they develop a new sexual awareness.

Regular practice of shambhavi mudra retards the degeneration of the pineal gland and is therefore recommended for children from the age of eight onwards. Shambhavi mudra is said to directly awaken ajna. When the mudra is practised, the pranas are raised by the force of the mudra to the frontal portion of the brain, irrigating and infusing this area with energy.

Yoga must also be practised in such a way that the very foundation, the very source of sexual energy is controlled at sahasrara chakra in the pituitary body. In kriya yoga, the first technique one practises is vipareeta karani mudra, and by means of this technique one learns to maintain complete control over the pituitary body, the centre from which the hormones flow.

Khechari mudra and the brain

The practice of *khechari mudra*, gesture of the tongue lock, exerts a controlling influence upon the network of endocrine glands throughout the body. This is achieved by regulating the production of the powerful secretions of the brain itself. These secretions are produced in tiny amounts to control the functions of the pituitary gland, thereby controlling the whole orchestra of glands associated with the centres below ajna. These dependent glands include the thyroid, mammary, thymus, adrenal and reproductive glands, as well as many other dependent processes which continually go on in the body.

Khechari mudra also influences the centres in the hypothalamus and brainstem which control involuntary actions such as autonomic breathing, heart rate, emotional expression, appetite and thirst. The hypothalamus has a strong connection with the thalamus and the RAS (reticular activating system), which assumes a vital role in the sleep and waking mechanisms and all degrees of central nervous system activities, including the ability to concentrate. The practice also influences the salivary gland and the faculty of taste, which are connected to the lower nerve plexuses involved in the digestive and assimilative processes, in turn allowing for some control over one's sexuality. In *Hatha Yoga Pradipika* the effects on the body are described (3:38–39):

रसनामूर्ध्वगां कृत्वा क्षणार्धमपि तिष्ठति ।
विषैश्चमुच्यते योगी व्याधिमृत्युजरादिभिः ॥

न रोगो मरणं तंद्रा न निद्रा न क्षुधा तृषा ।
न च मूर्च्छा भवेत्तस्य यो मुद्रां वेत्ति खेचरीम् ॥

The yogi who remains with the tongue going upwards for even half a second is freed from toxins, disease, death, old age, etc. One who accomplishes this khechari mudra is neither troubled by diseases, nor death, lassitude, sleep, hunger, thirst or unconsciousness.

This sloka concerning the powerful effects of khechari mudra on human psychophysiology and destiny is better understood when one knows about certain neuroendocrinal functions of the brain. During the practice of khechari mudra, a number of pressure points located in the back of the mouth and the nasal cavity are stimulated. These points influence the whole body. As the tongue is inserted into the nasal cavity, many tiny nerve endings are activated that allow for greater autonomic control. Even in normal life, with continuous practice of the simple version of khechari called *nabho mudra*, the sensations of hunger and thirst are reduced. One does not feel like eating or drinking and gradually the body adjusts accordingly. This can be experienced by experimentation.

Khechari mudra is just one example of how mudras, when practised properly for some time, can affect the physiology of the body and brain, in turn allowing access to parts of the brain and to human potentials that have previously remained dormant and unknown.

5

Mudra and Meditation

The human mind is a centre of consciousness. The more centred or one-pointed it is, the more powerful, blissful and harmonized it becomes. The greater the one-pointedness of mind, the greater the wisdom and knowledge of soul. On the yogic path the mind has to become like a bindu: infinitesimally concentrated, yet full of unlimited potential.

The secret lies in the simultaneous harmonization of the physical, psychic and mental energies of the human framework. This process automatically concentrates the mind to a perfect bindu. It is then that things start to happen which are beyond the normal comprehension of man. The blind begin to see for the first time.

From doing to being
Mudras are techniques that require very subtle awareness. They are introduced after some proficiency has been attained in asana, pranayama and bandha, and after gross blockages have been removed. Whole body awareness and integration of the body parts is the aim of these preparatory practices. Then when one comes to the practice of mudras, one can appreciate and feel what is going on at a subtle level. With mudra, the focus moves to cellular-level consciousness. There is a shift from the 'doing' techniques to the 'being' techniques.

43

Asanas and pranayama require a lot of manipulation and effort, a lot of 'doing'. Mudra techniques are much more within the scope of just 'being'. One can now flow with the energy that has been created in the previous practices and develop experiences that arise into the consciousness. Bandhas are used to slow down the physical and mental energy, thinking process, brainwaves and metabolism. Through mudras the cellular level is reached where prana is manufactured, stored and utilized. The manufacturing of energy is called anabolism, the building up of tissue. The breakdown of energy is called catabolism, the using up of all the stores. The aim of yoga is to store prana, to build up and hold as much energy as possible. So the 'doing' techniques utilize energy, while the 'being' techniques store it up.

Conscious awareness and sakshi bhava

Mudras establish a flow of prana in the body that keeps the mind attentively in place and anchors the awareness to the present, avoiding the natural tendency of the mind to wander here and there. It is at this stage that the mind has to assume the quality of *sakshi bhava*, becoming a silent observer and witness of what is going on. Mudra, like no other yogic practice, is recognized as an external instrument having the capacity to prepare the mind for meditation. It sustains the flow of thoughts with the right discipline, preparing one to recognize subtler and higher levels of perception. Whatever mudra is performed, the basic requirement is a state of deep relaxation so that rather than expanding the awareness outwards, one allows the expansion to emerge from within.

As the awareness deepens with the practice of mudras, the practitioner moves closer to the ultimate truth. In this context, to expand the awareness means to become aware of something that already exists, but which has not been acknowledged. With mudras nothing new is created, the apparatus of perception is simply altered so that new dimensions can become manifest at the individual's level of existence. Thus, mudras seal the universe into the human being.

44

Mudras start to work at annamaya kosha, influence the pranamaya kosha, and then directly or indirectly stimulate manomaya kosha, where the meditative process begins. The more the awareness is progressively intensified, the more one experiences subtler realms of existence. At the material level, the body is experienced as separate from its environment and from the mind. In the higher level of awareness, however, the boundaries between body, environment and mind become increasingly blurred. At this stage, the environment and mind are recognized simply as different frequencies of prana and vibration. Ultimately, the individual merges with the cosmos and realizes the oneness with the world.

Overcoming instinctive behaviour

Tantric literature states that once the dissipation of prana is arrested through the practice of mudra, the mind becomes introverted, inducing states of *pratyahara*, sense withdrawal, and *dharana*, concentration. When prana is in the process of rebalancing itself, there is an automatic experience of mental tranquillity. Therefore, most mudras are used for going deep into a meditative state. They aid the processes of pratyahara and dharana. However, that is just one level of experience. At a deeper level of the personality, the instinctive tendencies are being overcome.

The four basic instinctive tendencies are: i) fear ii) sexual urge iii) the desire for food, and iv) the desire for sleep. These are the corresponding physical manifestations of the mental vrittis that are being experienced on the level of consciousness. For example, the sexual urge is a desire, a force, a thought and an expression. It is experienced in the region of mooladhara. The form of consciousness here activates that physical part of the body known as the mooladhara-swadhisthana region.

Sleep does not affect any one organ in the body; however, it slows down the activity of the nervous system. As the activities cease, one moves through different states of consciousness or states of sleep, including different stages of drowsiness and lethargy, the dreaming state to deep sleep.

45

The desire for food actually stimulates the digestive system. Therefore, that vritti can be controlled through the digestive system by controlling the physical region of manipura. Similarly, by controlling the autonomic nervous system, the vritti of fear which causes palpitations, secretion of adrenaline and rapid breathing can be controlled.

Patterns of the mind

Yogic texts also state that mudras overcome the mental patterns and emotional reactions that impede meditation. According to the *Yoga Sutras* of Sage Patanjali, one is not able to know or comprehend the higher states of consciousness until the patterns of the mind, the *chitta vrittis*, cease their activity, when the mind is no longer affected by the play of the three gunas and varying moods, and when there is no longer a feeling of identification with the objective world. With reference to khechari mudra it is stated in *Hatha Yoga Pradipika* (3:48):

गोशब्देनोदिता जिह्वा तत्प्रवेशो हि तालुनि ।
गोमांसभक्षणं तत्तु महापातकनाशनम् ॥

The word 'go' means tongue (and also means cow). When it enters into the upper palate, it is 'eating the flesh of the cow'. It (khechari) destroys the great sins.

When the tongue is swallowed back up into the nasal cavity in khechari mudra, it is referred to as 'eating cow's meat' in hatha yoga. According to the sloka, the practice of khechari is said to destroy the great sins. What are these sins? They are not overt crimes, rather defects in character which are the cause of crimes. There are many variants of the great sins described in yogic and Buddhist texts alike. Some texts have defined them as: lust, greed, anger, fear, ignorance and jealousy. They are also known as the six enemies. Khechari mudra helps one to overcome the gross emotions and passions that compel a person to react with anger, greed, and so on. The very pattern of one's thoughts and desires can be overhauled, and in this way the 'sins' are destroyed.

46

It is important not to misunderstand sin in this context due to its religious connotations. Sin should be understood as something that is an obstacle to spiritual progress. These negative modes of mind that grip the body and force one to act in a certain way can become a powerful fetter that binds one to lower levels of awareness and hinders development. They are not to be suppressed, yet they have to be overcome, and mudras, such as khechari mudra, provide a direct method of doing so by helping one recognize their subtle forms. Becoming established in khechari mudra can bring about a change in consciousness so that one learns from mistakes and is able to manage these inner forces properly without any unnecessary residue of guilt and anxiety.

The effect of mudras on the quality of meditation can be verified by experiment. One can practise meditation of a passive type for six months, and then change the practice to an active type incorporating mudras like maha vedha and khechari mudra. The nature of the experiences will definitely alter.

Stability of energy and mind

The *Gheranda Samhita* states: *Mudraya sthirata chaiva* – "By practising mudras, stability is attained." This steadiness can be understood to mean the stability of pranamaya kosha and manomaya kosha, stability of energy and mind. For example, with the practice of *shambhavi mudra*, gazing at the eyebrow centre with both eyes, and *nasikagra drishti*, gazing down at the nose tip, the uncontrolled activities of both prana and mind cease and become steady. In this way, the mind quickly becomes focused and internalized. This is the main aim of mudras: to help attain an inner state in which external emotions and events do not scatter the mental state.

Maha mudra is another powerful technique that spontaneously supports meditation. Involving asana, kumbhaka, mudra and bandha it makes a strong pranic lock and stimulates the energy circuit linking mooladhara with ajna chakra. Practised prior to meditation, maha mudra reduces restlessness and helps to make the mind one-pointed and introverted. The whole system is charged with prana, which intensifies awareness.

Similarly, both shambhavi and khechari cause the external mind to 'turn off' and an inner awareness to awaken. This is described in *Hatha Yoga Pradipika* (4:38):

श्रीशांभव्याश्च खेचर्या अवस्थाधामभेदतः ।
भवेच्चित्तलयानंदः शून्ये चित्सुखरूपिणि ॥

In the shambhavi and khechari states, though there is a difference in the place of concentration or influence, both bring about ecstasy and absorption in void, in the experience of *chit sukha* or the pleasure of consciousness.

Khechari mudra induces a state of inner calm and stillness. The tongue is an organ that moves a lot, often unconsciously, especially when one talks. By folding it back into khechari mudra one stabilizes and fixes muscles that are normally never still. This act produces stillness and quiet throughout the whole system, and has a profound effect on the consciousness. A lot of energy that would normally be utilized in cortical activity is free for other functions.

The purpose of vajroli and sahajoli mudras is to reverse the natural downward flow of apana so that the pranic force flows upward through sushumna. When this is perfected, all the psychological, physical, mental and emotional desires are transcended; the external mind becomes instantly tranquil and the awareness enters the inner dimensions. Mental equanimity means a steady mind, peaceful and unflinching in every circumstance. It is stated in *Hatha Yoga Pradipika* (4:14):

चित्ते समत्वमापो वायौ व्रजति मध्यमे ।
तदामरोली वज्रोली सहजोली प्रजायते ॥

When the mind is in equanimity and (prana) vayu proceeds through sushumna, then amaroli, vajroli and sahajoli are attained.

Allowing prana to flow through sushumna is the primary aim, yet it is difficult to cope with that experience and positively sustain it. In this sense, vajroli and sahajoli are not physical practices, but indwelling attitudes or states of perfection.

Without withdrawing the sensory awareness and experiencing the inner world in meditation, it is impossible to appreciate the external. Without striving for the inner experiences it is meaningless to live for the external experience, for that is limited by the senses. The internal world is vast and limitless. The deeper one goes into dharana and dhyana, the more one can appreciate the purpose and beauty of life.

Single-minded concentration is the most important aspect in the practice of mudras. It is the essence of perfection in every form of yoga. One must develop awareness of the experiences, actions and thoughts in each and every moment. Thus, there is constant awareness in the deeper states of dhyana and samadhi also.

Shambhavi mudra: special place in meditation

Head mudras form an integral part of kundalini yoga and many are meditation techniques in their own right. The head mudras are practices related to the eyes, ears, nose, tongue and lips. Techniques included in this category are: shambhavi mudra, nasikagra drishti, khechari mudra, kaki mudra, bhujangini mudra, bhoochari mudra, akashi mudra, shanmukhi mudra and unmani mudra. All the mudras expand consciousness, however, for the aspirant whose mind remains disciplined and whose awareness remains alert when all internal and external barriers have been dissolved in samadhi, shambhavi is said to bring the greatest perfection. The *Hatha Yoga Pradipika* states (3:125):

अभ्यासे तु विनिद्राणां मनो धृत्वा समाधिना ।
रुद्राणी वा परा मुद्रा भद्रां सिद्धद्व प्रयच्छति ॥

49

For those who are alert and with the mind one-pointed (disciplined) in samadhi, rudrani or shambhavi mudra is the greatest mudra for bestowing perfection.

The word *shambhavi* is the name of the creative power of consciousness, Shiva. *Shambhu* means 'the one born of peace', and *bhava* means 'emotion', so shambhavi implies the elevation of human emotion into intense spiritual longing. Therefore, shambhavi is a mudra which instils peace. The physical aspect of the practice is also known as *bhrumadhya drishti*, which means 'eyebrow centre gazing'.

There are seven stages of shambhavi, according to the vedic system: i) with coordination of the breath ii) with breath retention iii) first dharana iv) second dharana v) third dharana vi) fourth dharana and vii) fifth dharana (see Chapter 11 for details).

Shambhavi mudra and psychic symbol: After pratyahara has been established, it is easy for the isolated awareness to be consumed by the internal mental modifications. Visionary and psychic experiences will manifest according to the samskaras and desires of the meditator, and their appearance is endless. These manifestations do not indicate a meditative state. It is a trance. Laziness and lack of discipline have been transferred from the external world of sensory perception into the internal psychic and mental realms. Meditation is to remain one-pointed and disciplined in the midst of these inner experiences as well, and this discipline must continue through the succeeding stages of samadhi.

For this purpose the inner gaze is to be fixed upon a particular psychic symbol in shambhavi mudra. This symbol is chosen by the aspirant according to their own inclination, or it may be assigned by the guru. That symbol becomes the focus of pure consciousness; it becomes a real illumined object in one's consciousness by one-pointedness and discipline. Otherwise, meditation does not occur and the samadhi attained is of tamasic quality. It is to be remembered that the awareness is being constantly assailed by psychic

50

experiences, visions and even divine beings, and that these experiences increase as meditation deepens. To hold on to the chosen symbol is very difficult, and the meditator fails many times in this regard. Nevertheless, one should press on to perfection in shambhavi mudra. It is stated in *Hatha Yoga Pradipika* (4:37):

अंतर्लक्ष्यविलीनचित्तपवनो योगी यदा वर्तते
दृष्ट्या निश्चलतारया बहिरधः पश्यन्नपश्यन्नपि ।

मुद्रेयं खलु शांभवी भवति सा लब्धा प्रसादाद्गुरोः
शून्याशून्यविलक्षणं स्फुरति तत्तत्त्वं परं शांभवम् ॥

If the yogi remains with the chitta and prana absorbed in the internal object with the gaze motionless, though looking, he is not seeing. This is indeed shambhavi mudra. When it is given by the guru's blessing, the state of shoonya arises. That is the real state of Shiva (consciousness).

Concentration becomes much easier through the practice of shambhavi, and an adept at the practice can control the brainwaves at will. The moment shambhavi mudra is practised, concentration takes place so there is union between ida and pingala nadi in ajna chakra. When these two nadis unite there is an explosion of light.

Concentration is perfect when the totality of awareness knows only the object upon which it is concentrated. Perfect concentration is meditation, perfect meditation is samadhi. It is stated in *Hatha Yoga Pradipika* (4:39):

तारे ज्योतिषि संयोज्य किंचिदुन्नमयेद् भ्रुवौ ।
पूर्वयोगं मनो युंजन्नुन्मनीकारकः क्षणात् ॥

With perfect concentration, the pupils fixed on the light by raising the eyebrows up a little, as from the previously described (shambhavi), the mind is joined and instantly unmani occurs.

When shambhavi is practised for an extended period of time, a small light appears. That light has then to be seen with the eyes closed and concentrated upon until nothing else exists. When samadhi is achieved through the practice it is called *unmani*, which literally means 'no mind'. It is the state beyond mind and thought where the mind is turned completely inwards.

Shambhavi mudra and eye movement: Meditation becomes samadhi when awareness merges with the object of meditation and duality dissolves. In that state, sense perception is completely non-existent, and the eyeballs turn upwards, spontaneously fixed in shambhavi mudra. This is an external sign of the inner mental tranquillity.

Scientists have discovered that mental fluctuations in the form of changing thoughts, ideas and images cause rapid flickering movements of the eyeballs. During dreaming sleep, when the awareness is completely withdrawn into the mental realm and dreams are occurring, rapid eye movements (REM) are also produced. Thus, by watching someone who is asleep, it is possible to know if they are sleeping deeply or dreaming. When a person is dreaming, there are fluctuations in the eyeballs, which can be seen, felt and also measured by machines. In deep sleep, the eyes may automatically assume shambhavi mudra. Similarly, during the waking state, when the external world is being perceived visually, the eyes are constantly blinking and following the external objects. For example, an anxious person's eyes are unsteady and by stilling the eyes, the uncontrolled fluctuations of an anxious brain can generally be overcome.

These eye movements have been correlated with fluctuations in the electrical discharge of the brain, especially with prominent bursts of high-frequency beta waves on the electroencephalogram (EEG). During practices of concentration and meditation, when lower frequency alpha and theta waves emerge in steady, fixed patterns, the eyeballs are found to become spontaneously steady and fixed. Likewise, by stilling the eyeball movements, either externally or internally, it is possible to bring the brainwaves into the meditative pattern and induce the experience of meditation. It is on this basis that shambhavi mudra is practised.

Spiritual experiences arising with shambhavi mudra: The attainment of the state of shambhavi requires no intellectual capacity or brainpower, only sincere application to the practice. However, it may produce profound experiences and should only be performed under the guidance of a competent teacher. It is stated in *Hatha Yoga Pradipika* (4:80):

उन्मन्यवाप्तये शीघ्रं भ्रूध्यानं मम संमतम् ।
राजयोगपदं प्राप्तुं सुखोपायोऽल्पचेतसाम् ।
सद्यः प्रत्ययसंधायी जायते नादजो लयः ॥

In my opinion, contemplation on the eyebrow centre leads to a mindless state immediately. It is a suitable method even for those with less intellect to attain the state of raja yoga. The laya attained through nada gives immediate experience.

Spiritual life and experiences are independent of academic ability and intellectual or mundane knowledge. Spiritual knowledge, power and experience exist on a different plane altogether. Even a debauchee can perceive the nada and dwell in the greater experience. Anyone who hears it should listen intently, excluding other experiences and thoughts so that the mundane state of consciousness becomes illumined.

When Swatmarama says that in his opinion, eyebrow centre gazing leads immediately to mindlessness, he is narrating from his own experience. Those who have become highly established in spiritual consciousness through hatha yoga and raja yoga gain control of the mind; they are able to transcend its modifications and enter into the samadhi states at will, and this is due to their ability to concentrate the power of their mind. The wild energy of the mind must be concentrated into the bindu, that infinitesimally small yet infinitely powerful point of focus, for the secrets of the world to be revealed.

6

The Relevance of Bindu

There is the moon and the sun and between them is the
Seed. This last is that being whose nature is Joy Supreme.
                                                    —*Hevajra Tantra*

The most subtle of the chakras is ajna. Beyond ajna and
even more subtle is bindu. It is not a chakra. The chakras
are associated with the human psychic framework. Bindu, on
the other hand, is the subtle centre from which the human
framework itself arises. Bindu is therefore the primary
manifesting source of the chakras themselves. The chakras
are within the realms and fetters of the mind; bindu is
beyond the mind.

Dimensionless centre

To the uninitiated, the subject of bindu may seem abstract
and incomprehensible; however, it is a profound aspect
of tantra yoga and other mystical systems that must be
understood to acquire depth of mudra sadhana. Though it
may appear to have little significance in terms of practical
yoga, it is the purpose of all yoga practices to induce
awareness of bindu. It is impossible to understand bindu
merely by discussion, reading or speculation, for it unites the
finite with the infinite.

Bindu means seed, small particle, semen or sperm, a
point or dot. The word 'bindu' comes from the Sanskrit

54

root *bind* which means 'to split' or 'to divide'. This means that bindu is the origin of individuality; it is the point where the oneness first divided itself to produce duality, the world of multiple forms. This division implies limitation in knowledge, action, and so forth.

How is the yogi to realize within himself the entire creation in all its diversity, which has been studied in a thousand disciplines? Physics, chemistry, history, biology and geology are just a few of them. Even a lifespan of academic study cannot keep abreast of all these fields of research. Yogically, these types of knowledge are not absolute, and instead are the various aspects of a single creative seed and source, like rays emerging from the sun. The realization of creation, time and space, including one's own body and mind, as the outpouring of the one cosmic maha bindu, is the attainment of a yogi.

How is the yogic aspirant to gain this experience of yoga? How to realize the one containing the many, and the unity within diversity? This feat is accomplished by realizing the bindu, the seed, within one's own body, mind and consciousness. By the outpouring of the bindu, one has become many. By its retention, many again become one.

Bindu refers to a point without dimension, a dimensionless centre. In Sanskrit texts it is often called *chidghana*, that which has its roots in the limitless consciousness. The word 'bindu' also means zero or voidness, *shoonya*. More correctly, bindu is the gateway to shoonya. This zero or voidness is not, however, a total nothingness. It is an emptiness that contains the fullest potential. In fact, the word 'shoonya' should be translated not as nothingness, but as no-thingness. There is a vast difference between these two words. The state of no-thingness is pure consciousness. Bindu is therefore a mysterious, ineffable focal point where the two opposites, infinity and zero, fullness and no-thingness, coexist. It represents the focal point of individuality, whether animate or inanimate. It is the cosmic seed from which all things manifest and grow. It is an infinitesimally small point of infinite potential.

Bindu sadhana leads to dissolution or nullification of mental fluctuations. With awareness of bindu, the mind becomes lucid, receptive and perfectly one-pointed; it becomes crystalline, a perfect reflector of pure consciousness. Concentration of mind implies that there is awareness of bindu and, conversely, piercing of the bindu as in kriya yoga, implies that there is perfect concentration of mind. At this stage, the path of yoga is transformed into the experience of yoga.

When the mind is concentrated on the bindu point, then one passes from the limited to the unlimited. One passes beyond the realms of the mind. This is the reason why concentration of mind is the essence of all yoga practices and spiritual life in general. It is by piercing the bindu that one passes into the realm of pure consciousness, into the realms of zero time, timelessness.

The nectar of bindu

Bindu is widely called the *bindu visarga*, 'the falling drop'. This indicates that bindu is one of the many drops of nectar that continually trickle down from sahasrara, the fountainhead. This *amrit*, nectar, irrigates life. It is the real 'water of life', it is bliss, and bindu is the abode of uninterrupted bliss. This is symbolized in Indian mythology by the river Ganges, coming down from the crescent moon.

Amrit does not flow constantly, only for a fraction of a second, and the moment this fluid flows into the body, the body and mind begin to change. One may be sitting anywhere and the consciousness begins to change, even if there is no awareness of it.

Yogic texts are pervaded by the theme of this immortal nectar, as well as the techniques and practices by which it can be trapped and consumed within the human body. In this context, the divinization of man is considered to be a process of physiology rather than a philosophical or religious idea.

Bindu is said to be the place where the moon resides and when it is full it sheds its nectar or ambrosial fluid down to

56

permeate the entire body, just as the external moon pours its light over the surface of the earth at the time of the full moon. In *Shiva Samhita* it is written (3:73):

राजदंतबिलं गाढं संपीड्य विधिना पिबेत् ।
ध्यात्वा कुण्डलिनीं देवीं षण्मासेन कविर्भवेत् ॥

When having firmly closed the glottis by the proper yogic method, and contemplating on the goddess Kundalini, he drinks (the moon fluid of immortality), he becomes a sage or poet within six months.

'Drinking the fluid or nectar of the moon' is drinking or assimilating the fluid released from bindu visarga. Bindu is always depicted as a full moon. The nectar produced in bindu is said to intoxicate the conscious mind and make the body resistant to toxins in the system. At a certain stage of spiritual evolution this is an inevitable process that takes place irrespective of the type of yoga one practises.

Drinking the nectar with khechari mudra

When one 'drinks' the nectar which drips down from bindu, one able to access a more subtle and refined level of energy. This allows the body to be nourished by a subtle form of prana. In *Hatha Yoga Pradipika*, this process is associated with khechari mudra (3:51):

मूर्ध्नः षोडशपत्रपद्मगलितं प्राणादवाप्तं हठा-
दूर्ध्वास्यो रसनां नियम्य विवरे शक्तिं परां चिंतयन् ।
उत्कल्लोलकलाजलं च विमलं धारामयं यः पिबे-
त्रिव्याधिः स मृणालकोमलवपुर्योगी चिरं जीवति ॥

Fluid drips into the sixteen-petalled lotus when the tongue is inserted into the upper throat cavity; the paramshakti (kundalini) is released and one becomes concentrated in the experience which ensues. The yogi who drinks the pure stream of nectar is freed from disease, has longevity, and has a body as soft and as beautiful as a lotus stem.

The sixteen-petalled lotus spoken of in the sloka is vishuddhi chakra. It describes the mechanism of consuming the nectarine flow by khechari mudra. When the tongue becomes flexible and can be inserted into the upper epiglottis, a nectarine secretion begins to flow. It drips from bindu visarga to soma, lalana and vishuddhi chakras. This is the technique of preservation and rejuvenation adopted by the yogis to gain radiant health, longevity and physical attractiveness.

This indicates the capacity of the yogi who has awakened vishuddhi chakra to assimilate both positive and negative aspects of life; to retain balance, health and equanimity in the midst of the dualities of pain and pleasure, light and dark, life and death, body and mind. Physiologically, the symbology has relevance to the thyroid gland in the front of the neck and its relationship with the pituitary gland. The thyroid gland is responsible for regulation of the body's metabolic rate. It differs from other endocrine glands in that it has the capacity to secrete and store the hormones synthesized by its secretory cells within the follicles of the gland itself, and these pooled secretions can be understood as the nectar of vishuddhi.

Thyroxine is essential in maintaining the normal activities of the central nervous system, body growth and movement, memory, thought process and speech, and emotional and behavioural stability. It also exerts important effects on the biochemistry of the liver, heart and skeletal muscles, is essential in the maintenance of the cells of the anterior pituitary, and has other important functions. Thus, thyroid imbalance has far-reaching effects on the whole body.

It is interesting to note that in *Hatha Yoga Pradipika*, Yogi Swatmarama mentions the body becoming as soft as a lotus stem with the trapping of nectar, as thyroxine maintains skin pliability and texture. Correct proportion of thyroxine is essential for balanced functioning of the body and mind. This is a part of the physiological aspect of the 'dripping of nectar', a phenomenon associated with the practice of khechari mudra.

The purpose of khechari mudra is to stimulate and awaken lalana chakra. Though it is a physical technique, it induces subtle changes on a psychic level, which is the effect of all mudras. *Lalana chakra* is a minor chakra closely associated with vishuddhi. It is located between bindu and vishuddhi, in the back of the nasopharynx, the inner cavity above and beyond the soft palate into which the nasal passages open. When khechari mudra is performed, one is attempting to turn the tongue up and backwards into this cavity to stimulate the flow of nectar by touching nerve endings located here. This centre is also referred to in the *Bible* (Judges 15:19):

> But God clave a hollow place that was in the jaw, and there came water thereout; and when he had drunk, his spirit came again, and he revived . . .

The water referred to in the text is not liquid water; it is bliss. When the nectar trickles down from bindu it is stored in lalana, a sort of glandular reservoir, before reaching vishuddhi chakra. Although this fluid is known as ambrosia, it actually has a dual nature and can act as poison as well as nectar. When it is produced in bindu and stored in lalana, it remains undifferentiated, neither poison nor nectar. As long as vishuddhi remains inactive, this fluid runs downward unimpeded, to be consumed in the fire of manipura, resulting in the processes of decay, degeneration and finally death in the body's tissues.

However, by a practice such as khechari mudra the ambrosia is secreted from lalana and passes to vishuddhi chakra, the purifying and refining centre. When vishuddhi is awakened, the divine fluid is retained and used, becoming the nectar of immortality. The secret of youth and regeneration of the body lies in the awakening of vishuddhi. Life becomes a source of joyful experiences.

There is a well known story about Meera Bai, one of the greatest saints and bhaktas of India. Her devotion to Lord Krishna was so intense that she lived in constant ecstasy through remembering him. Even when her mother-in-law fed her deadly poison she remained unaffected. People say that Lord Krishna turned the poison into rosewater or milk. Actually, her system was immune to it because of the flow of nectar from the bindu.

In Hindu mythology, Lord Shiva holds poison in his throat; the throat is the point where the poison is refined into a pure substance. This signifies that even poison can be readily digested when vishuddhi chakra is awakened. It means that at higher levels of awareness, vishuddhi and above, even the poisonous and negative aspects of existence become integrated into the total scheme of being. They are rendered powerless, as concepts of good and bad fall away. In this state of awareness, the poisonous aspects and experiences of life are absorbed and transformed into a state of bliss. It is stated in *Hatha Yoga Pradipika* (3:45):

नित्यं सोमकलापूर्णं शरीरं यस्य योगिन: ।
तक्षकेणापि दष्टस्य विषं तस्य न सर्पति ॥

The yogi's body is forever full of the moon's nectar. Even if he is bitten by the king of snakes (Takshaka), he is not poisoned.

An aiding factor in the release of the nectar during the practice of khechari mudra is the heat that is produced in the physical and subtle bodies. It is stated in *Hatha Yoga Pradipika* (3:49):

जिह्वाप्रवेशसंभूतवह्निनोत्पादित: खलु ।
चंद्रात्स्त्रवति य: सार: सा स्यादमरवारुणी ॥

When the tongue enters the cavity, indeed heat is produced and man's nectar flows.

This heat is extremely important for the release of the 'nectar from the moon'. Just as metal becomes liquid when it is heated, ice becomes water, and paraffin wax becomes liquid paraffin; so the nectar in the body which has solidified begins to run like a fluid when it is heated.

60

Rejuvenation and immortality

One of the significant benefits attained through the flow of nectar during the practice of khechari mudra is rejuvenation of the physical cells of the body. However, this effect is not common, nor is the purpose of this nectar to rejuvenate the physical body; it is simply a side effect of the perfected practice. When the lower centres metabolize the nectar of bindu, the body undergoes the process of decay, old age, disease and death. With the practice of khechari mudra, yogis reverse this process by stimulating bindu visarga and trapping the drops of hormone or amrit at vishuddhi.

When the hormone is retained in the vishuddhi region, it becomes purified and creates a different effect on the body. It does not combine with the acids of the stomach and become poison. It retains its purity and is distributed throughout the body after being percolated by the mucous membranes and salivary glands lining the mouth. Catabolism, the decaying process that involves the decay and degeneration of the blood vessels, cells and whole body, is arrested and a proper balance between anabolism, metabolism and catabolism is created. In this way the yoga practitioner achieves rejuvenation, *kayakalpa*. Kayakalpa means changing the total content of the body. Thus, the lifespan can thus be increased through the practice of khechari mudra.

According to Sage Gheranda, the body of a person who has perfected khechari is not influenced by fire, water or air. When the nectar or elixir of life is taken in a proper way, the body cannot be influenced by old age, death or any kind of harm, and it becomes as hard as a *vajra*, thunderbolt, and unchanging. Immortality is usually understood as indestructibility. In the yogic scriptures immortality means something else. Immortality here means that whatever one's age, fifty, eighty or a hundred years, the body does not age, its capacity is not reduced and the mental energy is not impaired in any way.

61

According to hatha yoga, if the practice of khechari mudra can be perfected, after two weeks the process of degeneration in the body is reversed. *Hatha Yoga Pradipika* says (3:44):

ऊर्ध्वजिह्वः स्थिरो भूत्वा सोमपानं करोति यः ।
मासार्धेन न संदेहो मृत्युं जयति योगवित् ॥

With the tongue directed upwards, the knower of yoga drinks the fluid of the moon. Within fifteen days physical death is conquered.

It takes a long time to perfect khechari, but one should consider the fact that during the process of perfecting it, the body is slowly readjusting itself, and once it is perfected, it will only take a short time to release the fluid from bindu.

Absorption of amrit with maha mudra

In *Yoga Chudamani Upanishad*, maha mudra is the method described to absorb the vital fluid (v. 65):

शोधनं नाडिजालस्य चालनं चंद्रसूर्ययोः ।
रसानां शोषणं चैव महामुद्राऽभिधीयते ॥

The method taught for purification of the entire nadi structure governing the movement of the moon and the sun and absorption of the vital fluid is maha mudra.

Both practices, maha mudra and maha bheda mudra, govern the movement of prana and bindu in the moon and sun centres. Regular practice prevents the bindu from falling and reverses the bindu even after it has fallen. This leads to greater mental and vital power, which can be utilized for regenerating the system or awakening the higher mental faculties.

The practices supercharge the whole system and induce a state of spontaneous meditation. By the combined practice of asana, pranayama, mudra and bandha in these techniques, the entire nadi structure is balanced, purified and awakened, thereby balancing the whole mind and body system. The flow of pranic energy in the sushumna channel is cleared and stimulated, increasing awareness, inducing clarity of thought and removing nervous depression.

Reversal of the flow of amrit with vipareet karani mudra

Vipareet karani mudra is performed in vipareeta karana asana, which is an inverted pose that turns the body upside down. In hatha yoga, vipareeta karani mudra is explained in the context of the sun and moon. The centre of *surya*, the sun, is manipura chakra in the solar plexus, and the centre of *chandra*, the moon, is in the region of the brain or ajna, lalana and bindu chakras. In this practice, the positions of the sun, or manipura, and the moon, or bindu, are reversed, so that the sun is above the moon. In *Gheranda Samhita* this symbolism is used (3:45–46):

नाभिमूले वसेत्सूर्यस्तालुमूले च चन्द्रमाः ।
अमृतं ग्रस्ते सूर्यस्ततो मृत्युवशो नरः ॥

ऊर्ध्वं च योजयेत्सूर्यं चन्द्रं चाप्यध आनयेत् ।
विपरीतकरी मुद्रा सर्वतन्त्रेषु गोपिता ॥

The sun plexus is located at the root of the navel and the moon plexus is located at the root of the palate. A person dies when the sun consumes nectar secreted by the moon, but when the chandra nadi consumes the nectar, there is no fear of death. Therefore, the sun is to be brought up and the moon is to be brought down. This is vipareeta karani mudra, which is secret by all standards.

In vipareeta karani, the normal downward flow of the nectar from bindu to manipura is reversed. It is redirected from manipura back to bindu, its source, which leads to the expansion of consciousness and revitalization of one's entire being. Thus, it is said that even the aged can regain their youth and vitality by the practice of vipareeta karani.

In *Gheranda Samhita*, the asana or position of the body is described, but the technique or method to follow while in the posture is not mentioned at all. This is because this sadhana is extremely secret, *sarva tantreshu gopita*. In *Hatha Yoga Pradipika* and in the tantric texts there are many wonderful statements regarding this reverse action. They say that from the moon the nectar emanates. When the sun consumes the nectar, the yogi becomes old. The body decays and one dies. Therefore, by constant practice, the yogi should try to reverse the process. The nectar that is flowing towards the sun should be reversed and sent back to the higher centres so it is not consumed by the sun, but is assimilated by the pure body. When the body has been purified by hatha yoga, pranayama and a pure diet, this nectar is assimilated by the body. As a result, a high mental state is experienced. When the nectar returns to its source in the higher centres of the brain, a sort of quietness is felt.

There was an illiterate saint in India in the fifteenth or sixteenth century who sung a cryptic song. In the song, a fluid flows from heaven though a cave. A lotus is seen, however, there is no lake. On that lotus is the mind, which is like a bird playing and flapping its wings. There is no moon but there is moonlight, and whichever way one looks there is nothing but light. The tenth door is opened, but the others are shut: the eyes, the nostrils, the mouth, the ears, the urinary and excretory orifices make nine gates and the tenth gate is on top of the head. The lock is broken, and when that happens, guilt, delusion, disease, everything is finished. This song is about vipareeta karani and the effect of amrit on the body.

Altered states of consciousness

When amrit is able to be absorbed by the body, the restless mind becomes quiet and one-pointed. Passions, desires, imaginations and dissipations just drop away. When it flows and is reabsorbed by the body, one's state of consciousness changes, just as when cannabis, LSD, peyote, or even alcohol are taken, a change or an altered state of consciousness occurs.

Even if one does not know how to meditate or does not have sufficient willpower, if a mudra like khechari is practised, after some time the state of the mind and flow of the prana change. One begins to feel high and the brainwave patterns alter. Even with the eyes open, one begins to have an altered experience. With the eyes closed one is able to have inner experiences. One can hear music internally. One can see the beauty of flowers in any season, anywhere. One can see the moon even when there is none. It is not hallucination; it is a real and conscious experience. The body becomes quiet and the mind steady. *Hatha Yoga Pradipika* states (4:47):

पुरस्ताच्चैव पूर्येत निश्चिता खेचरी भवेत् ।
अभ्यस्ता खेचरी मुद्राप्युन्मनी संप्रजायते ॥

> The sushumna being completely filled at the rear (upper palate) also is khechari. The practice of khechari mudra is followed by the state of unmani (consciousness devoid of mind).

The mind usually functions within the confines of time and space, ida and pingala, yet it is possible to transcend these two poles of duality. With the practice of khechari one can reach a state beyond karma, that is, cause and effect, time, death and disease. Time and space are concepts of the finite mind and perception. In yoga and tantra they are said to be the tools of Maya, Prakriti or Shakti. They are the laws of nature, and the finite mind is the product of nature. If one can expand the consciousness beyond the awareness of the finite mind and natural phenomena, the consciousness will enter the realm of the infinite. This is the state of superconsciousness, beyond duality and the finite mind. It is called kaivalya, nirvana, moksha, samadhi or Brahman. These are all synonymous terms indicating the final stage or accomplishment of raja yoga. Khechari mudra directly influences brain functions and awakens the higher centres of awareness. Normal brain functions undergo a transformation and restructuring so that supernormal functioning takes place. *Hatha Yoga Pradipika* elucidates (3:40–41):

पीड्यते न स रोगेण लिप्यते न च कर्मणा ।
बाध्यते न स कालेन यो मुद्रां वेति खेचरीम् ॥

चित्तं चरति खे यस्माज्जिह्वा चरति खे गता ।
तेनैषा खेचरी नाम मुद्रा सिद्धैर्निरूपिता ॥

One who knows khechari mudra is unafflicted by disease, unaffected by the laws of cause and effect (karma) and free from the bonds of time (death). Mind moves in Brahman (khe) because the tongue moves in space (khe). Therefore, the perfected ones have named this mudra khechari, moving in space or Brahman.

By maintaining bindu in the higher centres, khechari mudra leads to the expansion of finite consciousness and realization of Shiva, Brahman or Atman. This is a state that transcends the mind; it is samadhi. The many fragmentary experiences, seeming realities, individuals and distinctions one confronts, are only elements of a greater Self, which includes all diversities and relative contradictions within it. By holding on to the bindu of consciousness within, one perceives the world through the eye of Shiva, the one who wishes well to all beings and sees only unity amidst apparent diversity. At this stage, all distinctions fall away and one can see that all people are essentially the same: all are born by the same process, with the same hopes and aspirations, fears and desires. One realizes that all minds are only minute parts and expressions of a single collective mind. This state is called *manonmani*.

Fulfilling the purpose of life

It is stated in *Hatha Yoga Pradipika* (3:47):

गोमांसं भक्षयेन्नित्यं पिबेदमरवारुणीम् ।
कुलीनं तमहं मन्ये चेतरे कुलघातका: ॥

By constant swallowing of the tongue he can drink amara-varuni. I consider him of high lineage (heritage). Others destroy the heritage.

Amaravaruni is another name for amrit. *Amara* refers to immortality or the moon, and *varuni* is wine. Amaravaruni is the wine of immortality or of the moon.

Just as the result of the union between a man and a woman is the release of reproductive secretions, so the union of ida and pingala with sushumna in ajna chakra releases amaravaruni. At that time, one experiences the climax of spiritual experience, which is more fulfilling than any empirical experience. With the release of amaravaruni, the body is impregnated with spiritual or cosmic force and gives birth to higher consciousness or atman. The physical body is the feminine principle of Shakti. Mind is the masculine principle of Shiva, consciousness. The union of the two is realization of the indweller, the Self.

Yogi Swatmarama says that the person who can drink amaravaruni is from a worthy or high lineage. Those who live, procreate and die without attaining any spiritual knowledge have not been fulfilling the purpose of life or evolution. They are only continuing the generations of families. However, once a person endeavours to know the spirit or pure consciousness, the whole physical structure undergoes a rearrangement and even the genes of that person change. Consequently, the generations that follow are influenced by the achievements made in sadhana. The children of such a person, and their children, have a greater chance of achieving the same perfections. Therefore, the person who can drink amaravaruni is truly venerable to his family.

7

Sublimation

In the classical texts of hatha yoga, it is advocated that the reproductive secretions must be drawn up into the body so that bindu and rajas, or consciousness and energy for male and female practitioners, remain within the body. This enables the sexual impulses to travel up through the central nervous system to the higher centres of the brain, leading to sublimation of the same energy and expansion of consciousness.

There are two mudras that are specifically advised for this: vajroli and sahajoli. Men practise vajroli to regulate the hormones secreted from the testes, and women practise sahajoli to regulate the hormones secreted from the ovaries. The principle of preservation is that a man must contain his *veerya*, semen, and the female must contain her secretions, *rajas*. Abstention from sexual life is not advocated. This is an important point that must be clearly understood, as it is a scientific point. Tantra does not denounce sexual relationships, but it definitely says no to ejaculation. For that, vajroli and sahajoli have to be learnt. By retaining the energy produced at the lower centre, one has to direct it to the higher centre so that the experience does not become a physical experience, yet is experienced nevertheless.

At the end of the sexual act, there is an experience which originates in the higher centres, but it is experienced in the lower centre. If that experience can be maintained at the higher centre, then consciousness and energy are heightened. This is possible through the practice of vajroli and sahajoli. When delicious sweets are eaten, the change of consciousness does not take place in the tongue, as the tongue has no mind. The experience takes place at a higher centre, but one experiences the sweet taste in the tongue or mouth. It is the same with the sexual experience.

Celibacy has its own merits, but it is not good for all. It is opposing the processes of nature. Therefore hatha yoga came up with the principle of preservation. One who masters the method of preservation is a *brahmachari*. Even a married person and a householder can be a brahmachari if preservation is mastered. Preservation is important, the act is not important. Nature has provided the mechanism of seminal release but, although it is generally not known, nature has also provided a means to control this mechanism through various practices of hatha yoga. If the release of semen and ovarian hormones can be controlled, a new range of experience dawns. Those experiences are also endowed by nature, even if only a few people have gained them. Therefore, the techniques should not be considered to be against the natural order. It is stated in *Hatha Yoga Pradipika* (3:83):

स्वेच्छया वर्तमानोऽपि योगोक्तैर्नियमैर्विना ।
वज्रोलीं यो विजानाति स योगी सिद्धिभाजनम् ॥

Even one living a free lifestyle without the formal rules of yoga, if he practises vajroli well, that yogi becomes a recipient of siddhis (perfections).

According to this sloka, sexual life can be elevated from the sensual to the spiritual plane if it is practised in a particular way, and for this vajroli has been described. The text further states (3:103):

देहसिद्धिं च लभते वज्रोल्यभ्यासयोगतः ।
अयं पुण्यकरो योगो भोगे भुक्तेऽपि मुदिः ॥

By the yoga of vajroli practice, perfection of the body fructifies. This auspicious yoga even brings liberation alongside with sensual involvement (bhoga).

This important sloka states a basic concept of tantra that shatters puritanical ideas. According to tantra, *bhoga*, or sensual involvement, can be the means to yoga. Sense interaction can lead to higher awareness. In the tantric system, it is said that the husband and wife should practise tantra together and for that purpose they must master certain techniques. The man has to master vajroli and the woman has to master sahajoli.

The very idea that the ultimate experience can unfold through sensual experience is not one that many people have been able to accept. Some commentaries on the hatha yoga texts refuse to accept this as a part of the science of yoga and completely omit the slokas pertaining to vajroli and maithuna from the original text, stating that they are obscure and repugnant practices followed by only those yogis who lack the willpower to reach their goal otherwise. That, however, is a clouded perception.

Controlling the reproductive system
The function of the reproductive organs can be influenced and eventually controlled by vajroli and sahajoli mudras, when practised over a sustained period of time. They allow the practitioner to direct the influx of energy and the processes going on in the testicles and ovaries. Sexual energy should give one vitality and strength; it cannot just be denied and refused. It should make one confident, brilliant, and full of vigour and vitality. Vajroli achieves this by controlling the production of semen and the dissipations of mind and emotion. Similarly, the reproductive fluids as well as the mind and emotions of women are controlled in sahajoli. According to *Hatha Yoga Pradipika*, the control of semen by the mind is possible (3:90):

चित्तायत्तं नृणां शुक्रं शुक्रायत्तं च जीवितम् ।
तस्माच्छुक्रं मनःश्चैव रक्षणीयं प्रयत्नतः ॥

A man's semen can be controlled by the mind and control of semen is life-giving. Therefore, his semen and mind should be controlled and conserved.

Just as a man should be adept in the practice, the woman also has to be well practised and adept. There are few references in the hatha yoga texts specifying practices meant for women, but in *Hatha Yoga Pradipika* it is clearly stated (3:99):

पुंसो बिंदुं समाकुंच्य सम्यगभ्यासपाटवात् ।
यदि नारी रजो रक्षेद्वज्रोल्या सापि योगिनी ॥

If a woman practises vajroli and saves her rajas and the man's bindu by thorough contraction, she is a yogini.

Just as a man should practise gradual contractions of the urogenital muscles so should the woman. According to tantra that is sahajoli. *Hatharatnavali* states (2:93, 101–102):

सिंदूरसदृशं योनौ स्त्रीणामास्थायिकं रजः ।
ऋतुमत्या रजोऽप्येवं रजो बिंदु च रक्षयेत् ॥

ततः परं समर्थःस्यादूर्ध्वं आकुंचयेद्रजः ।
तस्याः शरीरे नादस्तु बिंदुतामेव गच्छति ॥

सबिंदुस्तद्रजश्चैव एकीकृत्य स्वदेहजौ ।
वज्रोल्यभ्यासयोगेन योगसिद्धिः करे स्थिता ॥

Rajas is permanent, like red lead, in the reproductive organ of a woman. The rajas should be saved during menstruation like bindu is to be saved. The woman should practise vajroli. After that she should draw up the rajas if possible. The nada in her body moves like bindu. Bindu and rajas produced in the body should be mixed through the vajroli practice of yoga. Then success is at hand.

71

Perfection of vajroli means being able to withdraw the seminal fluid during the height of climax. This involves the practice of contracting and controlling the muscles of the urogenital complex. Initially the muscles of the genital, excretory and urinary organs tend to contract simultaneously. The muscular contractions have to be isolated in three distinct areas. Eventually contractions become so forceful that upward suction is created. In the female body, the labia minora should move upwards with complete contraction. Practice of uddiyana bandha before vajroli creates greater suction and tighter contraction.

According to the *Shatkarma Sangraha*, there are seven practices of vajroli, although in general it can be said that there are two types; one is concerned with *maithuna*, sexual intercourse under prescribed conditions, and the other is a simple raja yoga form in which the urethra is contracted upward. It is the latter that is commonly taught and also used in kriya yoga.

The full practice involves years of preparation, which commences with the simple contraction of the urogenital muscles and later the sucking up of liquids. Only after the sixth practice is perfected can the seventh be successfully attempted by the yogi, that is, the practice included in maithuna, yogic intercourse.

Managing the mind

Release of reproductive secretions is not only a physiological process, the mind is also involved. Without mental involvement the release cannot occur. In vajroli, the role of sensory pathways, *jnanendriya*, and mental imagery in initiating sexual responses must be witnessed. Control of the mind begins by becoming aware of the process. By isolating awareness, the mind remains unexcited in the midst of sensory perception. When the mind can be witnessed in this way, excitation of the motor responses, *karmendriya*, can be controlled, and semen can be withheld. Control of the mind means control of the whole process.

By the practice of vajroli one can learn to control the physical mechanism but, alongside this, mental control must be developed. When the mind wanders in useless fantasy, energy is dissipated. When the mind is totally concentrated on a specific object, symbol or point, pranic movements are channelled and the bindu is maintained. In hatha yoga the mind has to be kept on the aim of the practices in order to induce total one-pointedness.

The sexual act is one means to totally concentrate and captivate the mind, but in tantra it should not be the ordinary experience. The experience has to be more than the gross or sensual one. Awareness and control have to be developed. The senses have to be used, but only as the means of awakening the higher consciousness, not the animal consciousness, and for this, the two mudras or other equivalent tantric practices must be perfected. Vajroli and sahajoli are perhaps the most powerful practices in the awakening of kundalini and higher consciousness. However, unless the practitioner maintains a sattwic state of awareness, they are useless.

Effects of vajroli and sahajoli

The purpose of vajroli and sahajoli mudras is to convert *retas*, sexual energy, into *ojas*, highly refined pranic or psychic energy. This process is called *urdhva retas*, the sublimation of sexual energy. Prana is the essence of both retas and ojas. Vajroli and sahajoli help to bring about sublimation of the grosser retas into the more refined ojas.

What this means is that sexual hormones and secretions are reassimilated into the body and the essence of the reproductive fluids, which is pure energy, is not wasted. Instead, it rises up to ajna, or even beyond to bindu, where it becomes more subtle, and combines with *anahad nada*, the unheard sound. As a result of this process, one becomes full of vitality, strength, confidence and brilliance. All the energy centres are stimulated, the sushumna nadi is awakened, the higher faculties of the brain are activated, and there is equilibrium in the mind and body. In fact, these mudras accelerate the rate of evolution. Due to the practice, the nervous input is not depleted, and the brain, which supplies energy to the sexual organs, is not drained of vitality. Thus, the energy level is higher after practising vajroli and sahajoli than it was before.

The outcome of the practices is the union of the negative and positive poles of energy within one's own body. It is not just a matter of control during maithuna that can awaken the higher centres. It is the appropriate combination of the opposite elements and energies. When hydrogen gas and oxygen combine there is an instant explosion. Similarly, in the physical body, when the positive and negative elements combine there is an explosion. When the union takes place in the nucleus of mooladhara chakra, kundalini shakti is released. At that time, if vajroli or sahajoli are practised, the energy rises up sushumna and the central nervous system to ajna chakra in the brain. The purpose of the practices is neither indulgence nor birth control, but they are specifically used to expand the consciousness. The experience has an impact that can last for hours, days or weeks. When the practices have been perfected, the expanded state of consciousness becomes a permanent experience.

In mundane life, the climax of sexual experience is one time when the mind becomes completely void of its own accord and consciousness beyond the body can be glimpsed. However, that experience is so short-lived because the energy is expressed through the lower energy centres. This energy, which is normally lost, is used in vajroli and sahajoli to awaken the dormant power of kundalini in mooladhara. When the sperm can be withheld, the energy can be channelized through sushumna nadi and the central nervous system, to the dormant areas of the brain and to the sleeping consciousness.

Tracing the bindu

The whole experience of vajroli can be understood from another perspective: that of bindu. As we saw in the last chapter, *bindu* is the drop of potential; it is the nectar of immortality, it is semen, and it is the essence of all

74

that is. During vajroli, it is not just the physical fluid that is withdrawn, but the esoteric bindu, and traced to its origin: a point in consciousness. The origin of bindu is not in the body, nor in the mind, but is experienced through the body and the mind. When mooladhara chakra awakens in maithuna, by performing vajroli the bindu of consciousness is raised, away from the sensual experiences. The manifestation of bindu is controlled, the experience is sustained and prolonged, and its source realized.

The bindu is the interface between matter, energy and consciousness. If one tries to focus one's awareness upon the experience in mooladhara, it is not just the semen that one is trying to isolate, or the consciousness, or the experience of energy that one is undergoing. It is the bindu, that is all. The bindu is withheld, withdrawn and redirected upwards by vajroli.

Where does the point of consciousness go when vajroli is performed? Does it retreat upward towards its source? Or was its source in mooladhara, and through vajroli it is being enticed to rise? Through vajroli, this bindu rises to ajna chakra. It manifests at the eyebrow centre and can be experienced at ajna. It is stated in *Hatha Yoga Pradipika* (3:100):

तस्या: किंचिद्रजो नाशं न गच्छति न संशय: ।
तस्या: शरीरे नादश्च बिंदुतामेव गच्छति ॥

Without doubt, not even a little rajas is wasted through vajroli, the nada and bindu in the body become one.

Ajna is not the source of bindu; however, through vajroli its form will manifest there. By sustaining vajroli, the bindu goes beyond ajna where it becomes subtler than audible sound or nada in the consciousness, *ashabda*. The sound, or *nada*, released from the chakras below ajna is traced back to its source where the bindu and nada are one. Its source is somewhere in the totality of consciousness; above, beyond and within; somewhere where the mind has dissolved and time and body cease to exist, where only consciousness remains in the form of soundless sound.

8

Necessity of Guru

Generally, a yoga practitioner will receive their first introduction to mudra in a meditation class when they are asked to adopt a hand mudra and hold it for the duration of the practice. For most people, their association with mudras begins and ends here, and at this level the practice does not make any significant demands on the practitioner. The rare few who wish to take to mudra sadhana, however, need to develop a very subtle level of perception and receive the practice from a guru. One can practise asana, pranayama or mudra through the means of books, but if one wants to progress further, a guru is necessary. Breath control is not the ultimate aim of pranayama. Divers can control their breath longer than any one of us, but they do not have awakened prana; that is an art, a science which has to be mastered. To reach such a level in one's practice, a guru is necessary every step of the way.

Necessity of guru

Mudra sadhana is a higher practice that leads to awakening of the pranas, chakras and kundalini, and which can bestow major *siddhis*, psychic powers, on the advanced practitioner. Thus, it should be introduced at the right stage of one's evolution and in a specific sequence. If this is not observed, it can induce opposite and negative effects instead of the desired ones. That is why this knowledge has always been

76

handed down directly from guru to disciple in its complete form.

When mudra or any other practice is passed on from the guru to disciple, it is able to bear fruit, as the guru's words are shakti that manifests in a concrete form. In *Hatha Yoga Pradīpika* it is written (3:129):

उपदेशं हि मुद्राणां यो दत्ते सांप्रदायिकम् ।
स एव श्रीगुरुः स्वामी साक्षादीश्वर एव सः ॥

One who instructs mudra in the tradition of guru and disciple is the true guru and form of Ishwara.

The external guru is the only means to understanding the internal guru. Of course, the inner guru, the *atman*, has no form or shape. However, in order to perceive it some form and identity must be assigned to it. Atman with form is known as Ishwara and guru is considered as the manifestation of Ishwara. Ishwara is commonly translated as God. To the yogi, however, *Ishwara* has no religious connotation; it is purely the highest state or experience. Sage Patanjali says in the *Yoga Sutras* (1:24):

क्लेशकर्मविपाकाशयैरपरामृष्टः पुरुषविशेष ईश्वरः ॥

Ishwara is a special soul untouched by afflictions, acts, their traces and their fruits.

That state of experience can be reached through guru, therefore it is said that guru is That. Externally, guru has a physical body, ego and mind just like anyone else, but the guru's individual consciousness is illumined by the light of atma. Guru has realized the inner guru. Therefore, by contemplating on guru's form and by following guru's words and instructions, that experience can also come to the seeker. For the disciple, the guru represents the supreme experience and existence, Ishwara.

Once the disciple has chosen the guru and the guru has recognized the disciple, only the meaning and application of the guru's advice and instructions, and the regularity of practice have utmost importance in the disciple's life. The interaction with the inner and outer personality of the guru is all-important in removing egocentricity. The deep-rooted and inherited *samskaras*, impressions, which stand as blockages to the greater flow of awareness and limit the expression of greater energy, must be systematically exposed and rooted out.

How is the guru to be approached? The disciple has to use any and every means to come closer to the light of the guru's awareness. One's aspirations and efforts will be noted by the guru, who will give specific cues that the disciple must be attuned to receive. There are two important capacities for an aspirant. One is the ability to discriminate and to recognize a fine guru and guide. The second is to surrender the ego and conditioning at the guru's feet. Aspirants who want to experience the greater consciousness have to submit their own psychophysiological personality before the guru. Only a fool will consent to an anaesthetic without trusting the surgeon. The guru-disciple relationship must be established by a process of trust and surrender if the practices are to bear the greatest fruit.

Attainment of siddhis

Hatha Yoga Pradipika indicates the necessity of the guru-disciple relationship in attaining siddhi and immortality through mudra practice (3:130):

तस्य वाक्यपरो भूत्वा मुद्राभ्यासे समाहित: ।
अणिमादिगुणै: सार्धं लभते कालवंचनम् ॥

By following explicitly his (guru's) words, and practising mudra, one obtains the qualities of anima, etc., and overcomes death/time.

Indeed, it is said that the perfection of asana and pranayama results in minor siddhis or perfections, such as vitality, good health, mental and emotional equilibrium, and clairaudience. However, perfection of mudras and bandhas results in the attainment of major siddhis such as *anima*, making the body small like an atom; *laghima*, making the body light; *mahima*, making the body large; *garima*, making the body heavy; *prapti*, capacity to reach anywhere; *prakamya*, unobstructed fulfilment of desire; *vashitva*, control over all objects; and *ishitva*, power to create and destroy.

It must be remembered, however, that siddhis of any kind are obstacles on the path to samadhi and can completely hinder one's spiritual evolution. Therefore, at this stage of sadhana the presence of the guru becomes that much more significant to safely steer one through the temptation to indulge in the siddhis.

Maintaining sanctity of commands

It is often stated that the instructions that a disciple receives from the guru are sacrosanct and they are not to be discussed with others. Every disciple is at their own level of evolution and what the guru advises is pertinent for that level. When you tell others what the guru has said to you, the energy, the *shakti* of that teaching becomes weak. Now the thoughts, emotions and beliefs of other people influence you, not the karma of the guru. Others have greater influence on you than the guru. Remember, the other disciples have received guru upadesha too. Let them follow their own instructions and guidance and you follow your own."

This is particularly relevant when it comes to higher sadhanas. Thus, *Hatha Yoga Pradipika* says of mudra (3:9):

गोपनीयं प्रयत्नेन यथा रत्नकरंडकम् ।
कस्यचिन्नैव वक्तव्यं कुलस्त्रीसुरतं यथा ॥

These must remain secret just like precious stones, and not be talked about to anyone, just as one does not tell others about his intimate relations with his wife.

The traditional texts repeatedly mention that the practices, the siddhis, or the sadhana should never be divulged to anyone. It is the guru's decision who should be given the knowledge. Indeed, the fact that it takes an incarnation of divinity itself to bestow the grace and instruction needed to unlock the secrets of mudra emphasizes the special powers of the practice. Clearly, there is more to mudras than can be learnt from books or the experience of others; the experience must be had for oneself.

Mudra Practice

9

Guidelines for Practice

Systematic approach
Even though most mudras are simple enough to be practised anytime, anywhere, to be able to tune into the subtlety of this science, a systematic and gradual approach is required when beginning the practice. Once proficiency has been acquired, one may use them in everyday situations to alter the state of body or mind. It must also be remembered that although some of the techniques are seemingly simple, many are strong pranic practices that have associated precautions, contra-indications and strict guidelines. Care is needed not to strain. In some cases the starting position is an advanced asana, and often there are a few techniques combined within one practice. In this case, the individual practices should be perfected before attempting the outlined technique. If these guidelines are not followed and there is an attempt to rush the process, the practices may not be effective or worse, undesirable results may arise, causing physical or mental imbalance.

Guidance
There are many nuances in the practice of mudras that cannot be described adequately in a book. Therefore, it is advised to seek proper guidance from a qualified teacher. Guidance of a guru is necessary for the more advanced practices of mudra, as discussed in Chapter 8.

Time of practice

Mudra sadhana should ideally be practised in the early morning, preferably between the hours of four and six, or during the hours before sunrise. At this time, the body and mind are calm and refreshed after sleep, and the pranas are balanced and ready to awaken. The mudras having a calming effect are beneficial to practise at night.

Place

As with any yoga practice, the place of sadhana should be calm and peaceful where one will not be disturbed. It should be somewhat isolated, away from people, noise and interruptions. One may practise in the open air or in a well-ventilated, clean and pleasant room. Avoid practising in the sun or wind. The soft rays of the early morning sun are beneficial; however, when they become stronger, the body may become overheated. Practising in a draught or wind may cause chills and upset the body temperature. Nevertheless, as mudras can be used to overcome mental and emotional states such as of anxiety and anger, they can be practised discreetly anywhere and at anytime.

Posture

Unless specifically stated otherwise, mudras may be practised in a comfortable meditation posture or lying in shavasana. While lying in shavasana, it may be necessary to place a thin padding under the head so that the neck and back of the head are comfortable.

Clothing

If clothing is worn during the practice, it should be loose and comfortable so there is no constriction. The clothing, blanket, pillow, mat and so forth should all be of a natural fibre, such as cotton or wool; synthetic fabrics and rubber are not good conductors of prana, therefore foam or plastic-coated mats are not recommended.

84

10

Hasta Mudra: Hand Mudras

The human hand is the most perfect instrument nature has made. It is so perfect that modern science, with all its technology, biomechanics, computer science and medicine, is still not able to design an adequate replacement for it. Complex and coordinated function of numerous tiny muscles in the hand is controlled by a large area in the motor cortex area of the brain. These muscles have a rich supply of motor neural endings, which enables them to perform very precise and complicated movements. The hand is also rich in sensory neural endings; there are numerous receptors of various kinds constantly emitting sensory impulses towards the higher structures of the nervous system.

Out of the fourteen acupuncture meridians, six have their points of origin or end on the fingertips: the lung meridian is located on the thumbs; the large intestine meridian at the tip of the index fingers; the heart constrictor vessel at the tip of the middle fingers; the triple heater meridian on the ring fingers; and the small intestine and heart meridian on the little fingers. These meridians also have other points along the fingers, palms and backs of the hands. Many of these are subject to stimulation in hand mudras. All this makes the hand a potent instrument for pranic interaction and communication, healing and many other processes.

The hand mudras presented in this chapter are meditative mudras. They redirect the prana emitted by the hands back into the body. This generates a loop of energy that moves from the brain down to the hand and then back again. Conscious awareness of this process rapidly leads to internalization. For meditation, the first stage is to adopt a comfortable meditative asana. Once the body and mind are relaxed, the awareness shifts to the hands placed in the chosen mudra. Holding the awareness on the mudra facilitates the process of internalization and provides the subtle change in perception that is needed for the practice of meditation. Techniques included in this category are:

- Jnana mudra (attitude of knowing)
- Chinmudra (attitude of consciousness)
- Yoni mudra (gesture of the source)
- Bhairava mudra (fierce or terrifying attitude)
- Hridaya mudra (heart gesture)
- Chinmaya mudra (attitude of supreme intelligence)
- Aadi mudra (primal or first gesture)
- Brahma mudra (attitude of all-pervading consciousness)

JNANA MUDRA (attitude of knowing) and
CHINMUDRA (attitude of consciousness)

The word *jnana* means intuitive knowledge, and *jnana mudra* is the gesture of intuitive knowledge. According to one of the dhyana slokas of the *Bhagavad Gita*:

प्रपन्नपारिजाताय तोत्रवेत्रैकपाणये ।
ज्ञानमुद्राय कृष्णाय गीतामृतदुहे नमः ॥

Salutations to Krishna, the bestower of all desires for those who take refuge in Him, who holds the whip in one hand and the other in jnana mudra, who distils the nectar of the *Bhagavad Gita*.

Sri Krishna was in the pose of jnana mudra while bestowing the knowledge of the *Bhagavad Gita* to Arjuna during the battle of the Mahabharata. Thus, jnana mudra is known as the mother of the great knowledge of the *Bhagavad Gita*.

The word 'chin' is derived from *chit* or *chitta*, which means 'consciousness', therefore *chinmudra* is the attitude of chitta or consciousness. Both mudras are most commonly used during the practices of meditation.

These hand mudras are not only very comfortable for meditative practices, but they also have various symbolic meanings. The three open fingers in jnana mudra and chinmudra represent the three gunas: sattwa, rajas and tamas. *Sattwa guna* represents qualities such as understanding and purity; *rajoguna* represents action, passion and movement; and *tamoguna* includes such qualities as inertia, laziness, darkness and ignorance. It is these three gunas to which the mind is always subjected. These three states have to be transcended in order to pass from ignorance to knowledge.

The index finger represents the individual consciousness, *jivatma*, and the thumb represents the spirit of all-pervading consciousness or reality. The index finger is folded into the root of the thumb, symbolizing the individual bowing down to Supreme Consciousness and acknowledging its unsurpassed power. At the same time, the index finger and the thumb touch each other, which shows that though they seem separate, the individual being is one with the Supreme. It symbolizes union, the culmination of yoga. The other three fingers are separated, symbolizing the separation between the individual consciousness and the three gunas of prakriti. Thus, separation of individual consciousness from the three gunas of empirical existence and its union with the Supreme Consciousness is the attitude a yogi adopts during the practice of chinmudra or jnana mudra.

Technique: Jnana mudra

Assume a comfortable meditation posture.
Fold the index fingers of both hands so that they touch the inside root of the thumbs.

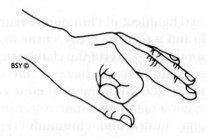

Straighten the other three fingers of each hand so they are relaxed and slightly apart.
Place the hands on the knees with the palms facing down.
Relax the hands and arms.
Folding the thumb over the index finger helps to retain the mudra.

Technique: Chinmudra

This mudra is very similar to jnana mudra, only the position of the hands is reversed, the backs of the hands being placed on top of the knees with the palms upward.

Variation: Jnana mudra and chinmudra are often performed with the tip of the thumb and index finger touching and forming a circle. Beginners may find this variation less secure for prolonged periods of meditation, as the thumb and index finger tend to separate more easily when body awareness is lost. Otherwise, this variation is as effective as the basic position.

Sequence: One of these two mudras should be adopted whenever practising meditation, unless otherwise specified.

Practice note: The effect of chinmudra or jnana mudra is very subtle and it requires great sensitivity on the part of the practitioner to perceive the change in consciousness established. With practice, however, the mind becomes conditioned to the mudra and when it is adopted, the signal to enter a meditative state is transmitted.

Benefits: Jnana mudra and chinmudra are simple but important psychoneural finger locks that make meditation asanas more powerful. The palms and fingers of the hands have many nerve root endings, which constantly emit energy. When the index finger touches the thumb, a circuit is produced that allows the energy that would normally dissipate into the environment to travel back through the body and up to the brain. When the fingers and hands are placed on the knees, the knees are sensitized, creating another pranic circuit that maintains and redirects prana within the body. In addition, placing the hands on the knees stimulates a nadi that runs from the knees, up the inside of the thighs and into the perineum. This nadi is known as *gupta* or the hidden nadi. Sensitizing this channel helps to stimulate the energies at mooladhara chakra. When the palms face upward in chinmudra, there is a slight stimulation of the nerves along the inside of the upper arms which helps to open up the lungs and chest cavity. When we begin to breathe in and out more easily, it is easier to control the mind. The practitioner may experience this as a sense of lightness and receptivity, which is absent in the practice of jnana mudra. Breathing also relates to the different mental moods, which can be controlled by regulating the breath.

Meridian effects: While performing jnana mudra and chinmudra, the energy flowing along the lung meridians to the thumb is transferred to the large intestine meridian. A link is created between the lung and large intestine meridians by connecting the point 'LI 1', on the tip of the index finger, to the point 'Lu 10', at the root of the thumb. In the variation of this mudra, in which the tip of the index finger joins to the tip of the thumb, point 'LI 1' is joined to the point 'Lu 11', at the tip of the thumb.

In the yin-yang relationship, the large intestine and lung meridians are coupled, respectively, so that the natural flow of energy, or prana, which goes from the lung to the large intestine meridian is enhanced in this mudra. According to yogic science, the lungs and the large intestine are two main areas where absorption of prana takes place. Therefore, by increasing the flow in their respective meridians, the body's vital energy is conserved and an overall increase in energy charge is experienced in the body and mind, enabling the practitioner to engage in meditative practice with a higher energy level. Stimulation of the lung meridian results in increased awareness, vitality and the ability to remain detached whatever the circumstances may be. The large intestine is facilitates detoxification on all levels. Physical, mental and emotional wastes are eliminated and deeper meditative states become gradually more accessible.

Chinmudra is also said to have an influence on abdominal breathing, and here it can be seen that there is a pranic connection between the lungs and abdomen through their respective meridians. In chinmudra, the hands are placed in the supine position, wherebythe inside of the upper arms, where the lung meridian travels, is gently stretched. This additional stimulation of the proximal portion of the lung meridian close to the chest helps to open up the area and induces a slightly deeper breathing pattern.

The hands press the kidney meridian at the point 'K 10' at the medial side of the knee; and the same meridian is stretched in the section that runs along the inner thighs. The kidney meridian intersects the governing meridian at the point 'GV 1' at the tip of the coccyx, indirectly spreading excitation into the governing meridian which runs through the perineal body, and stimulates mooladhara and swadhisthana chakras.

90

YONI MUDRA (gesture of the source)

According to *Kularnava Tantra,* Parvati asks Lord Shiva to explain the meaning of the 'names', such as guru, acharya, swami, yogi and yogini. In describing a yogi and yogini, Lord Shiva says (17: 21, 31):

योनिमुद्रानुसंधानात् प्रस्फुरंमंत्रवैभवात् ।
गीर्बाणगणपूज्यत्वाद्योगीति कथित: प्रिये ॥

Because he throbs with the glory of the mantra due to the practice of yoni mudra, and because he is adorable by the host of the gods (Girvana Gana) he is a yogi.

योनिमुद्रानुसंधानात् गिरिजापादसेवनात् ।
निर्लीनोपाधिबिभवाद् योगिनीत्यभिधीयते ॥

Because she practices the yoni mudra, attends upon the feet of Girija (the Divine Mother) and because of the glory of the total immersion without support, she is called a yogini.

The word *yoni* means 'womb' or 'source'. Therefore, *yoni mudra* is the attitude by which one invokes the primal energy inherent in the womb or source of creation.

Technique

Assume a comfortable meditation posture with the head and spine straight.

Place the palms of the hands together with the fingers

91

and thumbs straight and pointing away from the body.
Keep the pads of the index fingers together so that these two fingers form a triangle.
Turn the little, ring and middle fingers inwards so that the backs of the fingers are touching.
Interlock the little, ring and middle fingers.
Bring the thumbs towards the body and join the pads of the fingers and thumbs together to form the base of a yoni or womb shape.

Variation: Yoni mudra may also be performed by interlocking the middle, ring and little fingers without turning them inward. The thumbs may be crossed in front of the outstretched index fingers, or outstretched with the pads touching towards the body.

Benefits: The interlocking of the fingers in this practice creates a complete cross-connection of energies from the right hand into the left and vice versa. As well as balancing the energies in the body, it helps to balance the activities of the right and left hemispheres of the brain. Placing the tips of the index fingers and thumbs together further intensifies the flow of prana. This mudra makes the body and mind more stable in meditation and develops greater concentration, awareness and internal physical relaxation. It redirects prana back into the body, which would otherwise be dispersed through the hands and fingers. The elbows naturally tend to point to the side when performing this mudra which helps open up the chest area.

Meridian effects: In this mudra, all six meridians that end or start at the fingertips of one hand are joined to their symmetrical counterparts on the other hand so that the flow of the energy in the left and right side of the body is balanced. This leads to a balanced state of body and mind. The left lung meridian controls the flow in the right nostril, and the right lung meridian controls the flow in the left nostril. They are joined together when the thumbs touch each other, which equalizes the flow in both nostrils. This balances the flow of ida and pingala and the activity of both hemispheres of the brain.

All yin and yang meridians running along the arms and hands, which total six on each side of the body, are mutually connected in this mudra. Dissipation of energy through their end points is prevented, and the augmented flow of Qi is redirected primarily into the regions of the heart, head and brain, enhancing the mental power needed to achieve a meditative state, and simultaneously nourishing the heart space where the spiritual source resides and where it is to be realized.

In the variation of yoni mudra, the palmar (yin) sides of fingers are brought in close contact with the back side (yang) of fingers. This promotes harmony between yin and yang.

BHAIRAVA MUDRA (fierce or terrifying attitude)

According to the *Sri Vijnana Bhairava Tantra*, Bhairava is one of the forms of Shiva, and is said to be frightening and formidable. He is often depicted dancing in the cremation grounds, looking wild and fearsome. The consort of Shiva is Shakti. In this case Shakti is called Bhairavi, representing the power that manifests this particular aspect of existence. In the *Yajurveda*, a splendid hymn known as *Rudri* is entirely devoted to this *deva* or divine form, where he is named as the one who presides over the eight quarters of space and as the lord who protects. These eight quarters or directions of space are extremely important in any tantric sadhana or esoteric practice. If they are not taken care of, hindrances may occur. It is for this purpose that Rudra manifested as eight Bhairavas so that each quarter of space would be protected for the sadhaka who endeavours to enter the realm of transcendence. Bhairava acts as the guardian of the aspirant. Bhairava is also regarded as one of the violent forms of Shiva, associated with his fights against demons. The term 'demon' is used to personify characteristics or traits that one encounters on one's journey from gross to subtle spheres of consciousness.

In reality, the essence of Bhairava is not the nine forms. The state of Bhairava is immeasurable. One can have this inner experience for oneself when the mind is free from modifications or thought patterns. The atman of Bhairava, which is known as Bhairavi, is then experienced as the bliss of one's own inner awareness, a state whose form is fullness, free from all contradiction, which is the abode of the entire universe. There is an intimate relationship between Bhairava, the Supreme Awareness, and its cosmic counterpart, Bhairavi, the Supreme Energy. They are prakasha and vimarsha. Bhairava is *prakasha*, light, and Bhairavi is *vimarsha*, vibration and *nada*, sound. Together they give rise to the manifest phenomena through their interplay.

For the purpose of pranayama and meditation practice, this is a particularly comfortable mudra. What is easier than placing the hands one on top of the other in the lap, while sitting in a meditational asana? It is a mudra that people do almost automatically. It calms the nerves, introverts the mind, increases concentration and enhances meditation. It is also the mudra used to invoke energy in the practice of prana mudra (see Chapter 14).

Technique

Assume a comfortable meditation posture with the head and spine straight.

Place the right hand on top of the left, so that the palms of both hands are facing upward.

Both hands rest in the lap.

94

Close the eyes and relax the whole body, keeping it motionless.

Variation: When the left hand is placed on top of the right, the practice is called bhairavi mudra. Another variation mentioned in some texts is to touch the tips of the thumbs together.

Meridian effects: The yin meridians of the arm that run along the palm and palmar side of the fingers are the lung, pericardium and heart meridians. The yang meridians that run along the back of the hand and dorsal side of the fingers are the large intestine, triple burner and small intestine. The yang, or dorsal side of the right hand is resting on the yin, the palmar side of the left hand, connecting and balancing these two forces.

The position of the hands and fingers also create a link between the symmetrical meridians on the left and right sides of the body. For example, the left lung meridian is connected to the right lung meridian. This gently rectifies any imbalance between the left and right side of the body, induces a calm state of mind and smooth functioning of these important internal organs.

HRIDAYA MUDRA (heart gesture)

Hridaya mudra, or heart gesture, stimulates a nadi that affects the heart function. Many people suffering from heart problems practise this heart mudra every day and are benefited by it. The purpose of mudras is to awaken the nadis, to channel the flow of energy in a particular way so that it is not lost and a specific benefit is derived. In this mudra, energy is directed along a particular nadi that flows to the heart.

Technique

Sit in any comfortable meditation asana with the head and spine straight.

95

Place the tips of the index fingers at the root of the thumbs, as in chin and jnana mudras, and join the tips of the middle and ring fingers to the tips of the thumbs. The little finger remains straight.

Place the hands on the knees with the palms facing upward.

Close the eyes and relax the whole body, keeping it motionless.

BSY©

Awareness: Physical – on the breath in the chest area. Spiritual – on anahata chakra.

Duration: This practice may be performed for up to 30 minutes.

Variation: There is a variation, known as mritasanjivani mudra, in which the index finger is placed on the ball (the fleshy part of the palm at the bottom of the thumb), rather than at the root, of the thumb. All other aspects of the mudra are the same.

Benefits: This mudra diverts the flow of prana from the hands to the heart area, improving the vitality of the heart. The middle and ring fingers relate directly to nadis connected with the heart, while the thumb closes the pranic circuit and acts as an energizer, diverting the flow of prana from the hands to these nadis. Hridaya mudra is therefore beneficial for the heart. It is very simple and may be used safely and easily, even in acute situations. The heart is the centre of emotion. Hridaya mudra helps to release pent-up emotions and unburden the heart. It may be practised during emotional conflict and crisis.

Meridian effects: On the tips of the thumb, middle and ring finger are the acupuncture points 'Lu 11', 'Pc 9' and 'TB 1', belonging to the lung, pericardium and triple burner meridians, respectively. These points are joined together in hridaya mudra. In acupuncture they are used to restore consciousness and vital functions of the body in emergency situations. They are also used to calm the mind, revitalize body and mind, and treat headaches. Point 'LI 1' of the large intestine meridian on the tip of the index finger has similar properties and is being stimulated by pressing the tip of the index finger to the root of the thumb.

Pericardium meridian is stimulated through 'Pc 9' on the tip of the middle finger. Pericardium is the envelope of the heart, which has important functions in acupuncture physiology. One of them is to act as a protector of the heart, both in the physical and psychological sense. Physically, it controls the aorta from which the coronary arteries that nourish the heart muscles originate, as well as major blood and lymphatic vessels. Chinese medicine says that psychologically, the heart is the seat of the spirit and of emotions. In this sense, according to acupuncture science, hridaya mudra has a regulative effect on the heart on both levels, physical and psychological. That is why it is effective in preventing and aborting angina and in releasing charged emotions.

The triple burner meridian is also joined as a part of the quadrilateral circuit created by bringing the four fingers together in hridaya mudra. It is stimulated and exchanges energy through the point 'TB 1' on the tip of the ring finger. The upper burner, the upper third of the triple burner as an organ, governs the functions of the heart and the lungs. This is another route through which the heart gets energy in this mudra. Both the pericardium and the triple burner meridian, which belong to the 'extraordinary' organs with no material form, have an important overall balancing role in the body, which is of great medical significance in acupuncture. Both meridians are activated in hridaya mudra.

The heart meridian is stretched in the section that runs along the palm and little finger, when this finger is kept straight, as opposed to the other four fingers, which are folded. This contrast of the position of the little finger, which carries the heart meridian itself, can be understood in two ways, according to Chinese medicine. The first is that this opening of the heart meridian serves the purpose of opening the heart itself to receive the energy that is being generated by the mudra. The second is that the outstretched position of the little finger enables a negative energetic charge, in the form of positive ions, to be released from the heart meridian and its corresponding organ, the heart, which is then replaced by new energy created by the mudra.

CHINMAYA MUDRA (attitude of manifested consciousness)

The Sanskrit word *chinmaya* means 'manifested consciousness'; in other words, the phenomenal world that has arisen from the underlying consciousness. The four folded fingers in chinmaya mudra represent the finite aspects of the world. The closed fist shows that the phenomenal world seems to be severely limited, blind and unconscious. The thumb pointing forwards indicates the consciousness and the transcendental aspect of existence that pervades everything. It is often regarded as different or separate from the material world, yet it is really identical with and permeated with consciousness. The material world is linked intimately with consciousness. This is indicated by the contact between the index finger and the thumb.

Furthermore, the folded fingers represent the physical, energetic and mental aspects of life. This is not the complete picture of a human being, for there is also the consciousness. These aspects are intimately linked, yet it is the consciousness that is transcendental and capable of contacting infinity and the whole. This is indicated by the thumb, which points away

98

from the finitude symbolized by the four fingers. Thus the mudra symbolizes yoga: the realization that the individual, represented by the four fingers, is identical to and connected directly with consciousness.

The four fingers can also represent the gradual unfolding of higher states of awareness. That is, the little, ring and middle fingers represent different facets of the material world, from stones and trees to animals and birds, all becoming increasingly sentient. Eventually there is humanity, which appears to be no more than mind and body, yet it is humans alone who can develop the awareness to recognize the integral identity with consciousness. This is shown by the joining of the thumb and index finger.

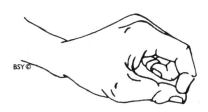

Technique

Assume a meditation asana.

Relax into the posture.

Hold the fingers in the same way as for jnana mudra.

Fold the three straightened fingers so that the tips touch or point towards the palm.

The index finger can either touch the root or the tip of the thumb.

Place the hands on the knees with the palms facing either up or down.

Benefits: This mudra influences prana and stimulates movement in the thoracic area, affecting respiration. It helps ventilate the middle lobes of the lungs and is used in hasta mudra pranayama (see Chapter 16). Energy is directed into the area of samana and prana between the navel and the throat.

Meridian effects: This mudra brings harmony between the yin and yang meridians that run along the arm; yin that projects inward is protected within the fist by folded fingers, and yang that tends to project outward is exposed on the outstretched outer surface of the hand. Thus the natural harmony between yin and yang, introversion and extroversion, is enhanced.

Points 'H 9' and 'H 8' are joined together by the little finger pressing the palm. In this mudra, the pericardium meridian envelops this portion of the heart meridian, on the outer surface of ring finger, protecting it in the same way as it does with the heart as an organ. The heart and pericardium meridians, which receive an additional energy charge in this mudra, are closely related to the brain and harmonize the central nervous system. Hence, a state conducive for meditation and expansion of consciousness is induced.

Deep, relaxed abdominal breath is enhanced by joining index finger and thumb, enhancing the energy loop of the natural transfer of Qi from the lung meridian to the large intestine meridian through their terminal and beginning points on these two fingers respectively. Relaxed breathing contributes to the steady flow of prana in the nadis in the thoracic area; this being the area that receives energy supply from the lung, pericardium and heart meridians which are stimulated in this mudra.

In addition, stimulation of the lung meridian results in increased awareness, vitality and the ability to remain detached. Stimulation of the large intestine meridian leads to a more efficient detoxifying action on all levels; physical, mental and emotional wastes are eliminated. The end result is that in the new state of harmony that arises deeper meditative states are easier to achieve.

In this mudra, the hands rest on the knees, pressing the point 'K 10' on the kidney meridian, which in turn has an internal connecting branch to the starting point 'GV 1' of the governing meridian. This meridian conducts the upward flow of energy from its origin in the perineal body, in the location of mooladhara chakra, up through the central spinal canal that corresponds to sushumna nadi, all the way to the top of the head, in the location of sahasrara chakra which is responsible for the expansion of human consciousness into transcendental realms.

AADI MUDRA (primal or first gesture)

This is the first mudra that human beings perform in the course of life; a newborn baby spontaneously holds the hands in aadi mudra.

Technique
> Assume a meditation asana.
> Relax into the posture.
> Fold the thumb into the palms of the hands; then slowly curl each finger over the thumb to make a fist.
> Place the hand on the knees with the palms either up or down.

Benefits: This mudra influences upper chest breathing and ventilates the upper lobes of the lungs, moving energy to the region of udana in the neck and head. At birth, the baby's diaphragm is weak, and breathing happens primarily in the thoracic area through the use of the intercostal muscles of the chest. This mudra enhances naturally the predominant thoracic breath and stimulates both prana and udana. The latter governs the function and development of sense organs which in this stage of life need to undergo fast and intense development. Harmonizing the function of sense organs has a calming effect on the nervous system. This mudra also increases the capacity of the upper lobes of the lungs. The leak, or loss of prana through palms and fingertips, which in open hands is substantial, is almost completely prevented.

Meridian effects: The distal portions of the heart and pericardium meridians, which run along the palmar side of the little and middle finger, envelop the distal portion of the lung meridian, which runs along the palmar side of the thumb. Transfer of Qi or prana between these meridians is stimulated and energy loss prevented. Hence, the function of the lungs is enhanced, especially in the upper lobes which receive an energy supply primarily from distal portions of the lung meridian. One of the important functions of the heart and pericardium organs, which is the maintenance of mental and emotional stability, clarity and harmony, is strengthened and exerts a soothing influence on the mind.

BRAHMA MUDRA (attitude of all-pervading consciousness)

In this mudra, an intimate relationship is experienced between the thumb, representing the Supreme Consciousness, and the four fingers, representing different levels of the individual existence. The fingers cover the thumb, yet the thumb exerts a strong influence on the fingers by keeping them connected with itself. This signifies that all dimensions of the individual being are being guided by the Supreme Consciousness, thus it is called the attitude of all-pervading consciousness.

Technique
Assume a meditation asana.
Relax into the posture.

Turn the thumbs inward across the palms and fold the fingers over the thumbs.

Then place the back of the hands on the thighs and bring the knuckles of the hands together.

The thumb side of the hand is away from the body; the fingernails are visible; the little finger side of the hand is close to the body.

Place both hands close against the body at the level of the pelvic bone.

Benefits: Brahma mudra stimulates full, deep yogic breathing, enhancing the movement of the diaphragm, chest and collarbones, and is very useful especially in pre-pranayama practices. All five elements, represented by five fingers, are brought together in one harmonious unit and their vibrancy in both the left and right side of the body is equalized by bringing both hands together. Pressing the hands against the pubic bone redirects pranic flow upward along the spine from the two lower chakras up to the higher ones. The flow of vyana is stimulated.

Meridian effects: As in aadi mudra, all three yin meridians in the hands, the heart, pericardium and lung, are stimulated. In addition, all three yang meridians, the large and small intestine and triple burner that run along the outer surface of index, little and ring finger respectively, are also stimulated by pressing the knuckles of both hands together, and resting the back of the hands in the lap. The loss of Qi through the distal acupuncture points located at the tips of the fingers is prevented, and the flow of both yin and yang energy is equalized and stimulated. In addition, by joining the knuckles of both hands together, this harmonizing effect on the yin and yang energies spreads to affect both the left and right side of the body, equalizing the energy field in the whole body. Pressure exerted by the hands on the pubic bone activates acupuncture point 'CV 6', whose Chinese name 'Qi Hai' translates as 'The Sea of Qi' and which is one of the main toning points in the body. It is used to boost the vital energy or electromagnetic field of the whole body, which corresponds to the enhancement of the flow of vyana in the yogic model.

11

Shirsha Mudra: Head Mudras

According to acupuncture, the head is the area where all the yang meridians meet. All yin meridians have their openings in specific sense organs, and all of them are represented on the surface of the tongue also. Thus, the concentration of acupuncture points on the head is very high. All this forms the basic foundation of the effectiveness of head mudras. Shirsha mudras form an integral part of kundalini yoga and many are meditation techniques in their own right.

Head mudras utilize the eyes, ears, nose, tongue and lips. Many of these practices, especially those involving the eyes and tongue, stretch the surrounding muscles in a way that does not normally occur throughout the day. Thus, extreme care should be taken not to strain. Mudras work on many different levels, physically and psychologically, and it is imperative that such practices are performed with patience and in a relaxed manner. A systematic approach should be adopted so that the preparatory and gentler techniques are perfected before moving on to more advanced practices. Generally, only one new mudra is practised and integrated at a time into a balanced sadhana program, under the guidance of a qualified teacher. Techniques included in the head mudras are:

- Shambhavi mudra (gesture of eyebrow centre gazing)
- Nasikagra drishti / Agochari mudra (gesture of nose tip gazing)

- Khechari mudra (gesture of the tongue lock)
- Akashi mudra (gesture of the inner space)
- Manduki mudra (frog gesture)
- Kaki mudra (crow's beak gesture)
- Bhujangini mudra (gesture of cobra respiration)
- Bhoochari mudra (gesture of gazing at nothingness)
- Shanmukhi mudra (gesture of closing of the six gates)
- Unmani mudra (the attitude of mindlessness)

SHAMBHAVI MUDRA (gesture of eyebrow centre gazing)

Shambhavi is the name of the wife or consort of Shambhu, Shiva. She has many other names, such as Parvati, Shakti, and so on, all of which have special significance in Indian mythology. It is believed that Shambhu taught Shambhavi the practice of shambhavi mudra and urged her to practise it diligently if she wanted to attain higher awareness. It is said that the practice of shambhavi mudra will stir Shambhu, the Superconsciousness, and make him appear before the sadhaka.

The practice is also known as *bhrumadhya drishti*. The word *bhrumadhya* means 'eyebrow centre', and *drishti* means 'gazing'. This name describes the practice exactly: eyebrow centre gazing. This practice, like agochari mudra, is widely quoted in the yogic scriptures. For example, the *Gheranda Samhita* states (3:76):

नेत्रान्तरं समालोक्य चात्मारामं निरीक्षयेत् ।
सा भवेच्छाम्भवीमुद्रा सर्वतन्त्रेषुगोपिता ॥

Direct your eyes towards the middle of the eyebrows. Reflect on your real nature. This is shambhavi mudra, the most secret of all tantric scriptures.

The same text devotes the next few verses to showering praise on this mudra. Among other things it says (3:78):

स एव ह्यादिनाथश्च स च नारायण: स्वयम् ।
स च ब्रह्मा सृष्टिकारी यो मुद्रां वेत्ति शाम्भवीम् ॥

106

The man who diligently practises and knows shambhavi mudra becomes Lord Shiva himself. He becomes Narayana (Vishnu), the sustainer of all and also Brahma, the creator of the universe.

This infers that by practising shambhavi mudra for a sufficiently long period of time, one can transcend the fetters of the individual ego. Gradually there is withdrawal of the individual awareness. As the individual awareness withdraws, the higher, expanded awareness takes its place. In this way, one sees the significance and essence behind everything, and realizes that one's real nature is far more than can normally be conceived.

Though this technique is called a mudra, it is also a meditative practice in its own right. The practitioner can perform shambhavi mudra, or agochari mudra, for a prolonged period of time to gain the same benefits and experiences as other meditational techniques. Shambhavi mudra should be practised after mastering agochari mudra, as it is a little more difficult. The ability to perform nose tip gazing helps in gaining proficiency in gazing at the eyebrow centre. If necessary, repeat the method that is described for nose tip gazing before moving on to the next practice.

Method of converging the eyes
Place one finger at the tip of the nose.
Focus both eyes on the fingertip.
Slowly move the finger upwards keeping the eyes 'glued' to the fingertip.
If this is done properly, shambhavi mudra can be practised quite easily. The eyes will automatically be drawn upwards to focus on the eyebrow centre.

Internal shambhavi mudra
When shambhavi mudra has been mastered with the eyes open, the same practice can be attempted with the eyes

closed. It is a more powerful practice, for the awareness is less likely to be externalized. It is an excellent method of introspection. The only drawback is that it is far easier to relax the eyes and stop doing shambhavi mudra without realizing it. In the external form of shambhavi, one can easily tell if the eyes are directed upwards or not by noting the V formation at the eyebrow centre. In the inner form, one must always be aware of the practice to ensure that the eyes are still facing upwards.

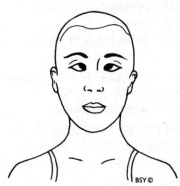

Technique
Stage 1: With normal breathing
Sit in a comfortable meditation posture.
Straighten the back and head.
Place the hands on the knees in chinmudra or jnana mudra.
Close the eyes for a short time and relax the whole body.
Relax all the muscles of the face, including the forehead, eyes and behind the eyes.
Breathe normally for the duration of the practice.
Slowly open the eyes and look straight ahead at a fixed point.
Fix the head in that position.
Then look upward and inward.
Try to focus both eyes at the eyebrow centre.
If this is done correctly, two curved images of the eyebrows can be seen, which merge with each other at the centre,

forming a V-shaped point at the root of the nose.

The head should not move.

Be aware of the V-shaped formation, which is the approximate location of the eyebrow centre.

If this V formation is not seen, it is a sure indication that the eyes are not converging as they should.

When a strain is felt, close the eyes for a few moments and relax them.

Then resume the practice.

Do not strain the eyes.

Initially the eye muscles will begin to feel strained after a few seconds. Therefore, each round should be performed for a short period only.

Practise 10 to 15 rounds.

Stage 2: With coordinated breathing

After mastering the eye movement, try to coordinate the movement of the eyes with the breath.

Breathe in slowly and look up and in towards the eyebrow centre.

Then breathe out slowly and lower the gaze.

Practise 15 to 20 rounds.

Stage 3: With kumbhaka

Once the eye movement is coordinated with the breath, gradually train the eye muscles to remain in shambhavi without any kind of eye tension.

Continue coordinating the eye movement with the breath.

Retain the breath either inside or outside, maintaining shambhavi mudra for the duration of the retention.

The head should remain straight throughout the practice.

Practise 10 to 15 rounds.

Stage 4: The five dharanas

There are five levels of experience in shambhavi, according to the vedantic approach, through which the image of the self is developed.

These experiences manifest as each stage is perfected.

This kind of imagination or visualization also helps to focus the mind to a greater extent, so that sublimation can take place.

The normal thoughts, ideas and visions, which constantly distract the concentration, must be eliminated so that a different kind of experience can arise. In the first visualization, or dharana, concentrate on the entire body in the form of agni, fire.

The whole body is to be viewed as an agni mandala.

Feel the body as fire.

This is not just a visual or mental imagination, but a sensorial experience.

The flames and heat can be experienced along the spine and the front of the body.

The different experiences of fire must be felt in the body. In the second dharana, concentration is on surya mandala.

Here the image of the sun is visualized in shambhavi mudra at the point between the eyebrows.

In the third dharana, the awareness is of chandra mandala, which is also called ajna mandala.

Here the symbol of ajna chakra is visualized at the gazing point in shambhavi.

In the fourth dharana, one visualizes light at the centre of ajna chakra.

This light does not radiate any sensation of heat or coolness. It is pure, white light.

In the fifth dharana, visualization is of lightning within the white light.

These are the five levels of experience in shambhavi mudra.

Start with 5 rounds and gradually increase to 10 rounds over a period of months.

Precautions: The eyes are very sensitive and consequently the final position should not be held for too long. If the nerves are weak, any strain can cause retinal detachment. Release the position when strain is experienced.

Contra-indications: People suffering from glaucoma should not practise this mudra. Those with diabetic retinopathy or those who have just had cataract surgery, lens implant or any other eye operation, should not perform shambhavi without the guidance of a competent teacher.

Practice note: In order to master shambhavi mudra, practise trataka. Trataka is not merely gazing at one point, although in the beginning the eyes must be kept fixed on something. Gradually the eyes become concentrated at the mid-eyebrow centre and shambhavi mudra develops, bringing ida, pingala and sushumna into union and triggering the flow of kundalini energy.

Benefits: Due to the different stages of experience that can be attained by this practice, it is highly regarded in all yogic, tantric and vedantic texts. It has been stated that one who becomes proficient in this technique can awaken ajna chakra. This enables one to transcend the faculties of the lower mind and establish oneself in higher consciousness. The physical benefits are strengthening of the eye muscles and gradual release of the tension that accumulates in the nerves and muscles of the eyes. Mentally there is reduction of anxiety, anger, worry and emotional stress. It is easier to achieve concentration, mental stability and the state of thoughtlessness by this practice than by other techniques for controlling the mind.

Meridian effects: The gaze and concentration are directed to the eyebrow centre where an extraordinary point is located. The Chinese name for this point is *Yintang*, and it translates to 'seal of the hall'. The term 'seal' is also used to define mudra. 'Hall' may be correlated with chidakasha, the space of *chitta*. Chidakasha is also defined as the dark space in front of the closed eyes. In the practice of shambhavi mudra, when the eyes are closed, it is on this space that the practitioner meditates. In some acupuncture texts, this point is connected with the possibility of inner vision. Otherwise, this point is used in the treatment of tension headaches, because it relieves tension and calms the spirit, dizziness, vertigo, hay fever, insomnia, etc.

Certain points of the urinary bladder, stomach and gallbladder meridians are located in the close vicinity of the eyeball. They are stimulated by the contraction of the eyeball muscles and the movement of the eyeballs. These points are used in the treatment of various eye disorders and disorders of the eye muscles. A branch of the heart meridian emerges from the heart, runs along the side of the oesophagus and ends in the eye. Through this branch of the meridian, eyeball movements in shambhavi mudra stimulate the heart which, according to acupuncture physiology, regulates emotions, and the mind from which awareness originates. In this way, shambhavi mudra calms emotions such as anger, increases the level of awareness and leads to higher states of consciousness. According to acupuncture physiology, the liver controls the eyes; it 'opens up in the eyes'. Thus, eyeball movements in shambhavi mudra influence the liver, which enables a harmonious and stable flow of energy throughout the body and mind, and may add to the balancing effect of shambhavi mudra.

NASIKAGRA DRISHTI / AGOCHARI MUDRA
(gesture of nose tip gazing)

Gazing steadily at the tip of the nose is known as *nasikagra drishti*. The word *nasika* means 'nose', *agra* means 'tip' and *drishti* means 'gazing'. This is an exact description of the technique, namely 'nose tip gazing'. It is also known as agochari mudra, which comes from the Sanskrit word *agocharam*, meaning 'beyond sensory perception', 'unknown', or 'invisible'. This mudra is so named since it enables the practitioner to transcend normal awareness.

This mudra is one of the oldest recorded yogic practices. It is depicted in the ancient ruins of Mohenjodaro, which was a flourishing society many thousands of years ago, even before the Vedas were recorded. The great archaeologist, Sir John Marshall, who did much exploration of this ancient site, says: "It (the statue) represents someone seemingly in the pose of a yogi . . . the eyelids are more than half closed and the eyes are looking downwards to the tip of the nose." One can only postulate that the ancient sculptor and the people of that time must have had great respect for this practice to depict it in stone for posterity.

Nasikagra drishti is very similar to shambhavi mudra. The main difference is that the eyes are focused on the nose tip instead of the eyebrow centre. It fundamentally gives the same benefits and the two mudras are equally good. They are both an integral part of kriya yoga and should therefore be mastered to a reasonable level of proficiency before starting to learn and practise kriya yoga.

Nasikagra mudra is mentioned in a number of ancient yogic texts, including the *Bhagavad Gita* and *Hatha Yoga Pradipika*. It seems so simple and inconsequential that one might easily regard it as insignificant. On the contrary, if practised for a long time with intensity it can induce high states of introspection and in turn, meditation. The *Bhagavad Gita* refers to nose tip gazing (6:13):

समं कायशिरोग्रीवं धारयन्नचलं स्थिरः ।
सम्प्रेक्ष्य नासिकाग्रं स्वं दिशश्चानवलोकयन् ॥

Let him hold his body, head and neck erect and still, gazing at the tip of his nose, without looking around.

This verse is from Chapter 6, which describes the method one should adopt to purify and steady the mind and make it one-pointed. The *Bhagavad Gita* says that by sufficient practice and by keeping the mind in a continual state of balance and concentration, one attains meditation and higher illuminative knowledge. This aspect is also described in the Chinese scripture called *T'ai Chin Hua Tzung Chih* translated by Wilhelm:

113

The expression 'tip of the nose' is very cleverly chosen. The nose must serve the eyes as a guideline. If one is not guided by the nose, one either opens the eyes too wide and looks into the distance so that the nose is not seen, or the lids shut too much so that the eyes are not seen. But when the eyes are opened too wide, one makes the mistake of directing them outwards; thereby one is easily distracted (by outer events). If they are closed too much, one makes the mistake of letting them turn inwards, thereby one easily sinks into a dreamy reverie (lost in thoughts; unawareness). Only when the eyelids are lowered properly, halfway, is the tip of the nose seen in just the right way. Therefore, it is taken as a guideline . . .

While gazing at the nose tip, one is actually activating mooladhara. The bridge of the nose represents the spinal cord: just as different centres in the body are represented in the brain, the different psychic centres are also represented along the bridge of the nose. At the top of the bridge is ajna and at the tip is mooladhara. Just as shambhavi mudra aims to activate ajna chakra by gazing at the eyebrow centre, nasikagra drishti aims to activate mooladhara chakra by gazing at the nose tip. Nasikagra mudra is a practice of hatha yoga that directly awakens the kundalini shakti in mooladhara.

Sitting either in siddhasana or siddha yoni asana, one gazes steadily at the tip of the nose. The eyes become slightly convergent and the two sides of the nose are seen. Concentration should be centred right in the middle. At first the vision will be unsteady and the eyes will tire quickly. With a little practice each day the eyes become accustomed. While gazing at the nose tip, concentration is on the movement of breath in the nostrils so that it can be determined which nostril the breath is flowing through. When both nostrils are open, that is, sushumna is flowing, the practice is taking effect. After five to ten minutes, one

114

closes the eyes and looks into the dark space in front of the closed eyes, the *chidakasha*. When a light is seen in the darkness, one concentrates on it. That is the light that can completely absorb the consciousness. It is stated in *Hatha Yoga Pradipika* (4:41):

अर्धोन्मीलितलोचन: स्थिरमना नासाग्रदत्तेक्षण-
चंद्रार्कावपि लीनतामुपनयन्नि स्पंदभावेन य: ।

ज्योतीरूपमशेषबीजमखिलं देदीप्यमानं परं
तत्त्वं तत्पदमेति वस्तु परमं वाच्यं किमत्राधिकम् ॥

Mind steady, eyes semi-open, gaze fixed on the nose tip, the moon (ida) and sun (pingala) suspended, without any movement (physical or mental), that one attains the form of light (jyoti) which is endless and is complete, radiant, the Supreme. What more can be said?

By external gazing at the nose tip, a vision of the inner light is aroused as the flow of shakti in the mind and body becomes concentrated. When the light switch is turned on, the light emanates from the bulb. The same applies in the physical body. When the kundalini shakti is released from mooladhara it is drawn up to ajna chakra, and there the inner light appears. When seen, that light should be concentrated upon as it is the essence of being, the inner light or *jyoti*. The purpose of practising nasikagra mudra is to arouse that experience. It is also said that when one concentrates on the tip of the nose, *divya gandha*, divine aroma, is experienced.

Though the gaze is directed towards the tip of the nose when the eyes are half-closed and the eyeballs are steady, the mind should be fixed only on the Self. In the *Bhagavad Gita* (6:25) Sri Krishna says: "Having made the mind abide in the Self, let him not think of anything else." Gazing at the tip of the nose will soon bring about such concentration of mind. Thus nasikagra mudra is considered an excellent form of trataka. Although the eyes are open, the aim of nasikagra mudra is to create introspection. The open eyes should not be aware of the outside world. Focusing them on the nose tip concentrates the mind, developing one's powers of concentration and inducing meditative states. It takes the practitioner into the psychic and spiritual planes of consciousness.

At first nasikagra mudra will seem a little strange and difficult, for it requires a fixed gaze at the nose tip. The eyes have to assume a position to which they are normally unaccustomed. With practice, however, the eye muscles adapt themselves to their new role, strengthening the eyes and in turn improving the eyesight.

Nasikagra mudra is an excellent technique for calming anger and disturbed states of mind. It is especially suitable in this respect, for it can be performed at any time during the day, which is when one is most likely to meet stressful and disruptive situations. Most other techniques require preparation and a special place for practice. The technique of nasikagra mudra can be practised at any time as it needs no preparation. This mudra can even be practised while sitting on a bus or a train. The ideal times for its practice are early in the morning and late at night. Just before sleep is an especially good time, as the calmness of mind it induces prepares one for deep, restful sleep.

Preparatory practice

It may be difficult at first to focus the eyes on the nose tip.

To overcome this, hold the index finger up at arm's length from the eyes and focus the gaze upon it.

Slowly bring the finger towards the nose, keeping the gaze steadily fixed upon it.

When the finger touches the tip of the nose, the eyes should still be focused on the finger.

Transfer the focus of the eyes to the nose tip.

Eventually this method becomes superfluous and the eyes readily fix on the nose tip at will.

116

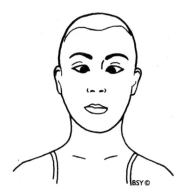

Technique
Stage 1: With normal breathing

Sit in a comfortable meditation posture.

Close the eyes and relax the whole body.

Breathe normally throughout the duration of the practice.

Open the eyes slightly and focus on the nose tip.

Keep the head straight.

Do not strain the eyes, but try to hold the gaze steadily at the tip of the nose.

If the eyes are correctly focused, a double outline of the nose should be seen.

These two lines converge at the tip of the nose, forming a V.

Try to hold the gaze at the apex of the V.

When a strain is felt, release the gaze and relax the eyes for a few seconds.

Then repeat the practice.

Gradually increase the duration as the eyes become accustomed.

Continue for up to five minutes.

Concentration should be centred in the very middle.

At first the vision will be unsteady and the eyes will tire quickly.

With a little practice each day, the eyes will become accustomed.

117

When gazing at the nose happens without the slightest difficulty, begin to develop awareness of the breath as well. Be aware of the breath flowing in and out at the nose tip and determine which nostril the breath is flowing through.

When both nostrils are open, that is, when sushumna is flowing, the practice is taking effect.

After five to ten minutes close the eyes and look into the dark space in front of the closed eyes, the chidakasha.

When a light is seen in the darkness, concentrate on it, because that is the light which can completely absorb the consciousness.

Try to become completely absorbed in the practice to the exclusion of all other thoughts.

Practice note: Stage 2 of nasikagra drishti is always practised with inner retention, not external retention. During inhalation and exhalation, the eyes remain closed.

Stage 2: With kumbhaka

Close the eyes and become aware of the breath at the nose tip.

Inhale with the eyes closed.

Retaining the breath inside, open the eyes slightly and gaze at the nose tip.

Concentrate on the point of the V.

Then release kumbhaka and breathe out slowly.

Close the eyes and relax them.

Continue the practice for five minutes.

Awareness: Physical – on the muscles of the eyes, and on relaxing them completely between rounds. Spiritual – on mooladhara chakra.

Time of practice: Nasikagra drishti may be practised at any time of day, although ideally it is performed early in the morning or late at night before sleep.

Contra-indications: People suffering from glaucoma should not practise this mudra. Those with diabetic retinopathy or who have just had cataract surgery, lens implant or other eye operations should not perform nasikagra drishti without the guidance of a competent teacher. Those suffering from depression should avoid this practice.

Effects: If practised for some time with awareness, nose tip gazing can induce high states of concentration and tranquillity of mind.

Meridian effects: According to yogic philosophy, there is a direct connection that exists between the nose tip, the sense of smell, and mooladhara chakra. Acupuncture theory helps to explain the connection of nasikagra drishti with mooladhara. Point 'GV 25' of the governing meridian is located at the tip of the nose and is stimulated by mental concentration in nasikagra drishti. The name of this point translates as the 'plain seam', which can also mean a plain or direct connection. 'GV 25' is one of the terminal points of the governing meridian; the first and terminal points of every meridian are very important and powerful points. The governing meridian is one of the two most important extraordinary meridians in the body, and it runs along the back median line. It emerges on the surface of the body at the perineum and then runs backwards towards the tip of the tail bone, the coccyx, and all the way up to the upper lip. The other major extraordinary meridian is the conception meridian which runs from the centre of the perineum, where the first point 'CV 1' is located, up along the frontal median line to end on the upper lip also. These two meridians, governor and conception, are joined together in a yin-yang relationship. This means that the flow of energy in both of them is closely interconnected and that when one of these meridians is stimulated, the change in the flow of energy spreads into the other. Stimulation of point 'GV 25', which happens by gazing at the nose tip, excites the governor meridian and influences the conception meridian. When excitation in the conception meridian reaches the point 'CO 1' at the perineum, mooladhara chakra is stimulated.

In the tantras, it is written that ajna chakra, whose external focusing point is the eyebrow centre, is directly connected with mooladhara chakra. This link can be explained through the relationship of the governor and conception vessels. If any awakening takes place in ajna it also takes place in mooladhara, and vice versa.

Traditional functions of the point 'GV 25' on the nose tip include the raising of yang, restoring energy and clearing the senses, which could refer to the increased power of concentration mentioned in the yogic explanation of this mudra. As increased energy flows towards the head, mental faculties are enhanced and meditative states can be reached easily. All yang energies and meridians in the body flow upward from the lower parts of the body toward the head. All yang energies are created from the yin, for yin is the earth, the basic source of everything. Point 'GV 25' raises the yang upward, yet at the same time stimulation also spreads into the conception meridian, which is yin. Stimulation of the point 'CO 1' triggers mooladhara chakra which corresponds to the earth element in yoga and is the basic source of prana.

KHECHARI MUDRA (gesture of the tongue lock)

Khechari mudra, the gesture of the tongue lock, is regarded as a very important practice in hatha yoga, raja yoga and vedantic texts, due to its effect on the body and mind (see Chapter 6). *Khe* means 'in the sky' and *chari* means 'one who moves'. Therefore, *khechari* means 'one who moves through space'. This name has been given to the mudra as it produces a state of mind in which the astral body is detached from the physical body. In such a state, the consciousness dwells in *akasha*, the space between the astral and physical bodies.

Nabho mudra, the sky gesture, is another name for the simple form of khechari mudra. It is an example of a simple raja yoga style technique. The mudras described in raja yoga are similar to those explained in hatha yoga. The practices of raja yoga, however, are given keeping in mind the normal physical condition of the body and the care that it needs, whereas the practices of hatha yoga are carried out by exerting force on the body and by changing its physical state. Khechari mudra is generally combined with ujjayi pranayama and other meditation practices. It is also used in conjunction with *kumbhaka*, or breath retention, as the intake of air can easily be stopped when the tongue is reversed like this. It can be practised with both internal and external breath retention. *Gheranda Samhita* praises it with (3:32):

यत्र यत्र स्थितो योगी सर्वकार्येषु सर्वदा ।
उर्ध्वजिह्व: स्थिरो भूत्वा धारयेत्पवनं सदा ।
नभोमुद्रा भवेदेषा योगिनां रोगनाशिनी ॥

Wherever one is and during all activities, a yogi should keep the tongue turned upward and retain the breath. Nabho mudra destroys all the disorders of a yogi.

Nabho mudra is suitable for most people, although it too takes a long time to perfect. The tongue is folded upward and backward so that the tip of the tongue is brought as far back as possible and lies in contact with the soft upper palate. It is kept there for as long as possible, from half a minute to ten or twenty minutes. Day by day, week by week, month by month, year by year, this is done, and slowly the tongue becomes flexible and elongated. Once it can enter into the epiglottis, the same result can be achieved as with the full hatha yoga practice of khechari mudra, which is described in the next section.

The direct concern of khechari mudra is to activate the psychic, physiological and endocrine processes responsible for cellular revitalization and longevity. If khechari mudra is correctly practised in conjunction with ujjayi over a long period of time, the tongue goes into the upper nasal orifice, which in the language of Kabirdas is called the 'cave of the sky', the place where *amrit*, the nectar of immortality, flows constantly. Perfection of this practice enables the yogi to trap the descending drops of amrit at vishuddhi, overcoming hunger and thirst, and rejuvenating the entire body.

Just below the crown of the head where the Hindu brahmins keep a tuft of hair, lies the centre of bindu. *Bindu* means 'drop'. This centre is so called because of a small gland there that produces a secretion which is converted into nectar (see Chapter 6). This crude secretion drops down into a refining centre in the throat, vishuddhi chakra, where it is purified. By practising khechari mudra for two to five years, these two important centres can be stimulated. When this occurs nectar will flow, rejuvenating the body. About this Kabir has written: "When this nectar is tasted, all fears, diseases, guilt and ignorance are burned away. Inside you will shine like the full-moon lit night." When the eyes are closed, what does one see? Only darkness. However, if the eyes are closed when the nectar is flowing, only light is seen. The whole brain, the whole consciousness is illumined. This is the aim of practising ujjayi with khechari.

Technique

Sit in any comfortable meditation pose, preferably padmasana or siddha/siddha yoni asana, with the head and spine straight and the hands in chin or jnana mudra.
Relax the whole body and close the eyes.
Fold the tongue upward and backward, so that the lower surface lies in contact with the upper palate.
Stretch the tip of the tongue backward as far as is comfortable.
Do not strain.
Perform ujjayi pranayama.
Breathe slowly and deeply.
Hold the tongue lock for as long as possible without straining.
At first there may be some discomfort and ujjayi pranayama may irritate the throat, but with practice it will become more comfortable.

When the tongue becomes tired, release and relax it, then repeat the practice.

Breathing: Gradually reduce the respiration rate over a period of months until the number of breaths per minute is 5 or 6. This may be reduced further under the guidance of a competent teacher.

Awareness: Physical – on the stretch of the tongue and the light pressure against the upper palate. Spiritual – at vishuddhi chakra.

Duration: Practise for 5 to 10 minutes. Khechari mudra may also be performed with other yoga practices.

Precaution: If a bitter taste is experienced during khechari mudra, the practice should be terminated. It is due to physical impurity and is experienced when there is too much kapha dosha, mucous element, in the body. As a general rule, if one goes through the process of hatha yoga, elimination of toxins and balancing of the doshas can be achieved, and the bitter taste will not be experienced. However, if the practice is taken up without purification, the bitter taste will remain.

Contra-indications: Tongue ulcers and other common mouth ailments will temporarily preclude performance of this practice.

Benefits: Khechari mudra stimulates a number of pressure points located in the back of the mouth and the nasal cavity. These points influence the whole body. A number of glands are also massaged, stimulating the secretion of certain hormones and of saliva. This practice reduces the sensations of hunger and thirst, and induces a state of inner calm and stillness. It preserves the vitality of the body and is especially beneficial for inner healing. Ultimately, this mudra has the potential to stimulate prana and awaken kundalini shakti. It is said that the practitioner of khechari mudra is not troubled by unconsciousness, hunger, thirst or laziness. Fear of any disorder or disease, old age and death vanishes as the body becomes divine. For such a one, it is said, "The

123

physical body is neither burnt in fire nor dried up by the wind. It can neither be made wet by water nor does poison have any effect on it." The body becomes graceful and charming, and samadhi is perfected. (See Chapters 4, 5 and 6 for specific effects of khechari mudra on the brain, meditation and bindu.)

Meridian effects: The kidney meridian terminates at the root of the tongue and is stimulated by the tongue lock in khechari mudra. Kidneys have extremely important vital functions. According to acupuncture physiology, they store the essence, corresponding to *ojas* in ayurveda, which controls growth, development, immunity and regeneration of the body. Kidney essence produces marrow and holds the fundamental yin and yang of the body. The kidneys, which are yin by nature, are coupled with the urinary bladder as their yang counterpart. Both organs govern the functions of the reproductive organs, adrenal glands and the autonomic nervous system. The kidneys act as a major controller of homeostasis in the body, ensuring physical and mental endurance, vitality and resistance. All of these functions are enhanced by khechari mudra, and they correlate with the benefits described from the yogic point of view.

The spleen meridian also terminates at the root of the tongue. The spleen is the major digestive organ in acupuncture physiology, which transforms nutrients and helps in the production of the blood. It also maintains the upward flow of energy, increases awareness and lucidity of thoughts. It also encompasses the functions of the cerebral cortex, all organs that secrete digestive juices, and the female reproductive glands. Some of these functions of the spleen can be correlated to the benefits of khechari as explained in yoga.

When the essence in the kidneys is strong and digestion well-regulated by the spleen, heat is properly accumulated in the body and the state of sound health and high resistance is attained. Proper nourishment of the brain ensures mental stamina and stability, clarity of thoughts and the power of introversion. The spleen is coupled with the stomach in the yin-yang relationship, therefore stimulation spreads from the spleen meridian to the stomach meridian. The stomach is called 'the sea of nourishment', and it has a major role in the production of heat in the body. In *Hatha Yoga Pradipika* it is said that khechari produces heat in the body. Stimulation of the stomach may be the mechanism behind this effect. Yogic texts also state that khechari mudra retards the feelings of hunger and thirst. These urges are dependent on the stomach according to acupuncture physiology.

The liver meridian passes through the nasopharynx, the nasal part of the oral cavity where the tip of the tongue enters in the final stages of khechari mudra, and thus is also stimulated. The liver is an important detoxifier of the body and may be the underlying cause of the purifying and revitalizing effect of this mudra. According to acupuncture, the liver also determines a person's basic attitudes, manifesting on deep levels. Khechari mudra causes profound changes in the realm of consciousness, which have repercussions on a deeper level of the personality also. The conception meridian is stimulated at the points 'C 23' and 'CO 24' at the front of the neck, which are excited by the contraction of throat muscles in khechari mudra. The proper flow of energy through this meridian ensures high vitality and resistance to diseases, as ascribed to khechari mudra in the yogic scriptures.

Hatha yoga technique

The hatha yoga technique of khechari mudra involves the gradual cutting of the fraenum and elongation of the tongue, and only those who have detoxified their body and are advised by the guru should attempt it. It is also not recommended for anyone needing to live an active life in society. Cutting the fraenum affects swallowing, making eating difficult, and without a special diet the health suffers.

It can also make speech quite indistinct. Therefore, the hatha yoga technique was traditionally only undertaken by those yogis who were totally dedicated to spiritual awakening and no longer involved in worldly life.

The procedure is described in *Gheranda Samhita* (3:33–35):

जिह्वाधो नाडीं संछित्य रसनां चालयेत्सदा ।
दोहयेत्रवनीतेन लौहयन्त्रेण कर्षयेत् ॥

एवं नित्यं समभ्यासाल्लम्बिका दीर्घतां व्रजेत् ।
यावद्गच्छेद्भ्रुवोर्मध्ये तदा सिध्यति खेचरी ॥

रसनां तालुमूले तु शनैः शनैः प्रवेशयेत् ।
कपालकुहरे जिह्वा प्रविष्टा विपरीतगा ॥

The nadi connecting the tongue and the root of the tongue, which is located underneath the tongue, is to be severed and the tip of the tongue is to be moved continuously. By applying butter and with the help of dohan kriya (the milking process) it is to be pulled with iron forceps.

With daily practise the tongue becomes elongated. Its length should be so increased that it can reach the eyebrow centre. Khechari mudra is then accomplished.

In this way the tongue should gradually be inserted into the root of the palate. By folding the tongue upward and backward, it should be taken right up to the nasal cavity. Keep the awareness fixed at the eyebrow centre at that time. This is khechari mudra.

In olden days, yogis used to say that the fraenum should be severed with the help of the root of a tree, or a sharp-edged leaf like tejpata (Cinnamomum tamala) which is pure, so there is no infection. It is also sometimes severed with the help of a rice stalk. In the *Yoga Tattwopanishad* it states that each time this is practised, the severing should be equivalent only to the thickness of a hair. This means that it should be a mere touch, a slight stroke.

In modern times some people have had the tongue severed through surgery. In this process bleeding takes place, but according to the *Yoga Tattwopanishad* and other yoga scriptures, the oozing of blood should not take place at all while perfecting khechari. The motive behind this statement cannot be known exactly, but it can be inferred that it is cautionary. In those days, if the region became septic, medicinal herbs might not always have been available. It would have been difficult for a person if there was no one close by with knowledge of medicinal herbs. It is also likely that with such gradual cutting, speech impairment will be minimal. Thus it says that severing of the tongue should be just equal to the thickness of a hair and there should be no bleeding. This means it is just like drawing a line. It should be a process in which the fraenum is cut daily or weekly, bit by bit.

The tongue is also to be gradually elongated by *dohan kriya*, the milking process. Two methods of dohan kriya are explained. One is outward massage of the tongue using a finger and the other is using forceps. The tongue is massaged in the same manner as in the milking process and it is pulled daily with a pair of forceps. There is a possibility of vomiting if the tongue is held with the fingers during dohan kriya, so forceps or a pair of tongs can be used to hold it firmly but gently.

Once the tongue has been sufficiently elongated and pranayama has been perfected, the tongue is folded back on itself and moved upwards into the nasal cavity. This is not an easy process, and at first it is necessary to push the tongue into position with the fingers. When the tongue is strengthened, it can be pushed right into the back of the nasal cavity by itself, and when prana is awakened in the body, the tongue will move into that position spontaneously.

When the tongue is inserted right up into the nasal cavity, the breath can be directed into either nostril by the tip of the tongue. The tip of the tongue will be able to block the right or left passage or be placed a little lower so that both nostrils are open. To actually elongate the tongue to the extent that it can move up to the eyebrow centre takes many years of consistent practice and the instructions of the guru should be followed carefully at each step.

Traditionally, the tongue is prepared for khechari mudra at an early age, twelve to sixteen years, during the period when the body is still developing so the adverse effects are not experienced. In fact, when performed at a young age, the severing of the fraenum is treated as a *samskara*, rite of passage, just as piercing of the ears or initiation into the sacred thread is a samskara, and is known as *jihva shodhana*, purification of the tongue. These rituals bring about purification at a subtle level and help in a balanced development of the personality.

Breathing

It is essential to perfect pranayama prior to the practice of khechari, for when the tongue goes upward, the nasal cavities can be closed and breathing is not so easy. In some of the yogic scriptures it is said that mastery of pranayama does not mean retaining the breath inside or outside, but simply suspension of the breath. It is believed that one who has perfected khechari mudra can suspend the breath for hours or days at a time. This is how yogis who bury themselves underground remain alive. However, not everyone can attain the capacity to retain the breath for such lengths of time, but a state akin to it is attained. If there are normally ten to fifteen breaths per minute, then in an advanced state of practice the breathing is reduced by half, which means only five to seven breaths per minute. Thus the speed and rate of breathing are reduced for hours at a time.

The aim of yogis is to reduce the breathing rate gradually, so that there is only one breath in and out in a minute. In this state, there should be no compromise in the normal functioning of the body, no feeling of breathlessness and no lack of oxygen. Therefore, for khechari it is essential to have control over the breath and to prepare the tongue.

The flow and taste of nectar

Various tastes are experienced in the mouth that reflect associated states of the body and mind. These are described in *Gheranda Samhita* (3:39–40):

नानारससमुद्भूतमानन्दं च दिने दिने ।
आदौ च लवणं क्षारं ततस्तिक्तकषायकम् ॥

नवनीतं घृतं क्षीरं दधितक्रमधूनि च ।
द्राक्षारसं च पीयूषं जायते रसनोदकम् ॥

Therefore, strange types of juices keep being produced, day in and day out, through the tongue of the practitioner. New blissful experiences manifest. In the beginning salty, alkaline, bitter and astringent tastes and then the taste of butter, ghee (clarified butter), milk, curd, buttermilk, honey, grapes or raisins and then nectar are produced.

In yogic texts it is also clearly instructed that khechari mudra should not be brought into use until the tongue becomes long and thin. When the tongue is inserted upward and backward, a taste is experienced; juices are secreted from the taste glands (buds) located on the palate and *kapala kuhar*, 'hole in the forehead'. At first, the mouth may be filled with an extremely bitter taste. Next comes an astringent taste, then salty and after that it is filled with a sweet taste. That means all types of tastes are experienced while doing this practice. When the tongue crosses the limits of the taste glands, various tastes are secreted that cannot be described. For instance, the taste of milk or butter, which is neither sweet, nor alkaline, nor salty, nor bitter, not even sour, and cannot be described. So the experience of these other tastes, which can be called natural flavours, occur as the glands become active. The secretion of saliva in the mouth is also gradually reduced while practising khechari so that saliva does not constantly need to be swallowed.

The particular tastes attributed to the nectar are related to the pancha tattwas. Each of the five tattwas: earth, water, fire, air and ether, creates a particular flavour when it

129

predominates. Tattwas represent specific pranic flows associated with the pancha pranas and each can be tasted when it is active. According to the flavour, the active tattwa can be known. Earth tattwa is characterized by a sweet flavour, water is astringent, fire is bitter, air is acidic and ether is pungent or hot.

Precautions

There is also a warning that khechari should not be practised by anyone who experiences a bitter taste in the mouth. If a bitter taste is produced and one keeps on practising khechari without paying any heed, that bitterness can become poison for the body. If the bitter taste persists, it also means that all the toxins and disorders of the body are not yet fully removed. If this happens, it is imperative to practise the hatha yoga shatkarmas all over again.

It is important to make the body completely free from all disorders. The indication of being free from disorders is absence of bitterness in the mouth. On rising in the morning, there is often a persistent bitter taste in the mouth, which means that the digestive system is unhealthy. It has been observed that when the bowels are clear, the bitter taste automatically vanishes.

Cease the practice for at least one month if an extreme bitter taste is experienced. Take care with the diet and lifestyle, and then try again.

AKASHI MUDRA (gesture of the inner space)

The word *akashi* means 'inner space'. Akashi mudra is awareness of the inner space. This practice induces mental tranquillity by withdrawing the senses. It renders the mind free of thoughts and leads to states of trance. Akashi mudra belongs to the group of techniques featuring gazing at an external focal point as a means to achieving dharana or the meditative state of relaxed concentration.

It is recommended that the practitioner be completely familiar with the practices of ujjayi, khechari, nasikagra drishti and shambhavi before commencing akashi mudra. At first, ujjayi pranayama may irritate the throat when performed with the head back. However, with practice, it will become more comfortable.

Technique
Sit in any comfortable meditation asana.
Close the eyes and relax the whole body for a few minutes.
Fold the tongue back against the palate in khechari mudra.
Practise ujjayi pranayama and shambhavi mudra.
Tilt the head backwards about 45 degrees.
Straighten the arms and lock the elbows, pressing the knees with the hands.
Breathe slowly and deeply in ujjayi.
Continue for as long as is comfortable.
Then bend the arms, while slowly bringing the head to the upright position.
Gently lower the eyes and practise nasikagra drishti.
Continue for as long as is comfortable.
Close the eyes, release khechari and ujjayi breath, resume normal breathing and relax.
Be aware of the inner space.
Then begin the next round.

Variation: Akashi mudra may also be practised with breath retention. Perform the practice as described above. Inhale while tilting the head backwards. Hold the breath inside, performing internal kumbhaka in the final position. Exhale while slowly returning the head to the starting position. From this position, practise external kumbhaka with nasikagra drishti, holding for as long as is comfortable.

Awareness: On ajna chakra.

Duration: Begin with one round and gradually increase to 5. Maintain the final position for as long as is comfortable, increasing the length of time in the mudra very slowly.

Precaution: As soon as faintness is felt, stop the practice. This technique must be practised slowly under the guidance of a competent teacher.

Contra-indications: People suffering from high blood pressure, vertigo, brain disorders or epilepsy should not practise this mudra.

Benefits: This practice combines the benefits of kumbhaka, ujjayi, shambhavi, nasikagra drishti and khechari. It aims at developing control over the senses, thereby inducing calmness and tranquillity. When perfected, it arrests the thought processes and induces higher states of consciousness.

When one concentrates on the nose and the sense of smell in the mudra, one is actually focusing the attention on the most primitive of all the senses, which is located deep down inside the primal brain. Vision, on the other hand, is the most developed sense. As the attention is drawn to the eyes, one is moving to a very highly developed part of the brain. Therefore, as one performs the rounds, one is continuously making a link between the higher brain and the lower brain.

There is a theory that at some stage along the evolutionary path, choices had to be made about which senses would be developed; for example, dogs developed smell much more actively that vision. In the brain, there are two main areas for vision. One is the occipital cortex, an area about the size of the hand that controls involuntary vision. One has no choice but to keep moving the eyes in order to continue receiving sensory information and input. The second area, which is located in the frontal lobe, is involved in voluntary vision. It helps in directing the eyes to look for a specific purpose, like looking ahead, in the same way as the purpose of the frontal lobes is thinking ahead, looking to the future. This is the physical level of the mental activity. This mudra fixes the eyes, stops involuntary movement, stops the use of energy and brings all the brain cells into entrainment. They go into a simple alpha rhythm.

If one closes the eyes, an alpha rhythm brainwave pattern will occur that is experienced as a relaxed state in the back of the head. However, when one focuses deeply in this mudra, this relaxed rhythm is not only occurring in the back of the head, but also in the frontal lobes. This is the main reason why akashi mudra is so tranquillizing; it stops the thinking process almost instantly. Thought and thought waves are intrinsically connected to metabolic activity in the cells, the rate of breathing, the rate of movement of the eyes and also the rate of movement of the tongue. These activities have a reflex in the frontal lobes, so that when movement is slowed down the brain is also slowed down, for example, during meditation.

Akashi mudra involves different forms of manipulation, either looking upward at the eyebrow centre and directing the energy to the higher centres in the brain, or looking downward at the nose tip, fixing the attention on the lower, more primitive centres in the brain.

Meridian effects: All the benefits of shambhavi, khechari and nasikagra drishti are experienced. In addition, in akashi mudra the head is extended backwards, which extends the conception meridian and compresses the governing meridian. This influences the flow of energy

133

in them. These two meridians play an essential role in the whole meridian network, and they run along the median line on the front and the back of the trunk, which are identical to arohan and avarohan psychic passages.

The overall synergistic effect of all the components of akashi mudra is the enhancement of the flow of prana in arohan and avarohan, which excites both mooladhara and ajna chakras, augmenting the pranic flow to chitta and increasing the level of awareness.

MANDUKI MUDRA (frog gesture)

The word *manduki* means 'frog-like', so *manduki mudra* is the frog-like attitude. Some of the texts define it as the mudra in which the sitting pose resembles the natural position of the frog, while other texts define it as the mudra in which the tongue movement resembles that of a frog. Both mudras are described below. The first technique is an advanced variation of nasikagra drishti, gesture of nose tip gazing.

The purpose of gazing at the tip of the nose is to calm the disturbances and fluctuations of the mind, and to balance ida and pingala, creating harmony between extroversion and introversion. This leads directly to meditation if it is perfected. An important aspect of manduki mudra is stimulation of mooladhara chakra. This occurs through the sitting pose of bhadrasana and the practice of nasikagra drishti. The sense of smell is also enhanced, as it is a faculty of mooladhara. Mooladhara chakra and the area of smell are one of the most powerful regions for storage and recovery of memory. A smell can trigger a memory from childhood. Smell is the most primitive of all the senses. This area is very deep inside the primal brain. Whether the faculty of smell is used wilfully and consciously or it happens naturally, there is a change in the energy structure at mooladhara, and the corresponding centre in the brain is affected by it. The awakening of mooladhara chakra in manduki mudra may lead to the experience of a divine aroma, in the same way that it does in nose tip gazing in nasikagra mudra.

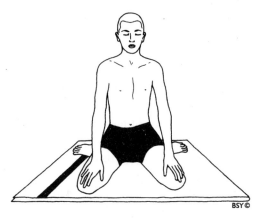

Technique
>Sit in bhadrasana (see Appendix).
>If possible to do so without straining, adjust so that the toes are pointing outward.
>The buttocks should rest on the floor.
>A folded blanket may also be placed underneath the buttocks to apply firm pressure to the perineum, stimulating the region of mooladhara chakra.
>Place the hands on the knees, holding the spine and head straight.
>Close the eyes and relax the whole body.
>This is manduki asana.
>Open the eyes and perform nasikagra drishti.
>When the eyes become tired, close them for a few seconds.
>Continue the practice for 5 minutes, until the mind and senses become introverted.

Breathing: Breathing should be slow and rhythmic.

Awareness: Physical – on the nosetip. Spiritual – on mooladhara chakra.

Contra-indications: Those with glaucoma, diabetic retinopathy or those who have just had cataract surgery, lens implant or other eye operations should not perform nasikagra drishti without the guidance of a competent teacher. Manduki asana should not be practised unless the ankles, knees and hips are very flexible.

Practice note: If it is difficult to sit in manduki asana, then sit in bhadrasana with the toes pointing inward and the soles upward. The buttocks should rest on the floor. If this too is difficult, place a folded blanket underneath the buttocks. This will apply firm pressure to the region of mooladhara. It should be performed in mild light so that the tip of the nose can be seen clearly.

Effects: Manduki asana is a counterpose for cross-legged meditative asanas. Manduki mudra activates mooladhara chakra. It calms the disturbances and fluctuations of mind and balances ida and pingala nadis, leading directly to meditation.

Meridian effects: The mechanisms set in action are similar to those in nasikagra drishti; however, the conception meridian is additionally stimulated by the pressure point 'CV 1' at the centre of the perineum, which is why the position of bhadrasana with toes pointing outward is recommended. A direct connection is established between the conception meridian and the governing meridian, stimulated by mental concentration on the point 'GV 26' at the nose tip. The effects of this connection are described in the section on nasikagra drishti. The hands are on the knees, connecting the upper yang part of the body with the lower yin part. The resulting balanced state has repercussions on the mind in the form of tranquillity and calmness.

Technique 2

This second technique is a simplified version of khechari mudra.

Close the mouth and then rotate the tongue to the right, left and up and down.

The rotation of the tongue to all sides is just like the

jumping of a frog; hence it has been named manduki mudra.

Effects: Manduki mudra stimulates secretion from the gland located at the bindu chakra. This secretion is known as *sudha* or *amrit*, nectar. The nectar is very useful for the health of a practitioner, providing strength and vitality to the body (see Chapter 6).

KAKI MUDRA (crow's beak gesture)

The word *kaki* means crow. Kaki mudra is so called because during inhalation the mouth is shaped like a crow's beak. It is claimed that regular practice of this mudra leads to the disease-free long life that is associated with the crow. This mudra is also considered to be a pranayama practice due to its close similarity to sheetali and sheetkari pranayamas.

During the inhalation the lips are pursed together, leaving a small tube through which the air may be inhaled. The tongue should be relaxed. Practitioners should be thoroughly familiar with nasikagra drishti prior to commencing this technique. The eyes must be kept open throughout the practice and nasikagra drishti should be continuous. If the eyes become tired, relax them for as long as necessary before recommencing the practice.

Technique

Sit in any comfortable meditation asana with the head and spine straight and the hands resting on the knees in either chinmudra or jnana mudra.

Close the eyes and relax the whole body for a few minutes.

Open the eyes and perform nasikagra drishti by focusing both eyes on the nose tip.

Try not to blink the eyes throughout this practice.

Purse the lips, forming a beak through which air may be inhaled.

The tongue should be relaxed.

137

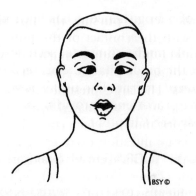

Inhale slowly and deeply through the pursed lips.
At the end of inhalation close the lips and exhale slowly through the nose.
Repeat the process for 3 to 5 minutes.

Awareness: On the flow and sound of the breath, and on the nose tip.

Sequence: This mudra is a cooling practice. It balances the temperature of the body when performed after heating pranayamas.

Time of practice: It may be performed at any time of day, although it is best performed early in the morning or late at night. It should not be performed in cold weather.

Precautions: Kaki mudra should not be practised in a polluted atmosphere or in excessively cold weather, as the normal filtering and air-conditioning function of the nose is bypassed. Care should be taken not to strain the eyes.

Contra-indications: People suffering from depression, glaucoma, low blood pressure or chronic constipation should avoid this practice. People suffering from diabetic retinopathy or those who have just had cataract surgery, lens implant or other eye operations, should not perform this practice without the guidance of a competent teacher.

Benefits: Kaki mudra cools the body and mind and soothes mental tensions. In addition to the benefits of nasikagra drishti, the act of pursing the lips in this practice, together with the contact of the indrawn air with the membranes of the mouth, stimulates digestive secretions, aiding the digestive process generally.

Meridian effects: The large intestine meridian curves around the upper lip and is stimulated by the contraction of the orbicularis oris muscle, which controls movements of the lips. The large intestine excretes physical wastes, which results in the purification of blood and mental wastes, which in turn calms the mind and soothes tensions. Kaki mudra triggers a kind of natural shankhaprakshalana mechanism that cleanses the entire digestive tract.

The stomach meridian makes the loop in the close vicinity of the lips and is gently stimulated by the contraction of the same muscle. In acupuncture physiology, the stomach encompasses the entire upper digestive tract all the way down to the middle portion of the small intestine, and thus the digestive process is enhanced with kaki mudra. Cool air is inhaled through the mouth, bypassing the nasal area where it is supposed to be warmed up through the contact with many tiny blood vessels in the nasal mucous lining. This cool air reaches the stomach and cools it down.

The superficial branch of the vital vessel, one of the eight extraordinary meridians, terminates encircling the lips. This meridian helps in the control of energy and blood throughout the whole body and has an important role in maintaining the state of high vitality and freedom from disease, which are also the qualities of a crow, after which this mudra is named.

The governing meridian ends inside the upper lip. The conception meridian terminates encircling the lips. Both meridians are stimulated in kaki mudra when the lips are pursed. They serve together as important reservoirs of energy which is used according to the needs of the body. Simultaneous toning of these yang-yin paired meridians results in an increased level of mental and physical energy, increased resistance to disease and environmental changes, as the constitutional energy is strengthened on a deeper level.

BHUJANGINI MUDRA (gesture of cobra respiration)

The subject of burping has long been controversial in various societies throughout the world. In China and during the middle ages of Europe, it was almost a ritual to end a meal by burping. This clearly showed that one had enjoyed the food. If a person did not burp, they were likely to be labelled ill-mannered or uncivilized. Burping was almost considered an art. This art has been lost in modern societies, as it is considered both crude and distasteful. Nevertheless, revival of this ancient practice is needed and the technique is known as bhujangini mudra. It is also known as *vatsara dhauti*, one of the shatkarma practices. The *Gheranda Samhita* says the following (1:15–16):

काकचञ्चुवदास्येन पिबेद्वायुं शनै: शनै: ।
चालयेदुदरं पश्चाद्वर्त्मना रेचयेच्छनै: ॥

वातसारं परं गोप्यं देह निर्मलकारकम् ।
सर्व रोगक्षयकरं देहानलविवर्द्धकम् ॥

Shape your lips like a crow's beak and drink air. Let the air swirl in the stomach for some time and then allow it to expel itself. Vatsara dhauti is a most secret technique to purify the body. It destroys all diseases and increases the gastric fire.

Under normal circumstances, burping brings an immediate sense of relief. It is a normal response which no one can avoid, for everybody tends to swallow air while eating. This is trapped in each mouthful of food and accumulates in the stomach. The amount of air swallowed, of course, varies greatly with eating habits, but it may be as high as half a litre. A little of this passes into the intestinal tract, but most of it is expelled by means of the simple expedient of burping.

Vatsara dhauti utilizes the same basic process, but instead of inducing air into the stomach by eating food, it is induced by voluntary effort. In other words, air is sucked into the stomach while inhaling. To many people, especially children, this technique will come almost naturally. In fact, they will have already practised it for the fun of hearing the resulting noise on expulsion, without realizing that they are performing an ancient practice of yoga.

The main reason for doing the practice is to clean the stomach of stale, foul-smelling gases. It also helps to eliminate and prevent hyperacidity and especially heartburn. Furthermore, many processes of digestion work far better when there is a liberal supply of oxygen in the stomach. Thus, it increases the digestive power of the body by improving the chemical reactions taking place within the stomach. When one considers that a large number of ailments arise from digestive disorders, the necessity for a healthy digestive system becomes obvious. Bhujangini mudra, or vatsara dhauti, is one method of attaining this end.

Bhujangini mudra can be practised as many times as one wants, however once or twice is sufficient just before eating. It can be done at any time of the day, yet preferably not during or immediately after a big meal. This practice is most useful, however, if performed just before eating a large or heavy meal as it stimulates the digestive system to work at a higher level of efficiency.

Technique

Sit in any comfortable meditation asana.

Close the eyes and relax the whole body, especially the abdomen.

Push the chin forward and a little upward.

Open the mouth or purse the lips together like a crow's beak in kaki mudra.

141

Suck in air through the mouth and draw it into the stomach, not the lungs.

This can be done in one sucking action, or in a series of gulps, as though drinking water.

Expand the stomach as much as possible to create a vacuum effect.

Fill the stomach as much as possible.

Then completely relax.

Hold the air inside for as long as comfortable, then expel the air by belching.

Practice note: This is not difficult, but may require a little practice. Choose whatever method is easiest.

Duration: For general purposes, 3 to 5 rounds are sufficient. For specific ailments, further rounds may be performed.

Sequence: This mudra may be practised at any time, but is particularly beneficial after the technique of shankhaprakshalana.

Benefits: Bhujangini mudra tones the whole stomach, removes stagnant wind and helps alleviate abdominal disorders. Retaining air in the stomach enables the practitioner to float in water for any length of time.

Meridian effects: In this mudra, strong stimulation is applied to both the stomach and spleen meridians, which are interlinked in one loop as coupled yang-yin meridians. These organs are stimulated directly, potentiating an overall toning effect upon them. The power of digestion, which is the principle function of the spleen, and the power of nourishment, the principle role of the stomach, are stimulated and digestive disorders are alleviated. As a result, vitality increases.

BHOOCHARI MUDRA (gesture of gazing at nothingness)

The word *bhoo* means 'earth', and *chari* means 'moving' or 'dwelling'. Thus the literal meaning is 'gazing at nothingness'. Bhoochari mudra may be performed as a preparation for meditation and as a meditation technique in its own right. The mudra is allied to nasikagra drishti, akashi mudra and shambhavi mudras, all three being forms of trataka. *Trataka* means 'steady gazing' and is a technique that involves gazing at an external focal point as a means to achieve *dharana* or the meditative state of relaxed concentration. Nasikagra drishti and shambhavi mudra are often combined with other yogic techniques or done specifically during one's sadhana. Bhoochari mudra, on the other hand, can be easily practised in everyday life.

The mudra is best performed facing a blank wall or an open space, such as the sky or a body of still water. This ensures that there are no visual obstructions to distract the attention. This is not essential, only preferable. It is an excellent, simple, and effective practice, which brings tranquillity and concentration of mind when done for a reasonable period of time with awareness. It can be done in any position and almost at any place. It can be done while standing, sitting or lying. It can be done in the privacy of one's own home, at work or at play, whatever is convenient.

At first, this simple practice is reasonably difficult for there are so many outer distractions that continually lure one's attention in other directions. As with every other yoga technique it is practice that makes perfect.

Technique

Sit in any comfortable meditation asana with the head and spine straight and the hands in chin or jnana mudra. Close the eyes and relax the whole body.
Open the eyes and raise the right hand in front of the face. The elbow should point to the side of the body.
Hold the hand horizontally, palm down, with the fingers together.
The side of the thumb should be in contact with the top of the upper lip.
Focus the eyes on the tip of the little finger and gaze at it intently for a minute or so, without blinking or flickering the eyes.

143

Try to maintain continuous awareness of the little fingertip.

After a minute or so lower the hand.

Continue to gaze into the place where the little finger was, without blinking.

Become fully engrossed in this point of nothingness.

Simultaneously, be aware of any thought processes.

When the focus dissipates, raise the hand and again concentrate on the tip of the little finger.

After some time, lower the hand and continue to gaze intently into the space, the nothingness.

Be aware of space only; there should be no registration of outer events in the field of conscious perception.

Continue the practice for 5 to 10 minutes.

Awareness: Physical – on the sensation of complete relaxation and stillness. Spiritual – on ajna chakra.

Contra-indications: People suffering from glaucoma, diabetic retinopathy or those who have just had cataract surgery, lens implant or other eye operations should not perform bhoochari mudra without the guidance of a competent teacher.

Benefits: Bhoochari mudra develops the power of concentration and memory. Just as shambhavi and nasikagra mudras increase concentration, bhoochari mudra takes one into a field of vision that is no longer focused on a point, but on the entire visual field. It tranquillizes and introverts the mind and is particularly beneficial for calming anger and stress. Whenever one is angry, bhoochari mudra can be practised and one can then feel the calming effect. It also develops mental stability and the state of thoughtlessness. It helps to awaken ajna chakra and induce meditative states. It takes the practitioner into the psychic and spiritual planes of consciousness.

Meridian effects: The thumb gently presses the point 'GV 27' of the governing meridian, which is located on the median tubercle of the upper lip. A similar mechanism to nasikagra drishti is put into motion, enhancing the natural upward flow of energy in the governing and conception meridians. The increased influx of energy in the head area enhances the processes of concentration, memory and introversion, as well as calming the mind.

The point of the thumb that touches the upper lip is the point 'Lu 11', the terminal point of the lung meridian. In this way the connection is made between the governor meridian, 'GV 27', and the lung meridian, 'Lu 11', the terminal point of the lung meridian. The lungs are greatly involved in regulating the body's overall energy and the connection between these two meridians contributes to an enhancement of the upward flow of energy in the governing meridian. In this way, the effects of the mudra are increased. The lungs also control the ability to mentally interact with the environment and the ability to remain detached. These functions can contribute to the introverting and tranquillizing effect of bhoochari mudra.

SHANMUKHI MUDRA (gesture of closing the six gates)

The word *shanmukhi* is comprised of two roots: *shat* means six and *mukhi* means gates or faces. Shanmukhi mudra involves redirecting the awareness inside by closing the six doors of outer perception: the two eyes, the two ears, the nose and the mouth. Furthermore, shanmukhi mudra is also known as *baddha yoni asana* (the locked source pose), *devi mudra* (attitude of the great goddess), *parangmukhi mudra* (gesture of inner focusing), *sambhava mudra* (gesture of equipoise) and *yoni mudra* (gesture of the source).

Shanmukhi mudra is used to withdraw the mind from the external environment and to focus it at bindu, the source, in order to experience psychic sound. In fact, shanmukhi mudra is an integral part of *nada yoga*, the science of subtle sound. Bindu is traditionally considered to be the centre or source of individual creation, from where the psychic vibrations first emanate. These vibrations are known as *nada*, or 'psychic sound'. They are the first manifestation of creation from the unmanifest source. By taking the awareness to bindu, one begins to experience the inner silence in which the psychic sounds are heard. Shanmukhi mudra is a mudra of introversion through which one experiences the different layers of psychic sounds. The six gates are the six doors of perception through which information is received from the outside world. In this mudra, these gates are closed, allowing the awareness to be redirected to the source.

One should not expect to hear subtle sounds immediately; practice is necessary. At first there may be no sounds or a confused jumble of sounds. Upon hearing one distinct sound, focus the awareness totally upon it. This may take a few weeks of practice. As sensitivity develops, subtler sounds will be heard. Shanmukhi mudra is also used to enhance visualization in other branches of yoga such as swara yoga, tattwa shuddhi and kriya yoga. It is also a beautiful mudra to use while doing japa.

Shanmukhi mudra is a comparatively difficult mudra, even though outwardly it appears simple. Much concentration is needed for its success. It is said that one must be perfectly established in brahmacharya for success in this mudra, and that it is very difficult to obtain even by the *devas*, gods. Therefore, one must realize the importance of this mudra and practise it very cautiously. *Sri Vijnana Bhairava Tantra* says (v. 36):

कररुद्धदृगस्त्रेण भ्रूभेदाद् द्वाररोधनात् ।
दृष्टे बिन्दौ क्रमाल्लीने तन्मध्ये परमा स्थिति: ॥

By using the hands (as tools) to block the entrances in all directions, the eyebrow centre is pierced and bindu (or light) is seen. Being gradually absorbed within that, the supreme state is realized.

Technique

Sit in siddha/siddha yoni asana if possible.
Otherwise take a comfortable meditation asana and place a small cushion beneath the perineum to provide pressure in this area.
Hold the head and spine straight.
Close the eyes and place the hands on the knees.
Relax the whole body.
Raise the arms and bring the hands in front of the face with the elbows pointing sideways.
Close the ears with the thumbs, the eyes with the index

fingers, the nostrils with the middle fingers, and the mouth by placing the ring fingers above and little fingers below the lips.

The fingers should gently but firmly close the six gates.

Release the pressure of the middle fingers and open the nostrils.

Inhale slowly and deeply, using full yogic breathing.

At the end of inhalation, close the nostrils with the middle fingers and practise antar kumbhaka.

Concentrate at bindu and listen to the inner sound or nada emanating from that region.

Retain the breath inside for as long as is comfortable.

After some time, release the pressure of the middle fingers and slowly exhale.

This is one round.

Inhale again immediately to start another round.

To end the practice, lower the hands to the knees, keeping the eyes closed, and slowly externalize the mind, becoming aware of external sounds and the physical body.

Breathing: This technique gives greater benefits when the practitioner can retain the breath for extended periods.

Awareness: Physical – on synchronizing the hand mudra with the breath. Spiritual – bindu, ajna or anahata chakra may be used for concentration. The important point is to introvert the senses.

Duration: Practise for 5 minutes to begin with. Gradually build the duration up over a period of months to 30 minutes.

Time of practice: Shanmukhi mudra is best practised early in the morning or late at night when there is maximum silence. Practising at this time awakens psychic sensitivity.

Contra-indications: People suffering from depression should avoid this practice.

Benefits: Shanmukhi mudra is also a technique of prana vidya where the energy which is emitted from the hands and fingers is absorbed by the nerve endings in the face. The energy and heat from the hands and fingers stimulates and relaxes the nerves and muscles in the face, which are very sensitive to any kind of external change. In this way, a circuit is created between the hands and eyes, nose, mouth and ears. Neurological connections are created between all of these senses, the awareness introverted, and enough pressure is applied to stimulate the flow of ida and pingala. The pressure on the sensory organs is the pingala aspect, while the sensory component is the ida aspect. Through this practice, areas of the cortex are consciously brought into relationships which would otherwise not normally occur. This accounts for the simultaneous potency of internalization and the maintaining of wakefulness. How it affects the inner sound, how it creates nada, is an experience outside the area of physiology. It is also good for those suffering from vertigo.

Meridian effects: The thumbs press the acupuncture points in the vicinity of the ear lobes around the external aperture of the auditory canal. These points are 'GB 2', 'TB 21' and 'SI 19' on the gallbladder, triple burner and small intestine meridian, respectively. They are all concerned with the functions of the inner, middle and external ear, and sound perception as well. These points are used in the acupuncture treatment of tinnitus. It could be possible that acupressure stimulation of these points enhances concentration on and perception of subtle inner sounds.

The index fingers press and gently stimulate the points around the eyes: 'UB 1', 'GB 1' and 'ST 1' on the urinary bladder, gallbladder and stomach meridians, respectively. They are all important for proper function of the eyes and are used in the treatment of various eye disorders.

The tip of the middle finger stimulates the terminal and important point of the large intestine meridian, point 'LI 20', close to the nostril. This point influences the functions of the nose and is important in treatment of nose diseases.

149

The ring and little fingers stimulate points 'GV 26', just above the upper lip, and 'CV 24', just below the lower lip, on the governing meridian and conception meridian respectively. These very powerful points are used when recovery of the consciousness is needed, for example, in the state of shock or an epileptic fit. This strong awakening property is gently triggered in shanmukhi mudra, to sharpen sound perception and a wakeful state of the mind.

UNMANI MUDRA (attitude of mindlessness)

The word *unmani* literally means 'no mind' or 'not thinking'. It may also be translated as 'the attitude of thoughtlessness' or 'meditation'. Unmani implies that state which is beyond thought, a state where all attachment to the world of objects is dispelled. In this state, the awareness functions without the hindrance of conflicting thoughts and analysis. This is known as *unmani avastha*, the state of no thought.

Sri Vijnana Bhairava Tantra describes unmani as a tantric mudra where the eyes are open, gazing outward, but the awareness or attention is turned inward (v. 120):

क्वचिद्वस्तुनि विन्यस्य शनैर्दृष्टिं निवर्तयेत् ।
तज्ज्ञानं चित्तसहितं देवि शून्यालयो भवेत् ॥

O Goddess, momentarily casting the gaze on some object and slowly withdrawing it with the knowledge and impression of that object, one becomes the abode of the void.

It says, at that moment one is looking inside and seeing something that is invisible to others present. This mudra is also known as bhairavi mudra in some texts.

Technique
Sit in any comfortable meditation asana.
Open the eyes fully, but without straining.
Inhale slowly and deeply.

150

Hold the breath inside.

Focus the awareness at bindu in the back of the head for a few seconds.

Exhale slowly, allowing the awareness to descend with the breath from bindu through the chakras in the spine: ajna, vishuddhi, anahata, manipura, swadhisthana, mooladhara.

The eyes should slowly close as the awareness descends. By the time the awareness reaches mooladhara, the eyes should be fully closed.

Even when the eyes are open, the awareness is looking within.

Do not try too hard, but allow the process to occur spontaneously.

Inhale deeply and begin the next round.

Continue for 5 to 10 minutes.

Contra-indications: Those who have just had eye operations, or who have glaucoma or diabetic retinopathy should not perform unmani without the guidance of a competent teacher.

Benefits: Unmani mudra calms stress and agitation, and induces a meditative state.

Meridian effects: The location of the chakras in the spine correspond to certain acupuncture points on the governing meridian, except for mooladhara chakra whose location corresponds to the point 'CV 1', the first point of the conception meridian. The conception meridian also has points at the front of the body which correspond exactly to the *kshetram*, or trigger points, of all the chakras. As awareness moves down along the chakra points in the spine, corresponding points of the governing meridian are stimulated mentally. As governing and conception meridians are closely related, both of them are stimulated. This increases the level of physical and mental energy in the system. Energy normally flows upward through the governing and conception meridians. Many powerful points are

151

stimulated in unmani mudra. To prevent too much energy flowing into the head and creating heat there, the downward movement of awareness creates a balancing effect and enables the mind to become more introverted. In addition to this, there are other points which are stimulated, such as 'GV 14', which corresponds to the location of vishuddhi chakra and is said to clear the brain and calm the spirit.

12

Bandha Mudra: Lock Mudras

The lock mudras combine mudra and bandha. They charge the system with prana and prepare it for kundalini awakening. If one makes a study of the different hatha yoga texts, there will surely be some confusion when it comes to mudras and bandhas. Some practices are referred to as mudras in one text and as bandhas in another. In different texts the same practices may be described, but they might also have different names. It is stated in *Hatha Yoga Pradipika* (3:6–7):

महामुद्रा महाबंधो महावेधश्च खेचरी ।
उड्डीयानं मूलबंधश्च बंधो जालंधराभिध: ॥

करणी विपरीताख्या वज्रोली शक्तिचालनम् ।
इदं हि मुद्रादशकं जरामरणनाशनम् ॥

Maha mudra, maha bandha, maha vedha, khechari, uddiyana, moola bandha and jalandhara bandha, vipareeta karani mudra, vajroli and shakti chalana, verily, these are the ten mudras which destroy old age and death.

In particular, one could easily be confused about jalandhara, uddiyana and moola bandhas. In the ancient tantric scriptures these practices were defined as mudras, not bandhas. Then during the periods when tantric practices were prevalent, it seems they were not considered as separate practices, but their combination was called maha mudra.

When the system of hatha yoga was culled from the tantric practices, some of the practices were redefined, and mudras and bandhas were separated. Now jalandhara, uddiyana and moola are defined as bandhas, but their combination becomes a mudra.

When bandhas are combined with mudra and pranayama, they awaken psychic faculties and form an adjunct to higher yogic practices. These practices combine asana, pranayama and mudra, and are not suitable for beginners. Purification of the body, mind and nadis is necessary before including these practices in one's daily sadhana. To ensure that these techniques are practised appropriately and without causing physical, mental or pranic imbalances, proper guidance from a qualified teacher is essential. Techniques included in this category are:

- Maha mudra (great psychic attitude)
- Maha bheda mudra (the great separating gesture)
- Maha vedha mudra (the great piercing gesture)

MAHA MUDRA (great psychic attitude)

Maha mudra is formed from two words 'maha' and 'mudra'. *Maha* means great, and *mudra* means psychic attitude. Therefore, *maha mudra* means 'the great psychic attitude'. Before commencing maha mudra, the practitioner should be proficient in the techniques of khechari, shambhavi, moola bandha and kumbhaka, and have practised them for some time. This practice should not be attempted without expert guidance.

Hatha yoga technique

Sit in utthanpadasana with the right leg outstretched (see Appendix).
Keep the back straight.
Relax the whole body.
Practise khechari mudra.
Take a deep breath in.

Exhale and bend forward.

Clasp the right big toe with both hands.

Keep the head erect, and the back straight.

Slowly inhale, tilting the head slightly back.

Perform shambhavi mudra and then moola bandha (see Appendix).

Hold the breath inside and rotate the awareness from the eyebrow centre, to the throat, to the perineum.

Mentally repeat, 'ajna, vishuddhi, mooladhara'.

The concentration should remain at each chakra for only 1 or 2 seconds.

Repeat the rotations between ajna, vishuddhi and mooladhara for as long as you can retain the breath comfortably.

To finish the practice, release shambhavi and moola bandha.

Slowly exhale, returning to the upright position.

This is one round.

Breathing: One round is equivalent to 2 complete breaths. The length of the breath should be extended gradually and the rotations continued for as long as the breath can be retained comfortably.

Duration: Practise 3 rounds with the left leg folded, then with the right leg folded, and then with both legs outstretched.

Sequence: This practice should ideally be done after asana and pranayama and before meditation.

Time of practice: In the early morning while the stomach is completely empty.

Contra-indications: People suffering from high blood pressure, heart complaints or glaucoma should not perform this practice. Those with diabetic retinopathy or who have just had cataract surgery, lens implant or other eye operations should not perform the practice without the guidance of a competent teacher. Maha mudra should not be performed without prior purification of the body. Impurity is indicated by any symptoms of accumulated toxins, such as skin eruptions. The practice of maha mudra generates heat and should be avoided in hot summers. Do not practise during active menstruation or pregnancy.

Benefits: Maha mudra combines the benefits of shambhavi mudra, khechari mudra, moola bandha and kumbhaka. It stimulates the energy circuit, linking mooladhara with ajna chakra. The whole system is charged with prana, which intensifies awareness and induces spontaneous meditation. Energy blockages are removed.

Effects: Maha mudra combines the benefits of shambhavi mudra, khechari mudra, moola bandha, kumbhaka and utthanpadasana. Physiologically, maha mudra stimulates the digestive capacity. It is stated in *Hatha Yoga Pradipika* (3:16):

न हि पथ्यमपथ्यं वा रसा: सर्वेऽपि नीरसा: ।
अपि भुक्तं विषं घोरं पीयूषमपि जीर्यति ॥

For one who practises maha mudra, there is nothing wholesome or unwholesome. Anything can be consumed, even the deadliest of poisons is digested like nectar.

Through the practice of maha mudra, digestion and assimilation of both food and prana are stimulated. Although it is said that the practitioner can even consume deadly poisons and be unaffected, it would surely take many years of practice to achieve this state. The benefits of maha mudra are equal and above those of mayurasana, and maha mudra is essentially more dynamic on a pranic and psychic level.

Pranically, maha mudra generates circulation of energy in the chakras. It clears the nadis and particularly stimulates the flow of sushumna. The whole system is charged with prana, which intensifies awareness and induces spontaneous meditation. The prana from the hands goes into the toes, creating a circuit. Pressure is exerted on vajra nadi and there is focusing on the ocular nerves. Along with contraction, a circuit is created in the movement of energy from mooladhara to ajna. Therefore, the mudra stimulates the channels of prana, circulates the movement of prana within the body and awakens prana. In the *Yoga Chudamani Upanishad* it is said (v. 65):

शोधनं नाडिजालस्य चालनं चंद्रसूर्ययो: ।
रसानां शोषणं चैव महामुद्राऽभिधीयते ॥

Maha mudra is a practice which purifies the entire network of nadis, balances ida and pingala and absorbs *rasa* or health-giving fluid so that it pervades one's entire being.

The practice increases one's vitality and harmonizes all bodily functions. It also increases one's awareness and brings about clarity of thought. Psychologically, it develops the mind and inner awareness, and psychically it arouses receptivity. Its effects can be strongly felt on a psychic level. Maha mudra rapidly eliminates mental depression, as it removes all energy blockages which are the fundamental cause of the problem. The practice stills the mind and body, and increases one's sensitivity to subtle experiences. It is therefore a highly recommended and powerful preparatory practice for meditation. It is stated in *Hatha Yoga Pradipika* (3:14 and 18):

इयं खलु महामुद्रा महासिद्धै: प्रदर्शिता ।
महाक्लेशादयो दोषा: क्षीयंते मरणादय: ।
महामुद्रां च तेनैव वदंति विबुधोत्तमा: ॥

कथितेयं महामुद्रा महासिद्धिकरा नृणाम् ।
गोपनीया प्रयत्नेन न देया यस्य कस्यचित् ॥

Maha mudra removes the worst afflictions (the five kleshas) and the cause of death. Therefore it is called 'the great attitude' by the ones of highest knowledge. Thus maha mudra has been described as the giver of great siddhis. It must be kept secret and not disclosed to anyone.

Meridian effects: Shambhavi mudra increases power of perception in chidakasha by stimulating the point 'Ex 1'. In addition, the converging movement of the eyeballs stimulates points 'St 1', 'UB 1', 'GB 1' on the stomach, urinary bladder and gallbladder meridians, improving the power of digestion and elimination.

Moola bandha directly stimulates 'CV 1' point on the conception meridian. The starting and terminating points of the meridians are considered powerful switches that strongly influence the flow of energy. The conception meridian is closely connected with the governing meridian and together they control and direct the flow of energy and the polarities of yin and yang through the whole meridian network. They actually run through the arohan and avarohan psychic passages, removing energy blockages and connecting all six chakras by awakening sushumna.

Khechari mudra extends the root of the tongue, stimulating the energy flow in the kidney and spleen meridians. Firstly, this increases the capability of the kidneys to store the essence, which is the equivalent to *ojas*, and leads to vitality, stamina and resistance. Secondly, the power of digestion, absorption and assimilation is strengthened.

In utthanpadasana, the long portion of the urinary bladder meridian along the back of the leg and the back is stretched, especially if the back is kept straight. Along the spinal column, and simultaneously along this meridian, there are pairs of acupuncture points that are considered important because they significantly influence the functions of all internal organs. These points can be linked to the pairs of spinal nerves that, after branching out of the spinal cord, perform essentially the same action. Strong stimulation of this meridian has an overall homeostatic effect on the all organs and systems.

Extension of the right leg stimulates the pranic flow in payaswini nadi that runs through the spinal cord in proximity of pingala and sushumna and terminates at the right big toe.

MAHA BHEDA MUDRA (the great separating gesture)

Maha bheda mudra means the 'great separating gesture'. This is a powerful practice for uniting with the inner being or self. The *Gheranda Samhita* describes maha bheda mudra under hatha yoga, however, another version is practised in kriya yoga in which the rotation of awareness is practised differently. In hatha yoga, while sitting in utthanpadasana and holding the big toe, bahir kumbhaka is performed along with maha bandha and nasikagra drishti. Holding this position, the awareness is rotated through the three chakras where the locks are applied: in moola bandha energy is locked into mooladhara, in uddiyana bandha awareness is of manipura, and in jalandhara bandha awareness is of vishuddhi. Thus, before commencing this practice, the practitioner should be familiar with the techniques of jalandhara, uddiyana and moola bandhas and bahir kumbhaka. Furthermore, this practice should be attempted only under the guidance of a competent teacher. This practice is described in *Gheranda Samhita* as (3:41–44):

रूपयौवनलावण्यं नारीणां पुरुषं बिना ।
मूलबन्धमहाबन्धौ महबेधं विना तथा ॥

महाबन्धंसमासाद्य कुम्भकं चरेदुड्डीन ।
महाबेध: समाख्यातो योगिनां सिद्धिदायक: ॥

159

महाबन्धमूलबन्धौ महाबेधसमन्वितौ ।
प्रत्यहं कुरुते यस्तु स योगी योगवित्तमः ॥

न मृत्युतो भयं तस्य न जरा तस्य विद्यते ।
गोपनीयः प्रयत्नेन वेधोऽयं योगिपुंगवैः ॥

In the same way that the beauty, youth and elegance of a woman are useless without a man, similarly moola bandha and maha bandha are also fruitless without maha bheda. First practise maha bandha, then while performing uddiyana bandha retain the air through kumbhaka. This has been called maha bheda. The yogis who perform maha bandha and moola bandha along with maha bheda daily are considered the best of all yogis. They are neither affected by old age nor the fear of death. The best of the yogis should keep it secret.

Technique

Assume utthanpadasana as described for maha mudra.
Keep the back straight.
Relax the whole body.
Take a deep breath in.
While exhaling, lean forward and clasp the right big toe with both hands.
Retain the breath outside and perform jalandhara, uddiyana and moola bandhas.
Rotate the awareness successively from the throat, to the abdomen, to the perineum, mentally repeating, 'vishuddhi, manipura, mooladhara'.

160

The awareness should rest on each chakra for only 1 or 2 seconds and then move to the next in a smooth flow.

Repeat the rotations between vishuddhi, manipura and mooladhara for as long as you can retain the breath comfortably.

To finish the practice, release moola bandha, uddiyana and jalandhara.

When the head is raised, inhale and return to the upright position.

Exhale and relax.

This is one round.

Breathing: One round is equivalent to 2 complete breaths. The length of the breath should be extended gradually and the rotations continued for as long as the breath can be comfortably retained.

Duration: Practise 3 times with the left leg folded, then with the right leg folded and then with both legs outstretched.

Sequence: After asana and pranayama and before meditation.

Time of practice: In the early morning while the stomach is completely empty.

Contra-indications: Precautions and contra-indications for kumbhaka, moola, uddiyana and jalandhara bandhas apply. People suffering from high blood pressure or heart complaints, cervical spondylosis, high intracranial pressure, vertigo, colitis, stomach or intestinal ulcer, diaphragmatic hernia or abdominal problems should not perform this practice. It should not be performed without prior purification of the body. Maha bheda mudra generates a lot of heat and should be avoided in hot summers. Do not practise during active menstruation or during pregnancy.

Effects: The benefits of maha bheda mudra are similar to maha mudra. It has a profound influence at a pranic level, specifically influencing mooladhara, manipura and vishuddhi chakras, manipulating and harnessing the

161

energies within them to induce concentration of mind and meditation. Maha bheda supplements and follows maha mudra; together they supercharge the whole body-mind complex, which enables a very powerful flow at the physical, mental and pranic levels. There is circulation of fresh energy in the body, mind and senses. Consciousness becomes extremely subtle and deep. One of the main benefits of this mudra is to achieve a high state of consciousness while maintaining awareness of consciousness in a normal form. This is the aim and purpose of maha bheda mudra. Maha bheda enables yogis to become *siddhas*, perfect and knowledgeable. A person who does all three practices of maha bandha, moola bandha and maha bheda daily is known as a *yogavit*, or yoga adept.

Meridian effects: Jalandhara bandha strongly stretches the cervical portion of the governing meridian, while at the same time it compresses the cervical portion of conception meridian. This stimulates the natural energy interchange between these interlinked and very important pranic flows, which correspond to the arohan and avarohan psychic passages that link all the chakras. In uddiyana bandha, another area of strong compression is added in the abdominal portion of the conception meridian, invigorating an already established energy loop between it and the governing meridian.

In moola bandha, the muscular contraction and subsequent stimulation of 'CV 1' of the conception meridian increases the quantum of pranic flow in the loop of the conception and governing meridians. The synergy of all these pranic modifications results in a quantum change in pranic levels. It also brings the perpetual flux in the flow of yin and yang energies in the conception and governing meridian loop into perfect balance. Due to the very nature of yin and yang, when they are in perfect balance, this allows the practitioner to be pranically and psychically stable, one-pointed and active at the same time, due to the awareness being rotated through the chakras. One's consciousness can soar high, while at the same time there is an awareness of one's normal consciousness.

MAHA VEDHA MUDRA (the great piercing gesture)

Maha vedha means 'the great piercer'. Through this practice the kundalini shakti is forced into sushumna and up to ajna chakra by gently beating the buttocks on the floor. The purpose of maha vedha mudra is to pierce mooladhara chakra and channel the kundalini energy upwards. This hatha yoga technique should not be confused with the similarly named practice of maha bheda mudra described above, which is similar to maha mudra. The technique described in the following sloka of *Hatha Yoga Pradipika* is quite like the kriya yoga technique of tadana kriya (3:26–28):

महाबंधस्थितो योगी कृत्वा पूरकमेकधी: ।
वायूनां गतिमावृत्य निभृतं कंठमुद्रया ॥

समहस्तयुगो भूमौ स्फिचौ संताडयेच्छनै: ।
पुटद्वयमतिक्रम्य वायु: स्फुरति मध्यग: ॥

सोमसूर्याग्निसंबंधो जायते चामृताय वै ।
मृतावस्था समुत्पन्ना ततो वायुं विरेचयेत् ॥

The yogi, in the position of maha bandha, should inhale, make the mind steady and stop the movement of prana by performing the throat lock.

Placing the palms of the hands on the ground, he should slowly beat the buttocks gently on the ground. The prana (then) leaves the two nadis (ida and pingala) and enters into the middle channel (sushumna).

Ida, pingala and sushumna become united and verily, immortality is attained. A death-like state occurs; then the breath should be exhaled.

163

This is a powerful practice for introverting the mind. It awakens psychic faculties and the kundalini which resides in mooladhara chakra. The effect of maha vedha on *brahma granthi*, the psychic knot in the region of mooladhara, is revealed in *Shiva Samhita* (4:23–24):

अपानप्राणयोरैक्यं कृत्वा त्रिभुवनेश्वरि ।
महावेधस्थितौ योगी कुक्षिमापूर्य वायुना ।
स्फिचौ संतडयेद्धीमांवेधोऽयं कीर्तितो मया ॥

वेधेनानेन संबिध्य वायुना योगिपुंगव: ।
ग्रंथिं सुषुम्णामार्गेण ब्रह्मग्रंथिं भिनत्यसौ ॥

Oh goddess of the three worlds! When the yogi, while performing maha bandha, causes the union of the prana and apana and, filling the viscera with air, drives it slowly towards the buttocks, it is called maha vedha.

The best of the yogis having, through the help of the pranas, pierced with this perforator the knot which is in the path of sushumna, should then pierce the knot of Brahma.

All the practices of hatha yoga that help to relax the body and mind, and that stimulate pranic capacity slow down the ageing process. Maha mudra and maha vedha mudra are powerful techniques that introvert the mind and awaken psychic faculties. They affect the pineal and pituitary glands and thus the whole endocrinal system. By activating the pineal gland, the pituitary is kept under control, hormonal secretions are regulated and catabolism is curtailed. Consequently, the symptoms of old age are either annihilated or reduced. In *Hatha Yoga Pradipika* it is said (3:29):

महावेधोऽयमभ्यासान्महासिद्धिप्रदायक: ।
वलीपलितवेपघ्न: सेव्यते साधकोत्तमै: ॥

This is maha vedha, and its practice bestows great perfections. Wrinkles, grey hair and the trembling of old age are evaded, thus the best of practitioners devote themselves to it.

Hatha yoga technique

Sit in padmasana (see Appendix).

If padmasana has not been perfected, one will not be able to practise properly.

Relax the body and keep the eyes closed.

Place the palms of the hands on the floor beside the thighs with the fingers pointing forward or make fists with the knuckles facing down.

Inhale slowly and deeply through the nose.

Retain the breath inside and perform jalandhara bandha.

Raise the body by placing all the weight on the hands, straighten the arms.

Gently beat the buttocks on the ground from 3 to 7 times, keeping your awareness in mooladhara.

Then rest the buttocks on the floor, release jalandhara bandha, sit quietly and exhale slowly and deeply.

This is one round.

Let the breathing return to normal, then again inhale and repeat the process.

Practise three rounds in the beginning.

After a few months the rounds can be gradually increased up to 5, but no more.

165

When beating the buttocks one must be gentle.

The buttocks and the backs of the thighs should touch the ground simultaneously.

The spine must be kept straight and jalandhara bandha maintained.

When the practice is complete, sit quietly and concentrate on mooladhara chakra for a few minutes.

Breathing: Inhale deeply in the starting position. Retain the breath inside while raising and lowering the buttocks. Exhale only after the body has been finally lowered to the floor.

Awareness: Physical – on retaining the breath while lightly beating the buttocks. Spiritual – on mooladhara chakra.

Sequence: After asana and before meditation.

Precautions: Beat the buttocks very gently. It is important to use a thick mat to avoid injury. Do not let the coccyx (tailbone) land directly on the floor. The backs of the legs and buttocks should hit the floor simultaneously. This cushions and distributes the impact over a wide area.

Contra-indications: People who have any inflammatory disease, infection or general complaints in or around the pelvic area should avoid this practice. Those with heart problems, high blood pressure, sciatica or weak or injured knees should not attempt this practice. Do not practise during active menstruation or pregnancy.

Practice note: If padmasana has not been mastered this practice can be performed with the legs outstretched, although this method is less effective.

Benefits: This is a powerful practice for introverting the mind. It awakens psychic faculties and the kundalini which resides in mooladhara chakra.

13

Adhara Mudra:
Perineal Mudras

In the region of the perineum, where there are many nerve endings, there are two main nadis known as the *vajra nadi*, corresponding to the sciatic nerve, and *brahma nadi*, which runs through the centre of sushumna. Both of these nadis are specifically stimulated or acted upon when the perineal mudras are practised. These techniques redirect prana from the lower centres to the brain (see Chapter 7). Mudras concerned with sublimating sexual energy are in this group. Brahma represents the creative aspect, the sexual urge, desire. With the practice of these mudras, the flow of apana within brahma nadi is reversed, and all the psychological, physical, mental and emotional desires are transcended. Apana is reversed and begins to move in brahma nadi in the other direction.

The techniques have been described in stages, starting with the practices suitable for beginners. These techniques not only contract the perineal and anal muscles, but also stimulate mooladhara and swadhisthana chakras. Tension which is released by performing such practices may result in emotions, thoughts and memories surfacing in the mind. Therefore, along with a systematic approach, cultivation of a witnessing attitude is an important aspect of these practices. Techniques included in this category are:

- Ashwini mudra (horse gesture)
- Vajroli/sahajoli mudra (thunderbolt/spontaneous psychic gesture)
- Vajroni mudra (thunderbolt gesture)

ASHWINI MUDRA (horse gesture)

Ashwini means horse. The practice resembles the movement a horse makes with its sphincter immediately after evacuation of the bowels. Ashwini mudra can be done in almost any asana, including any of the meditational asanas. It should definitely be performed while holding sarvangasana. Not only does this mean that two practices can be done at the same time, but this is a highly beneficial combination. Technique 2 of ashwini mudra can also be integrated with nadi shodhana pranayama, so that the anal contraction is during the retention of breath.

It is impossible to confine the muscular contraction only to the small area of the anus. Other pelvic muscles and muscles associated with the sexual organs will also contract. However, as much as possible, concentrate on the contraction at the anus. At first this is difficult, but with practice becomes easier and easier.

Technique I: Rapid contraction

Sit in any comfortable meditation asana.
Close the eyes and relax the whole body.
Become aware of the natural breathing process.
Take the awareness to the anus.
Rapidly contract the anal sphincter muscles for a few seconds without straining, then relax them.
Confine the action to the anal area.
Contraction and relaxation should be performed 10 to 20 times, smoothly and rhythmically.
Gradually make the contractions more rapid.

Technique 2: Contraction with antar kumbhaka

Sit in any comfortable meditation asana.

Close the eyes and relax the whole body.

Inhale slowly and deeply while simultaneously contracting the anal sphincter muscles.

Practise *antar kumbhaka*, internal breath retention, while holding the contraction of the anal sphincter muscles as tightly as possible without strain.

Exhale while releasing the contraction of the anus.

Perform 5 to 10 rounds.

Awareness: Physical – on anal contraction and relaxation. Spiritual – on mooladhara chakra.

Duration: There is no limit on the duration of practice. It is only limited by the time that is available. However, beginners should not overstrain their muscles. Increase the duration of the practice as the anal muscles become stronger and control is gained over them.

Contra-indications: People with high blood pressure or heart disease should not practise with antar kumbhaka.

Benefits: This practice strengthens the anal muscles. It prevents the escape of pranic energy and redirects it upward for spiritual purposes. Many people have weak anal muscles (sphincters). This is closely associated with such widespread ailments as constipation and piles (haemorrhoids). Ashwini mudra helps to stimulate intestinal peristalsis, which is a wavelike motion that propels the stool through the intestines to the anus for evacuation. Therefore, it is a great help in alleviating constipation and thus improving the general health and wellbeing of the practitioner.

Piles are characterized by an accumulation of blood in the region of the anus. The practice of ashwini mudra helps to squeeze this stagnant blood away from the anus. This process is intensified if the mudra is combined with sarvangasana. Ashwini mudra physically draws the blood away from the anus and sarvangasana allows the blood to drain downwards back to the heart. Every sufferer of piles should definitely practise this combination daily. Those people who suffer from prolapse of the anus or rectum should also do ashwini mudra. By strengthening the associated muscles, these ailments will slowly disappear.

For those who are seriously intending to practise kriya yoga in the future, ashwini mudra should definitely be performed and mastered. In this manner, sensitivity will be developed in the anal area, as well as the ability to isolate the muscles from other muscular systems in the pelvic region. This is important for eventual mastery of moola bandha.

Meridian effects: The governing meridian originates in the pelvic cavity, descends and emerges on the surface of the body at the perineum. From there it runs backwards, passing through the anus and continues towards the tip of the coccyx. It continues up along the spinal column to communicate with the kidneys in the lumbar region. It then ascends to the brain, reaches the crown of the skull and from there it descends along the front median line across the forehead and nose, to terminate at the upper lip. The connection of this meridian with mooladhara and the other chakras is obvious. It is stimulated at the very beginning by the contraction of the anal sphincter muscles. The result is that the natural upward flow of energy in this meridian is increased. This also means the kidneys receive an additional energy supply, due to their connection with the governing meridian.

The governing meridian is related to mooladhara chakra in two ways. First, it emerges from the pelvic cavity of the perineal area, which is the exact location of mooladhara in the physical body. Second, it is connected with the conception meridian which also emerges at the centre of the perineum and has its first point 'CV 1' at that location, representing a direct link with mooladhara chakra.

Connection of the governing meridian, which is stimulated by ashwini mudra, occurs at the point 'GV 4' which is called 'the door of life'. This connection is important because, according to acupuncture, the kidneys have certain properties that correspond to

170

properties of mooladhara chakra. They store the essence that controls all growth, development and reproductive functions. They produce bone and spinal marrow and govern the bones and teeth. The kidneys store the original energy, primal energy of man, and hold the fundamental yin and yang of the body. They are the foundation of all life in the body.

The local effects of the stimulation of the points on the governing meridian in the vicinity of the anus are used in the treatment of various disorders of the anorectal region, which are mentioned in the yogic explanation of ashwini mudra.

VAJROLI/SAHAJOLI MUDRA
(thunderbolt/spontaneous psychic gesture)

The word 'vajroli' is derived from the root *vajra*, which means 'thunderbolt' or 'lightning'. It is also the weapon of Lord Indra and means 'the mighty one'. Vajra in this context refers to the vajra nadi which governs the urogenital system. It is the energy flow within the spine which governs the sexual systems of the body and is the force which moves upward with the power of lightning. It is also the second innermost layer of sushumna nadi. In tantric sadhana this energy is not suppressed, but it is awakened and redirected. Vajroli and sahajoli mudra are practices that specifically sublimate sexual energy into *ojas*, or vitality, and kundalini shakti (see Chapter 7 for more details).

There are two types of vajroli: one involves *maithuna*, sexual intercourse under prescribed conditions, and the other is a simple technique that involves contraction of the urethra. Vajroli in the context of maithuna was never meant for the general public because the first requirement for the practice is a passionless state of mind. Very few people today can fit into this category. Only those who have entered the highest states of samadhi know what a passionless state is. These practices result in greater personal power

171

and if used by selfish people they will incur catastrophes upon themselves and others. The purpose of liberating the energy through vajroli is to go beyond personal identity and the limitations of the ego. If yoga is practised only to gain psychic power, or if vajroli is an excuse for any lesser fulfilment, the practices are being misused. Therefore, in *Hatha Yoga Pradipika* it says (3:95):

अयं योग: पुण्यवतां धीराणां तत्त्वदर्शिनाम् ।
निर्मत्सराणां वै सिध्येत्र तु मत्सरशालिनाम् ॥

Verily this yoga is perfected by virtuous and well-conducted men who have seen the truth and not those who are selfish.

A novice will not be able to find a guru to teach him the traditional method of this practice. Nor will a guru teach any person who is untrustworthy or cannot understand the purpose of the practices. Likewise, one has to be careful when reading about these practices as interpreted by non-yogis because incorrect descriptions have surely been given. Precisely for this reason many people have a misconception concerning vajroli. Only those who can comprehend the subtle laws of tantra, kundalini, energy and consciousness can appreciate its significance and necessity. The *Hatharatnavali* says (2:74–75):

वज्रोलीं कथयिष्यामि गोपितां सर्वयोगिभि: ।
अती तद्रहस्यं हि न देया यस्य कस्यचित् ॥

स्वप्राणैस्तु समो यस्मात् तस्यैव कथयेद्ध्रुवं ।
पुत्रस्यापि न दातव्या गुरुशिष्यक्रमं विना ॥

Now I will talk about vajroli which is kept secret by all yogis. The secret process of this should not be revealed to an unsuitable person.

The person whom the guru feels to be like his own prana, verily it should be told to him. It should not be given even to one's own son without the guru-disciple tradition.

Hatharatnavali further states (2:103–104):

अज्ञात योगशास्त्रेण वज्रोलीं स्त्री तु नाभ्यसेत् ।
अयं योग: पुण्यवतां धन्यानां तत्त्वशालिनां ॥

निर्भत्सराणां सिध्येत न तु मत्सरशालिनां ।
सर्वेषामेव योगानां अयं योग: शुभंकर: ॥

The lady who does not know the science of yoga should not practise vajroli. This yoga is successful to the courageous and the pious yogis who have an insight into reality.

Success in yoga can be achieved only by those who are in no way selfish. It cannot be achieved by self-seeking ones. This yoga is auspicious among all the yogas.

Preparation for vajroli, therefore, must specifically be done under the guidance of a guru and not just any teacher. In reality, this form of vajroli is rarely taught and therefore, even though instructions and techniques are given, it should not be attempted out of curiosity.

According to *Hatha Yoga Pradīpika*, sahajoli is an essential part of vajroli, just as jalandhara is part and parcel of uddiyana. It is a practice performed by both the man and woman which entails the application of ash.

Simple form of vajroli and sahajoli mudra

It is the simple raja yoga form of vajroli that is commonly taught and used in kriya yoga. Vajroli mudra is a practice for men involving gradual contractions of the urogenital muscles. The equivalent practice for women is known as sahajoli mudra, in which the entire vaginal passage has to be contracted. The word 'sahajoli' is from the root *sahaj*, meaning 'spontaneous'. Thus, *sahajoli mudra* is the psychic gesture of spontaneous arousing. Vajroli and sahajoli mudra are preferably performed in siddhasana and siddha yoni asana respectively, so before beginning the practice it is necessary to first perfect the relevant posture.

Technique

Sit in siddha/siddha yoni asana, or any comfortable meditation posture with the head and spine straight.

Place the hands on the knees in chinmudra or jnana mudra.

Close the eyes and relax the whole body.

Take the awareness to the urethra.

Inhale, hold the breath inside and draw the urethra upward.

This action is similar to holding back an intense urge to urinate.

The testes in men and labia in women should move slightly upward during this contraction.

Confine the contraction to the urethra.

Hold the contraction for as long as comfortable, starting with a few seconds, and gradually increasing.

Exhale, releasing the contraction, and relax.

Awareness: Physical – on isolating the point of contraction, avoiding generalized contraction of the pelvic floor. Spiritual – on swadhisthana chakra.

Duration: Begin with 3 contractions, slowly increase to 10.

Contra-indications: Vajroli/sahajoli mudra should not be practised by people suffering from urethritis as the irritation and pain may increase.

Benefits: Vajroli/sahajoli mudra regulates and tones the entire urogenital system. It helps overcome psychosexual conflicts and unwanted sexual thoughts. It conserves and redirects energy, enhancing meditative states.

Meridian effects: The conception meridian emerges from the pelvic cavity at the centre of the perineum where its first point 'CV 1' is located. Then it runs forward and upward to the mid-point of the superior border of the pubic bone, where its second point 'CV 2' is located. This is also the *kshetram*, or trigger point, of swadhisthana chakra. This point is very close to the muscles which are contracted in vajroli mudra, and thus gets stimulated during the practice. The conception meridian is stimulated in the

174

same way. The upward flow of energy in the conception mudra is enhanced. The governing meridian also receives stimulation, and contributes to the overall increase in physical and mental energy. The conception mudra, as the name suggests, influences conception, the reproductive organs and sexual function on all levels: physical, mental and emotional. Through stimulation of the flow of energy in this meridian, vajroli mudra increases the amount of energy that is available for all these processes. This is the acupuncture explanation of how vajroli mudra alleviates various disorders related to reproductive organs and psychosexual conflicts.

Practice note: Two asanas which help develop the practice of sahajoli are naukasana and namaskarasana:

1. Perform naukasana with the arms and fists clenched strongly. While holding this position, contract the vagina also. The practice has to be done holding the breath inside. When this can be performed with ease, contract the whole body, starting with the contraction of the vagina.

2. Assume the starting position of namaskarasana with the arms outside the legs and the hands flat on the floor. Contract all the muscles of the vagina and hold the contraction for as long as possible, while retaining the breath inside and performing shambhavi mudra.

Complete practice of vajroli

Stage 1: Sit in siddhasana and practise uddiyana, increasing gradually until it can be held for one and half minutes.

Stage 2: Eliminate the acidity of the urine through the diet, water and dry coriander seeds. For the latter, dry coriander seeds are soaked overnight in a glass of water. The following morning, the seeds are strained and the water drunk 30 minutes before breakfast. This continues until the acidity is eliminated, which may take up to a month.

Stage 3: Practise interrupted urination while in the starting position of namaskarasana. The time needed to perfect this stage is approximately six months.

Stage 4: By contracting the urethra and drawing it upwards, practise sucking the urine back up. This stage may take one or two years to master.

Stage 5: Once the technique in stage 4 is mastered, hold back the ejaculation of urine up to one minute.

Stage 6: Progressively increase the period of holding back the ejaculation until permanent retention is achieved.

Stage 7: Once stage 6 has been achieved, the awareness and concentration is directed to the chakras.

In the hatha yoga tradition a tube or catheter is inserted into the penis for practising this stage of vajroli mudra. First, air is drawn into the bladder, then water, later oil, honey and finally liquid mercury. According to some authorities, it is neither essential nor advisable to use any liquid other than water. Instead of drawing further viscous liquids into the bladder, pure water may be used while varying the suction exerted by increasing the height to which the liquid is raised. This is briefly described in *Hatha Yoga Pradipika* (3:86):

यत्नतः शस्तनालेन फूत्कारं वज्रकंदरे ।
शनैः शनैः प्रकुर्वीत वायुसंचारकारणात् ॥

By slowly drawing in air through a prescribed tube inserted into the urethra of the penis, gradually air and prana traverse into the vajra kanda.

The *Hatharatnavali* states that vajroli/sahajoli should be done by men and women. However, this particular practice is specifically for men. The complete method of practice is not given in *Hatha Yoga Pradipika*, however, in *Hatharatnavali* (2:80–85) there are detailed descriptions.

Just as a man prepares for vajroli by practising contractions and then drawing up air and water through a catheter via the urethra, a woman can also practise in a similar way. Instead of inserting a catheter into the urethra, however, a tube is inserted into the vagina so that a portion of it extends outside. She then sits on a bucket of water or bathtub and practises uddiyana bandha. If water is not sucked into the vagina through this process, then nauli is practised. When this has been perfected, the water is retained inside for as long as possible and nauli is performed. This cleanses the vagina of old secretions.

When these practices are perfected, the tube is discarded and water is taken in directly. When the water can be retained inside only by the practice of moola bandha and without uddiyana, the perineal muscles associated with moola bandha and vajroli/sahajoli have become strong.

Variation of vajroli and sahajoli mudra

According to other texts, vajroli and sahajoli have been described in an entirely different way. With regard to vajroli the full details may have been omitted. It states that one has to balance the body on the buttocks and place the feet behind the head. The arms remain in front of the body and palms on the ground. In this position the urinary complex is compressed and automatic contraction of the urogenital muscles occurs. However, it is not specifically stated that these muscles are, or should be, contracted. Neither is the retention of reproductive fluid hinted at.

The variation of sahajoli mudra has been described as follows:

Technique

Wash the legs and feet thoroughly, and then sit in siddha yoni asana.

Contract the muscles of the vagina and then relax them. Repeat this several times in succession.

When the vaginal muscles become stronger, contract the inner part of the vagina and hold the contraction.

Gradually increase the contraction of all vaginal muscles until it becomes more intense and deep.

When deep contraction has been achieved, begin to contract the vaginal muscles, raising the opening from the heel.

177

Then bring the heel up close to the vaginal opening, and relax the muscles so that the heel enters the vagina. Continue to contract and raise the vagina, then relax and lower it, until the heel enters approximately two centimetres into the vagina.

When this stage has been mastered, repeat the contractions while sitting in bhadrasana and gorakshasana.

VAJRONI MUDRA (thunderbolt gesture)

Learned ones have named this mudra vajroni as it enables the flow of energy which provides life. In tantra, the panchamakara sadhana prescribes vajroli mudra for men, sahajoli mudra for women and vajroni mudra for celibates. With these mudras one achieves *urdhva retas tattwa*, sublimation of sexual energy, so that the downward-flowing energy can be converted into upward-flowing energy. Thus, in tantra this practice carries great significance.

From the verses on vajroni mudra in *Gheranda Samhita*, it cannot be ascertained exactly how this practice is done; however, this mudra is linked with an asana called *brahmacharyasana*, celibate's pose. When classified as an asana, it is called brahmacharyasana and when classified as a mudra, it is called vajroni mudra.

Technique

Sit with the legs together and outstretched in front of the body.

Place the palms of the hands on the floor on either side of the hips with the fingers pointing forward and the elbows straight.

Adjust the position of the hands, bringing them slightly forward, until the centre of gravity is found.

Push down with the arms, using the abdominal muscles to lift the buttocks, legs and feet from the floor.

In the final position only the palms of the hands remain on the floor.

The whole body is supported and balanced on the hands alone.

The legs should be horizontal and straight; the spine may curve slightly.

Do not strain.

Hold the position for as long as is comfortable.

Slowly lower the buttocks and legs to the floor.

Relax for a few moments with the legs outstretched before performing the next round.

Practise up to 3 rounds.

Breathing: Inhale while seated on the floor. Retain inside while raising and balancing the body. Exhale while returning to the floor.

Awareness: Physical – on the tension in the abdomen, hips, leg and arm muscles, or perineum. Spiritual – on mooladhara or manipura chakra.

Sequence: Follow with shavasana or advasana.

Contra-indications: This mudra should not be practised by people with high blood pressure or any heart ailment or hernia.

Benefits: The mudra strengthens the abdominal organs and muscles, as well as the thighs and arms. The muscles of the perineum contract strongly while this mudra is performed, automatically inducing vajroli mudra, ashwini mudra and moola bandha. Consequently, it is an important mudra for the conservation of sexual energy for spiritual purposes.

Effects: During the practice of this mudra the entire body, including the urinary tract, rectum, muscles of the thighs, all muscles of the legs, feet and waist are contracted and moola bandha occurs spontaneously. A strong locking of moola bandha is important. This locking influences vajra nadi giving this practice its name, vajroni mudra.

The practice has similar effects as vajroli mudra, that is, control over the flow of reproductive fluids. It is said: *Aitad yoga prasadena bindusiddhirbhaved dhruvam* – "The

179

practice of yoga which enables siddhi or perfection of bindu is *veerya siddhi* or control over the semen." It is normal for men to have night emissions which may disturb them. During sleep, when there is no longer control over thoughts and feelings, passion may surface and night emissions occur. This is a natural process, but some fear that energy is wasted in this way. For control of this, vajroni mudra is practised. When semen is conserved, the life force in the chromosomes is also preserved and this life force influences the chakras.

That is why it is further said: *Siddhai bindoumahayatane kim na siddhyati bhootale* – "A human being can achieve victory over the earth element by means of bindu siddhi." Mooladhara chakra is the centre of reproduction and the earth element. Normally, the energy of mooladhara chakra is externalized and discharged. Conservation of this energy is helpful in the awakening of kundalini. That is why, in the asana category, vajroni is known as brahmacharyasana or the posture in which one can acquire celibacy.

Meridian effects: The governing meridian emerges at the perineum and passes through the anal sphincter, point 'GV 1'. The natural upward flow of energy through the governing meridian is augmented by the strong contraction of this sphincter in ashwini mudra, which in this practice happens spontaneously. The governing meridian, which runs up along the spine, connects all the chakras with its upward energy flow. This meridian connects to the kidneys through point 'GV 4'. The kidneys store essence, or ojas, that governs all growth, vitality, lustre and reproductive power. The influx of energy triggered in the governing meridian reaches the kidneys, and the essence, or ojas, is protected.

Point 'CV 2' in the area of the pubic bone on the conception meridian is contracted in vajroli or sahajoli mudra. The natural upward flow in this channel is also stimulated from its very base. This meridian governs processes of conception, reproduction and sexuality. When the energy flow in it is abundant, these processes are harmonious. Activation of the point 'CV 1' on this meridian by moola bandha augments this effect.

The resulting yin-yang harmony within the conception-governing meridian energy loop can also facilitate redirection of the downward flow of reproductive fluids.

14

Kaya Mudra: Postural Mudras

These practices utilize physical postures combined with a specified breathing technique and focus of concentration. These practices are not suitable for beginners, even if the posture can be performed physically. A certain amount of purification of the body, mind and nadis is necessary before attempting the postural mudras. Proper guidance from a qualified teacher will ensure that the techniques are undertaken with full awareness and in an appropriate and correct manner. Techniques included in this category are:

- Prana mudra (gesture of invocation of energy)
- Yoga mudra (gesture of psychic union)
- Shakti chalana mudra (gesture of moving the energy)
- Tadagi mudra (gesture of barrelled abdomen)
- Pashinee mudra (gesture of noose)
- Vipareeta karani mudra (gesture of inversion)

PRANA MUDRA (gesture of invocation of energy)

Prana is the vital energy that sustains not only the individual body, but also creation at every level. Prana exists in sentient beings as the energy that drives every action, voluntary and involuntary, every thought, every level of the mind and body. In this practice, with the help of the breath and hand gestures, the quantum of prana in the body is enhanced, to the point that it radiates out to the whole environment, in an

182

invocation of peace. Therefore, this practice is also known as *shanti mudra*, or peace mudra.

Technique

Sit in any comfortable meditation posture, preferably padmasana or siddha/siddha yoni asana with the hands in bhairava mudra.

Close the eyes and relax the whole body, especially the abdomen, arms and hands.

Stage 1: Keeping the eyes closed, inhale and exhale as deeply as possible, contracting the abdominal muscles to expel the maximum amount of air from the lungs.

With the breath held outside, perform moola bandha while concentrating on mooladhara chakra in the perineum.

Retain the breath outside for as long as is comfortable.

Stage 2: Release moola bandha.

Inhale slowly and deeply, expanding the abdomen fully. Draw as much air into the lungs as possible.

Simultaneously raise the hands until they are in front of the navel.

The hands should be open with the palms facing the body, the fingers pointing towards each other, but not touching. The upward movement of the hands should be coordinated with the abdominal inhalation.

The arms and hands should be relaxed.

While inhaling from the abdomen, feel the prana or vital energy being drawn from mooladhara chakra to manipura chakra.

Stage 3: Continue the inhalation by expanding the chest and raising the hands until they are directly in front of the sternum at the centre of the chest.

Feel the pranic energy being drawn up from manipura to anahata chakra while inhaling.

Stage 4: Draw even more air into the lungs by slightly raising the shoulders and raise the hands to the front of the throat in coordination with the breath.

Feel the prana being drawn up to vishuddhi.

Stage 5: Retain the breath inside while spreading the arms out to the sides.

Feel the prana spreading in a wave through ajna, bindu and sahasrara chakras.

In the final position, the hands are level with the ears. The arms are outstretched but not straight, and the palms are turned upward.

Concentrate on sahasrara chakra and visualize an aura

Stage 1

Stage 2

Stage 3

184

of pure light emanating from the head.

Feel that the whole being is radiating vibrations of peace to all beings.

Retain this position, with the breath held inside, for as long as possible without straining the lungs in any way.

While exhaling, repeat stages 4, 3, 2, 1, and slowly return to the starting position.

During exhalation, feel the prana progressively descending through each of the chakras until it reaches mooladhara.

At the end of exhalation, perform moola bandha and feel the prana returning to mooladhara chakra.

Relax the whole body and breathe normally.

Breathing: Increase the duration of inhalation, retention and exhalation slowly.

Be careful not to strain the lungs. When the practice

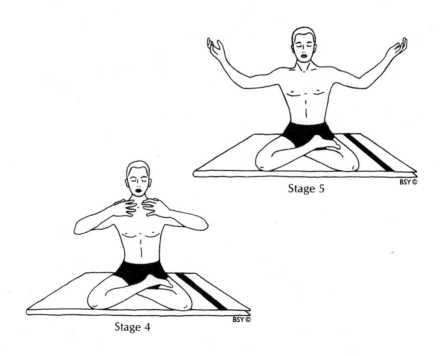

Stage 5

Stage 4

185

has been perfected, visualize the breath as a stream of white light ascending and descending within sushumna nadi.

Awareness: The awareness should move in a smooth and continuous flow from mooladhara to sahasrara and back to mooladhara, in coordination with the breath and the movement of the hands.

Sequence: Prana mudra is best practised after asana and pranayama and before meditation, but it may be performed at any time.

Time of practice: Ideally, practise at sunrise while facing the sun.

Benefits: Prana mudra awakens the dormant *prana shakti*, vital energy, and distributes it throughout the body, increasing strength, health and confidence. It develops awareness of the nadis and chakras, and the subtle flow of prana in the body. It instils an inner attitude of peace and equanimity by adopting an external attitude of offering and receiving energy to and from the cosmic source.

Meridian effects: Through moola bandha, the root of the conception meridian, the principal yin pool in the energy network, is activated. Then, by deep exhalation, its abdominal portion is compressed, triggering an increased upward wave of prana along its course that corresponds to the arohan psychic passage. Floating on the yang quality provided by the deep inhalation, raising the arms carries the yin between the palms and the front of the body, which are yin parts, all the way up. By opening the arms, the yin aspects, the inner sides of the arms and the palms, expose the totality of the raised yin to the cosmic yang, the cosmic prana, enabling the human energy network to absorb it freely, up to capacity.

YOGA MUDRA (gesture of psychic union)

The word *yoga* means 'union', and a *mudra* is described as a 'mental or physical expression of an inner feeling' or 'attitude'. However, it is not only an expression of a feeling, but if properly used it is also a means of invoking inner power and realization. This mudra is so called because it unites the individual consciousness with the Supreme Consciousness, or the outer nature with the inner nature. Although yoga mudra is also practised as a part of the padmasana group, with the name yogamudrasana, it has never actually been considered to be an asana. In yoga mudra, the forward bend is used to bring the legs into position, thereby exerting a slight pressure on the perineum, which opens sushumna.

There are a few reasons why yoga mudra is so comforting. Firstly, it brings the body in touch with the ground. Touching the front of the body with the legs is very comforting. The resulting pressure along the abdomen and chest has a very calming effect on the adrenal system, as in shashankasana and pranamasana. Also, in this posture the front of the body is protected while the back is exposed. The back of the body is harder; it is the soft front that needs protection. So, in yoga mudra one takes a very protective attitude in which one comes into contact with the earth and closes oneself off, exposing the back.

In padmasana, the heels press against the groin and create a spontaneous contraction of the relaxed muscles towards the centre, creating a semi-nauli effect. In nauli the muscles are pushed together, here they are relaxed.

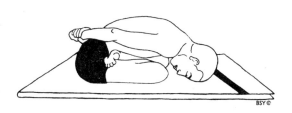

187

It is the heels which press the muscles towards the centre. This nauli effect is important in yoga mudra. In other cross-legged postures the nauli effect and resulting stimulation of manipura kshetram is absent.

Technique
Sit in padmasana (see Appendix).
Take hold of one wrist behind the back.
Close the eyes and relax the whole body.
Bring the awareness to mooladhara chakra; a slight moola bandha may also be performed.
Inhale slowly and feel the breath gradually rising from mooladhara to ajna chakra.
Retain the breath for a few seconds and concentrate on ajna chakra.
Exhale slowly while bending forward from the hips.
Synchronize the movement with the breath, so that the forehead just touches the floor in yogamudrasana as the air is fully expelled from the lungs.
Simultaneously, feel the breath gradually descending from ajna to mooladhara chakra.
Retain the breath outside for a few seconds while concentrating at mooladhara chakra.
Inhaling, raise the trunk to the vertical position.
Be aware of the breath moving upward from mooladhara to ajna chakra.
All the movements should be performed in a harmonious, smooth and synchronized manner.
Remain in the upright position, holding the breath for a few seconds and concentrate on ajna chakra.
Exhale slowly, moving the awareness back down the spine to mooladhara chakra.
This is one round.
Immediately start another round, performing a light moola bandha with the breath held outside and the awareness at mooladhara chakra.

188

Beginners may take a few normal breaths before starting the next round.

Perform 3 to 10 rounds.

Variations: In a variation of yoga mudra, the awareness is held at manipura chakra rather than moving from mooladhara to ajna. In both variations, the hands may also be placed: i) on the heels of the feet, with the elbows pointing out to the sides, ii) palms down on the soles of the feet, iii) palm to palm with the fingers pointing upward in the middle of the back in *hamsa* or swan mudra.

Breathing: The respiration should be as slow as possible without the slightest strain.

Awareness: Physical – on synchronizing the movement of the body with the breath. Spiritual – on mooladhara and ajna chakras.

Sequence: This practice may be followed by any backward bending asana such as bhujangasana or ushtrasana.

Contra-indications: People suffering from sciatica, high blood pressure, pelvic inflammatory disease or any other serious abdominal ailment should avoid this practice.

Practice note: If one cannot sit comfortably in padmasana, the practice can be done in vajrasana. This is like the technique of shashankasana with the hands clasped behind the back. If there is difficulty bending forward due to stiffness in the back, it will easier to bend forward into shashankasana. If there is difficulty in bending forward in vajrasana, due to the legs supporting the entire trunk, then separate the knees slightly, allowing the chest to come closer to the floor. That is also a very comfortable posture and the same results are experienced.

Benefits: The practice massages the abdominal organs and stretches the back, contributing to good general health. In addition, it is an excellent preparatory practice for meditation, engendering a sense of relaxation and tranquillity. Yoga mudra is the best antidote for anger, anxiety, tension, mental pressure, fatigue, lethargy, drowsiness or dullness. It develops awareness and control

189

of psychic energy and is used to awaken manipura chakra. It should be practised first thing in the morning, so that the prana begins to flow through the chakras and the entire chakra system becomes active.

Meridian effects: Pressure is applied to the perineum, at the point of 'CV 1', where the conception meridian emerges close to the surface of the body. Elongation of the whole spine that occurs in the forward bend of yoga mudra stretches and stimulates the governing meridian, which runs along the back median line. The natural upward flow of energy in both of these meridians is enhanced. This extra supply of vital force to the head helps the body and mind to prepare for meditation.

All the meridians that traverse the abdominal area: the spleen, liver, kidney, stomach and conception meridians are compressed in the forward bend of yoga mudra. This occurs after they have already been compressed in the legs and perineum in the posture of padmasana. The strong stimulation applied in this way explains the regulative effects that yoga mudra has on the abdominal organs and the adrenal glands.

The meridians on the left and right side of the body are criss-crossed on two places in this mudra; the meridians that run along the arms are criss-crossed at the area where one hand holds the opposite wrist and in the position of padmasana the meridians that run along the legs are also criss-crossed. The links between the meridians of the left and right side of the body, created in this way, have a balancing effect on the energy that flows throughout the body.

In yoga mudra, first the flow of energy in both upper and lower extremities is equalized. Then, in the forward bend, the trunk is put into close contact with the extremities. The final position of yoga mudra represents a perfect, self-contained gesture that expresses the eternal balance of yin and yang. Yang is active, extrovert edand is represented by the back and upper part of the body. Yin is passive, introverted and represented by the front and lower part of the body. In yoga mudra the yang upper part of the body is in close contact with the yin lower part. The back of the body, which is yang, is stretched and exposed, facing the outside world, in absolute accordance with the nature of yang. The front of the body, which is yin, is protected and hidden, in accordance with the nature of yin. The head, which is extremely yang, is in close contact with the earth which represents yin. Thus, there is a state of absolute interconnection and balance in yoga mudra. Everything is as it should be; in a perfect and balanced state of union, yoga.

SHAKTI CHALANA MUDRA (gesture of moving the energy)

There are different techniques of shakti chalana mudra. Both methods attempt to awaken kundalini shakti. Technique 1 has been described in *Gheranda Samhita*.

Technique I

Take a clean, soft piece of white cloth about 10 cm wide and 23 cm long.

Secure it around the navel region by tying it around the waist with a thin cotton or jute thread, so that it does not slip.

Knotting the cloth is prohibited as the size of the knot would interfere with the practice.

Instead of tying the cloth with a knot, ensure that it is wrapped tightly but without obstructing the blood circulation, and then secure it by tying it in place with a thread.

Sit in siddhasana/siddha yoni asana with holy ash applied on the body.

Inhale deeply, taking the breath not into the chest, but into the abdomen, the region of apana.

Retain the breath for 5 seconds.

191

Next, with the help of uddiyana bandha bring apana upward, uniting it with prana.

Due to tying a cloth over the navel region, the pressure of air inside the body will start moving towards the rectum, where ashwini mudra is performed to direct the energy upwards.

Release ashwini mudra, followed by uddiyana bandha, and gently exhale.

Breathing: After inhaling, retain the breath for 5 seconds. After releasing ashwini mudra and uddiyana bandha, exhale.

Duration: Up to seven or nine rounds is enough.

Precautions: This mudra should not be practised with the body naked. With a cloth wrapped around the abdomen, sit in a quiet secluded place to practice shakti chalana mudra. Furthermore, do not practice without the guidance of the guru. All variations of shakti chalana mudra require expert guidance.

Benefits: A practitioner of this mudra is said to achieve *vigraha siddhi*, perfection of the body, is relieved of all physical disorders and the power of reception is highly developed.

Technique 2

Sit in siddhasana/siddha yoni asana.

Keep the eyes closed throughout the practice.

Inhale slowly and deeply through the right nostril and perform internal breath retention, antar kumbhaka.

Perform moola bandha as tightly as possible, concentrating on the area of contraction.

Hold the breath and moola bandha as long as possible. Exhale slowly.

Perform jalandhara and uddiyana bandha.

Then practise 'churning' nauli, moving the rectus abdominis muscles clockwise in a circular motion from left to right, then directly back to the left and again circling to the right side, counting the number of rotations up to ten.

192

Before inhaling, come back to uddiyana, slowly release uddiyana and jalandhara bandhas.

Only after the head is raised should inhalation proceed very slowly.

This is one round.

Duration: Though it is stated in the texts that shakti chalana should be practised for ninety minutes, this will not be possible, nor is it advisable. Initially, five rounds can be practised. After seven months of continual practice gradually increase the number of rotations per round. Up to twenty rotations per round can be performed. Increase one rotation every two or three days. The number of rounds can also be increased very gradually up to ten rounds over a period of one year.

Meridian effects: Through the synergy of the combined effects of moola bandha, uddiyana banda, jalandhara bandha, nauli, antar kumbhaka and bahir kumbhaka, the amount of energy that flows through the conception and governing meridians increases to a high extent and overflows into the entire meridian network, supercharging it with vital force.

TADAGI MUDRA (gesture of barrelled abdomen)

The word *tadagi* literally means 'water pot', which resembles the shape of the extended abdomen.

Technique

Sit with the legs stretched out in front of the body and the feet slightly apart.

The legs should remain straight throughout the practice. Place the hands on the knees, keeping the head and spine straight.

Close the eyes and relax the whole body, especially the abdominal area.

Lean forward and grasp the big toes with the thumbs, index and second fingers.

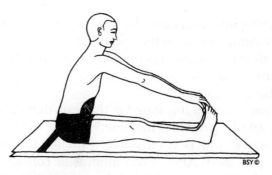

Keep the head facing forward.

Inhale slowly and deeply, expanding the abdominal muscles to their fullest extent.

Retain the breath inside for a comfortable length of time without straining the lungs in any way.

Exhale slowly and deeply while relaxing the abdomen. Maintain the hold on the toes.

Repeat the breathing up to 10 times.

Then release the toes and return to the starting position. This is one round.

Duration: Practise 3 to 5 rounds

Awareness: Physical – on the abdomen. Spiritual – on manipura chakra.

Contra-indications: Pregnant women and those suffering from hernia or prolapse should avoid this practice.

Practice note: Release the hold on the toes between breaths if the position becomes uncomfortable.

Benefits: Tadagi mudra relieves tension stored in the diaphragm and pelvic floor, tones the abdominal organs and stimulates blood circulation to these areas. The nerve plexuses in the visceral area are stimulated and toned. Bending forward and extending the stomach stretches the diaphragm and pelvic floor, and creates pressure throughout the trunk of the body. This stimulates *manipura chakra*, the centre of energy distribution, and raises the level of prana generally.

Meridian effects: The liver and spleen meridian have their origin at the big toe. The liver is responsible for the harmonious flow of energy throughout the body. It also controls the eyes and vision, which are under the influence of manipura chakra. The liver meridian passes through the pelvic floor and also through the diaphragm. When the flow of energy through this meridian is harmonious, relaxation of the pelvic floor and diaphragm occurs.

In acupuncture physiology in general, the human body is viewed in a standing position with the arms raised upward above the head. The flow of energy in meridians is described according to this posture. Therefore, the hands and fingers are the uppermost part of the body, and as such are considered as extra yang. The feet and toes are the lowermost parts, and are extra yin. In tadagi mudra the fingers are holding the big toes, creating a loop which links the upper and lower parts of the body, ensuring the balance of yin and yang.

PASHINEE MUDRA (gesture of noose)

The word *pash* means 'noose' and *pashinee* means 'bound in a noose' which reflects the physical form of the mudra. Pashinee mudra is a variation of *halasana*, the plough pose. In pashinee mudra, as well as bringing about the general benefits of an inverted posture, the neck muscles are given a powerful stretch, the cervical vertebrae loosened, the associated nerves toned and the thyroid and parathyroid glands in the throat are squeezed and massaged.

The thyroid gland is an important part of the endocrinal system. Amongst other hormones, the thyroid gland produces thyroxine, a powerful hormone which affects practically every cell in the body. Its main function is to regulate the rate at which food and oxygen are utilized by the various cells of the body. This gland also has a profound influence on physical, emotional and mental development. In a healthy person, the correct amount of thyroxine hormone is produced and secreted to meet their particular

195

needs. This is clearly shown by abundant energy and the ability to work and play without undue fatigue.

There are various reasons why the thyroid ceases to function correctly. The main reasons are: lack of iodine, bad or sluggish blood circulation, and emotional stress. The inverted position of the body in pashinee mudra directs a good blood flow to the thyroid gland under the action of gravity. Furthermore, the curvature of the neck in the final pose tends to restrict the normal flow of blood to the brain through the external carotid arteries. This flow is redirected into the thyroid gland. Thus for the duration of the asana, the thyroid is flushed and nourished with an extra supply of blood, which helps to improve its functioning.

Pashinee mudra and other variations of halasana are excellent preparation for vipareeta karani mudra.

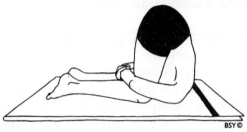

Technique
Assume halasana (see Appendix).
Separate the feet by about half a metre.
Bend the knees and bring the thighs towards the chest until the knees touch the ears, shoulders and floor.
Wrap the arms tightly around the back of the legs.
Relax the whole body in this position and close the eyes.
Breathe slowly and deeply.
Maintain the position for as long as is comfortable.
Slowly release the arms and come back into halasana.
Lower the legs and relax in shavasana.

Awareness: Physical – on the stretch of the neck. Spiritual – on mooladhara or vishuddhi chakra.

196

Sequence: This mudra should be followed by a forward bending asana.

Contra-indications: As for sarvangasana and halasana (see Appendix). People suffering from any spinal condition should avoid this practice. Precautions for inverted postures apply.

Benefits: Pashinee mudra brings balance and tranquillity to the nervous system and induces pratyahara, sensory withdrawal. It stretches the spine and back muscles, and stimulates all the spinal nerves. It massages the abdominal organs.

Meridian effects: The effects and mechanisms set in motion in this mudra are similar to those that are active in yoga mudra. In addition, in the inverted posture of pashinee mudra, the natural upward flow of Qi in the governing and conception meridian is enhanced, which helps to induce pratyahara.

Both the urinary bladder meridians, left and right, that run parallel to the spine and down the back sides of the legs, are strongly stretched in pashinee mudra. Important pairs of points, called 'back shu' points, which correspond to particular internal organs, are located along the urinary bladder meridian. The end result of both processes is a profound influence on the major internal organs.

The strong combination of the stretch and pressure applied by the forward bend on the neck occurs at the point 'GV 14' where the cervical and thoracic spines meet. Properties of this point include tranquillizing the mind and calming the spirit. This may relate to the introverted state of pratyahara which this pose induces.

VIPAREETA KARANI MUDRA (gesture of inversion)

The continual rotation of awareness and breath between the chakras takes this practice from being an asana to being a mudra whereby one increases the awareness of prana and redirects it. When it is used as a mudra, the pranic

197

dimension is augmented. With the rotation of awareness, the concentration and mental faculties are directed to a particular pathway in one's being. As one's awareness evolves, one can feel the actual movement happening at various levels.

Physiologically, the limbic system is linked up with the cortex. When vipareeta karani mudra is practised for a period of time, the awareness gradually moves through the brain circuits, from the limbic system up through the thalamus towards the cortex. The limbic system controls the unconscious and involuntary functions of the body: all the activities which go on automatically. It is also known as the pleasure centre. In this way, one becomes more conscious of all these involuntary functions, and gradually links them up. This develops control over pleasure, sexuality and all the other basic vegetative functions of the body.

In vipareeta karani mudra, there is a point where the legs are perfectly balanced. When the legs are brought up, suddenly something clicks into place and one becomes perfectly balanced. At this point, the pressure comes off the legs and automatically there is a sensation of opening in the throat. This is called an alignment of joints and angles, which opens up certain nadis and chakras. In the inverted posture, the weight of blood coming down into the brain is used to create pressure.

The inverted position, while draining the lower body, simultaneously enhances blood flow to the brain, especially the cerebral cortex and the intracranial glands, the pituitary and pineal. Cerebral insufficiency and senile dementia are counteracted. However, elderly people are not advised to commence inversion in later life because of the possibility of stroke. Inversion also profoundly influences the entire vascular network. The constant dragging force upon the arteries and veins continues throughout life, but is released completely during inversion. Regular practice prevents atheriosclerosis (arterial degeneration) by restoring vascular tone and elasticity.

Vipareeta karani mudra has a powerful draining influence on the visceral organs. Due to the force of gravity, the lower dependent parts of these organs tend to pool blood, and the body fluids also aggregate in the dependent parts of the body such as the pelvis and legs. Vipareeta karani flushes these dependent parts, returning pooled cellular fluid to the circulation. This cannot be induced in the upright or lying positions, and this is why inversion is so powerful physiologically. Inversion of the body also counteracts visceroptosis (protrusion of the abdominal organs), haemorrhoids, varicose veins and hernia, all of which are mediated by the downward force of gravity.

Inversion also reverses the polarity of the electromagnetic field created within the upright body. The energy field generated by the electrical activity of the brain is integrated with the geomagnetic field of the earth's surface. This has a revitalizing influence upon the human aura.

The most appropriate time to practise any inverted asana is in the morning after evacuating the bowels and bathing are complete. At that time the body is relaxed and rested. Later in the day, when food has been consumed and the body is at peak activity, different hormonal secretions are flowing throughout the system. If these flow down to the throat and head, imbalance may be created. The practice may be performed in the afternoon after first relaxing in shavasana for ten minutes, provided the stomach has been empty for more than three hours and one has not been doing strenuous physical work.

If one has constipation, it is advisable to empty the bowels first by drinking warm saline water or practising laghoo shankhaprakshalana. Then vipareeta karani helps relieve the tendency to further constipation. It is a powerful practice and is better done when the body is completely healthy. However, it can be used in the case of hypoactive thyroid to rebalance the functions.

The metabolic rate may increase when this mudra is practised for extended periods. If this happens, the food intake

199

should be adjusted accordingly. One of the initial positive effects of vipareeta karani is an increased capacity to digest and assimilate food. Digestive secretions and appetite are increased, therefore a moderate diet should be taken at regular intervals. Food should be taken after practising hatha yoga. If food is not taken, meaning if one fasts, the gastric acids and digestive enzymes will burn the lining of the stomach and duodenum. However, this is unlikely to happen when vipareeta karani is practised for a few minutes.

There are a number of basic rules which must be followed if one practises any of the hatha yoga techniques, and these are often omitted in the texts. It is therefore important to learn under expert guidance. The practices have a specific effect on the body and mind which has to be watched by the guide or teacher. All practices of hatha yoga will release internal heat in the course of time.

Technique

Assume vipareeta karani asana (see Appendix).
Bring the legs over the head so that the eyes look straight up at the feet.

200

Close the eyes and relax the whole body.
This is the starting position.
Fix the awareness at manipura chakra in the spine, directly behind the navel.
Inhale slowly and deeply with ujjayi pranayama.
Simultaneously, feel the breath and consciousness moving from manipura to vishuddhi chakra.
While exhaling, maintain the awareness at vishuddhi.
At the end of exhalation, immediately bring the awareness back to manipura and repeat the same process.

Awareness: Physical – on the inverted posture and the movement of the breath. Spiritual – on manipura and vishuddhi chakras.

Duration: Practise up to 7 rounds at first, or until discomfort arises. If pressure builds up in the head, end the practice. Gradually increase the number of rounds up to 21 over a period of months. The length of the inhalation and exhalation will increase spontaneously over time, as the practice becomes more comfortable.

Sequence: At the end of the daily practice program and before meditation. Do not perform after vigorous exercise or for at least 3 hours after meals. Upon completion of the practice, it is advisable to do a counterpose such as matsyasana, bhujangasana or ushtrasana (see Appendix).

Time of practice: Vipareeta karani mudra should be practised daily at the same time, preferably in the early morning.

Contra-indications: This inverted practice should not be performed unless the body is healthy. People suffering from high blood pressure, heart disease, enlarged thyroid or excessive toxins in the body should not perform this practice. Precautions for inverted postures apply.

Benefits: This practice gives all the benefits of vipareeta karani asana. It balances the activities of the thyroid. The posture reverses the downward and outward movement of energy, revitalizing and expanding the awareness. The flow of prana in ida and pingala nadis is balanced, resulting in an equal flow of breath in the nostrils. The balancing effect also helps to prevent disease on the physical and mental planes.

Meridian effects: Important points on the governing meridian that correspond to the location of the above-mentioned chakras are stimulated mentally, as the awareness ascends and descends. This thoroughly stimulates the governing meridian which runs along the back median line. This has repercussions on its coupled yin counterpart, the conception meridian also, which runs along the front median line, from the perineum to the lips. These two meridians are important reservoirs for the vital energy in the body. The conception and governing vessel are the confluence of all the yin and yang meridians, respectively, supplying the Qi when it is deficient and absorbing the surplus of it when it is excessive, thus maintaining balance in the whole system. The natural flow of Qi in both these meridians is in an upward direction. The force of gravity normally impedes this flow to some extent. In the inverted position of vipareeta karani mudra, the natural upward flow through these meridians is enhanced. The overall effect of all this process includes increased mental and physical energy, increased resistance to diseases and environmental influences, calming and cleaning of the mind, alleviation of bronchial disorders and a strengthening of the constitutional energy on a deep level, which could also be described as rejuvenation, in agreement with the effect ascribed to the mudra in classical texts such as *Hatha Yoga Pradipika* and *Gheranda Samhita*.

Variation

Assume the inverted position of the body.
Make the legs vertical.

Close the eyes and relax.

Become aware of the breath.

Practise slow, rhythmic ujjayi breathing, which should be natural due to the slight constriction at the throat.

Be aware of each inhalation and exhalation.

Bring the awareness to mooladhara chakra point, at the perineum.

This is the starting point of every round.

While inhaling, the breath flows from mooladhara to manipura.

While exhaling, the breath flows from manipura to vishuddhi.

Then bring the awareness straight back to mooladhara.

This is one round.

Begin with 10 rounds and slowly increase up to 21.

Practice note: In this variation the awareness is rotated between three regions: i) mooladhara, the perineal base ii) manipura, the lumbar base and iii) vishuddhi, the base connecting the body to the brain. The consciousness is moved from one base to the next with inhalation and exhalation. The movement of consciousness is always from mooladhara to vishuddhi, not the reverse. One becomes mentally aware of these bases when there is a pause momentarily between the inhalation and exhalation. In another variation of vipareeta karani mudra, ujjayi pranayama and khechari mudra are performed while adopting vipareeta karani asana.

15

Therapeutic Mudras

Many mudras can be used to remedy ailments of the physical body. Most are simple to perform hand mudras, yet they have a definite effect on the pranic body, which then influences the physical body and the mind. It is not necessary to sit in a meditative asana to practise these mudras, however, it is recommended that a comfortable sitting or lying position is adopted. It is also advisable to have the eyes closed in order to tune the awareness to the subtle changes taking place within the body and mind, such as any changes in the breath, body temperature, prana, thoughts and emotions. Sensitivity to these changes will develop over time with regular practice. Techniques included in this category are:

Tattwa mudras
- Prithvi mudra (gesture of the earth element)
- Apas mudra (gesture of the water element)
- Agni mudra (gesture of the fire element)
- Vayu mudra (gesture of the air element)
- Akasha mudra (gesture of the ether element)

Purifying and releasing mudras
- Shivalinga mudra (attitude of transformation)
- Kshepana mudra (gesture of elimination)
- Suchi mudra (needle gesture)

- Mushti mudra (fist gesture)
- Kubera mudra (attitude of Kubera)

Stimulating and strengthening mudras
- Rudra mudra (attitude of Rudra)
- Garuda Mudra (attitude of Garuda)
- Vajra mudra (gesture of the thunderbolt)
- Bhramara mudra (bee gesture)
- Linga mudra (gesture of the primal symbol)
- Makara mudra (crocodile gesture)

Revitalizing mudras
- Uttarabodhi mudra (attitude of the highest enlightenment)
- Hakini mudra (attitude of Hakini)

Balancing and harmonizing mudras
- Matangi mudra (attitude of Matangi)
- Kaleshwara mudra (attitude of Kaleshwara)
- Hridaya mudra (heart gesture)

TATTWA MUDRAS

The *pancha tattwas*, or five elements, are *akasha* or ether, *vayu* or air, *agni* or fire, *apas* or water, and *prithvi* or earth. However, these elements should not be mistaken for physical or chemical elements. Prithvi is not the earth one sees around oneself. Water is not the water one drinks or bathes with, nor is fire that which one burns to keep warm. Rather, they should be regarded as a consequence of subtle emanations which are created by different energy or pranic vibrations. These elements have a major influence on the personality, mind and emotions. They also govern and dominate specific parts of the body and are symbolized in each finger. Although there is some variation in the classical texts, generally it is believed the thumb represents fire, the index finger represents air, the middle finger represents ether, the ring finger represents earth, and the little finger represents water. The tattwa mudras are based on knowledge of these five elements.

Touching the tips or the base of any finger with the pad of the thumb causes the related element to increase. Conversely, touching the base of the thumb with the tip of the finger causes the related element to decrease. Through these two simple methods, as well as other more intricate hand mudras, the elements in the human body can be increased or decreased, bringing them to their optimal levels which calms the mental turmoil and cures physical sickness. Mudras never generate an excess of energy, they simply seek an optimal balance of prana. When the elements are at their highest level of normalcy, the human body, mind, emotions and spirit can be elevated to higher levels. The following is a selection of mudras that harmonize the tattwas.

PRITHVI MUDRA (gesture of the earth element)

The earth element is governed by mooladhara chakra. *Moola* means 'root' or 'foundation' and is associated with the qualities of stability, solidity and strength. In the body it is the solidity in the cellular structure of the bones and other organs, and it creates weight and density. It is also associated with *apana prana*, the downward moving energy that supports the functioning of the excretory and reproductive systems. Prithvi mudra increases the earth element within the body and rectifies any disturbances or illnesses associated with deficiencies of the earth element. Furthermore, on a subtle level, prithvi mudra can restore equilibrium and trust.

Technique
Place the tip of the thumb and ring finger together.
Extend the other fingers.

APAS MUDRA (gesture of the water element)

Apas tattwa is governed by swadhisthana chakra and can be described as a vast quantity of intensively active matter which emerges out of the water element. In the physical body, apas is the first tangible tattwa to emerge as matter, in the form of blood, mucus, bile, lymphatic fluid, and so on. Thus it is known to also control the fluids in the body. Thus, this mudra is also known as bhudi mudra, *bhudi* meaning 'fluid'. Apas or bhudi mudra subtly increases the water element within the body. It helps to restore or maintain equilibrium in the fluid balance and rectifies related problems in regards to the fluids under the influence of apas.

Technique 1

Place the tip of the thumb and the little finger together. Extend the other fingers in a relaxed way.

The following is a variation which decreases the water element, represented by the little finger. It especially helps with congestion of mucus or secretion in the frontal sinuses, lungs and the digestive tract from the stomach to the large intestine.

Technique 2

Bend the little finger of the right hand until the tip touches the ball (the fleshy part of the palm at the

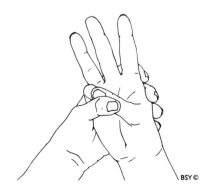

207

bottom of the thumb) of the right thumb, and place the
right hand thumb on top of it.
Cup the right hand with the left hand.
Place the left thumb on the right thumb and little finger
and press down gently.

AGNI MUDRA (gesture of the fire element)

Manipura chakra governs the fire element. Fire is necessary
for the human body just as the sun is essential for life. Fire is
the force that results in dynamism, energy and willpower. In
the physical body, agni tattwa regulates the fire of digestion,
appetite, thirst and sleep, and it either increases or destroys
them. Therefore, agni tattwa has to be controlled. Fire can
also be dampened by an excess of the earth element. This
can lead to imbalances such as mental dullness, lethargy and
heaviness. To rectify this imbalance, agni mudra stimulates
the fire element while simultaneously pacifying the earth
element. The thumb represents the fire element while the
ring finger represents the earth element.

Technique
Place the ring finger at the root of the thumb and press
down lightly with the thumb.
Extend the other fingers.

VAYU MUDRA (gesture of the air element)

The air element is governed by anahata chakra. Vayu has
been translated as air, or anything in gaseous form, and has
the nature of wind. Vayu tattwa represents kinetic energy in
all its diverse forms. In this sense it even includes the prana
in the body. The innate quality of vayu is movement through
contraction and expansion, and it controls these qualities in
the body through the pancha pranas. Ayurvedic medicine
describes many types of physical disorders that are caused
by an excess of the air or wind element. These include gout,

208

sciatica, flatulence, rheumatism and trembling in the hands, throat and head. Such conditions are often due to bad posture, disturbed bodily functions, toxins in the intestines, psychological or emotional problems, or an imbalanced lifestyle. This mudra assists in alleviating excess wind.

Technique

Bend the index finger so that its tip touches the ball of the thumb.

Then press the thumb lightly on to the index finger.

Extend the other fingers in a relaxed way.

AKASHA MUDRA (gesture of the ether element)

Vishuddhi chakra is related to *akasha tattwa*, the ether or space element. Akasha signifies that which provides the space for matter to become existent. It is the subtlest of the elements, all-pervading and motionless. Akasha tattwa is responsible for creating the idea of space, and in the human body it controls the space surrounding the different organs. It is responsible for the entire range of gross, subtle and causal sound perception conveyed through the ears. There are many diseases and illnesses associated with an imbalance of the ether element, especially those to do with the ears. Thus, this mudra relieves earaches and other ailments of the ears that are associated with the ether element.

Technique

Bend the middle finger until it touches the ball of the thumb.

Lightly press down on the middle finger with the thumb.

The other fingers are extended.

PURIFYING AND RELEASING MUDRAS

SHIVALINGA MUDRA (attitude of transformation)

A shivalingam symbolizes consciousness, or Shiva, in perpetual union with energy, Shakti. The part of the shivalingam that extends upwards is the symbol of the Shiva tattwa while the base, called *peeth* or *argha*, is the symbol of Shakti. In this mudra the hands are placed in the shape of a shivalingam.

Shiva is also the name of one of the gods of the sacred trinity, who is entrusted with the work of destruction and transformation. The other two gods, Brahma and Vishnu, are responsible for creation and preservation. The trinity represent the three aspects of life: creation, preservation and destruction. By destroying the old, Shiva makes new beginnings possible. This cycle of life occurs internally on subtle levels as well as externally within nature.

In terms of acupuncture, the water element is being affected on the outer edge of the hand and palm. According to traditional Chinese medicine, the water element is associated with various processes such as cooling, decay, transmutation and storage. The upright thumb channels an inflow of energy, which is absorbed through the lungs. The breath, as well as food, nourishes the store of energy in the body.

This mudra is said to support transformation by ridding the body of old energy and allowing new energy,

210

new inspiration to take its place. It alleviates tiredness, dissatisfaction, listlessness and depression, and also facilitates the process of healing.

Technique

Fold the fingers of the right hand into the palm and extend the thumb upwards.

Place the fingers of the left hand together and make a bowl shape with the hand.

Place the right hand on top of the left, with the thumb pointing upwards.

Position the hands at the level of the abdomen, with the elbows pointing outward and slightly forward.

KSHEPANA MUDRA (gesture of elimination)

Kshepana mudra stimulates elimination. The word *kshepana* means 'throwing' or 'expelling'. It does this not only through the large intestine, but also through the lungs and skin, via exhalation and perspiration, respectively. A high proportion of the body's waste products are eliminated through the skin. Often toxins accumulate in the skin and cause boils and pimples.

According to traditional Chinese medicine, the large intestine and lung meridians run along the index finger. Perspiration is also said to be a function of the lung energy; the lung energy dilates the sweat glands and skin pores to induce sweating and to release heat and toxins. Kshepana mudra clears blocked energy in the lungs and large intestines and promotes the release of physical and mental tension.

Technique

Interlace the fingers with the palms gently touching.

Let the fingers rest on the back of the hands.

Straighten the index fingers and rest them against each other.

The thumbs are crossed and resting in the hollow of the other thumb.
If in a seated pose, rest the hands in the lap and point the index fingers to the ground.
In shavasana, rest the hands on the front of the body and point the index fingers in the direction of the feet.
Let the elbows rest on the ground keeping the arms relaxed.

SUCHI MUDRA (needle gesture)

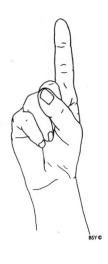

This gesture is named suchi mudra because the index finger points upward like a needle. The technique described below is a way to use suchi mudra that enhances its effects, which is to relieve constipation and aid elimination. Rapid elimination of waste materials from the body is essential for health and wellbeing. Constipation causes a build-up of waste products in the bowels, which are then reabsorbed into the bloodstream. Such toxicity affects both the body and mind; mental conflicts are often a reflection of the condition of the digestion system.

212

Technique

Clench both fists and hold them in front of the chest.
This is the starting position.
When inhaling, stretch the arms out to the sides and point the index fingers upward.
Hold this tension for a few breaths and then return to the starting position.

MUSHTI MUDRA (fist gesture)

Mushti mudra is another mudra that helps to alleviate constipation. It enhances the functioning of the stomach's process of digestion, represented by the thumb. This particular variation of mushti mudra has the additional feature of the thumb pressing down gently on the ring finger. According to acupuncture, the liver meridian runs along the ring finger. Thus, this form of mushti mudra balances the liver, alleviating both physical and psychological problems associated with the liver.

Technique

Fold the fingers into the palms.
Place the thumbs over the ring fingers.

KUBERA MUDRA (attitude of Kubera)

Kubera is the god of wealth and treasure. This mudra is said to assist in the attainment of goals and fulfilment of wishes. As a therapeutic mudra, it opens, decongests and cleanses the frontal sinuses.

Technique

Place the tip of the thumb, index finger, and middle finger together.
Bend the other two fingers so they rest in the middle of the hand.

213

STIMULATING AND STRENGTHENING MUDRAS

RUDRA MUDRA (attitude of Rudra)

Rudra is the ruler of manipura chakra. Manipura chakra is the centre of dynamism, energy, willpower and achievement. It is often compared to the dazzling heat and power of the sun, without which life on earth would not exist. Manipura chakra radiates and distributes pranic energy throughout the entire human framework; without it each person would be lifeless and totally devoid of vitality. It is also compared to a blazing fire, since it burns up and assimilates the energy in food in the same way that a fire burns up wood and releases the inherent energy. The absorption of energy takes place at different levels. At grosser levels it absorbs the nutrients of foods for the upkeep of the physical body, and at a more subtle level it absorbs the more subtle essence of food to refuel the pranic body. Rudra mudra strengthens the digestive organs. They in turn strengthen the whole body and mind.

Technique
Place the tips of the thumb, index and ring finger together.
Keep the other two fingers extended.

GARUDA MUDRA (attitude of Garuda)

Garuda is the mystical king of birds and the powerful and mighty vehicle that Vishnu rides. Garuda mudra, while subtle, is also powerful. It has the power to stimulate blood circulation, which invigorates and nourishes the organs. The placement of the hands stimulates the pelvic, abdominal and chest region sequentially. Combined with the breath, this mudra relaxes and releases tension related to these areas and is helpful in alleviating menstrual and stomach pain. This energizing mudra helps to remove

214

fatigue and generally raises the energy levels. Due to its powerful stimulating effect, caution is advised for those who have high blood pressure.

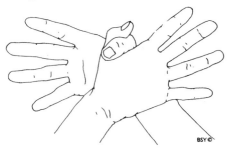

Technique

Place the palm of the right hand on top of the back of the left hand.
Interlace the thumbs.
Place the hands on the lower abdomen.
Remain in this position for 10 breaths.
Next, place the hands on the navel centre.
Remain in this position for 10 breaths.
Place the hands on upper abdomen.
Remain there for another 10 breaths.
Move the hands up and place them level with the sternum, slightly away from the body.
Turn the palms in the direction of the shoulders and spread the fingers.
Remain there for a few seconds.
This is one round.

VAJRA MUDRA (gesture of the thunderbolt)

The *vajra* or thunderbolt is said to be the weapon of Indra, the king of gods. Like the force of lightning, vajra mudra stimulates circulation of blood and lymph, enabling the organs and systems of the body to function more effectively and efficiently. Circulation is essential for the proper functioning of the cardiovascular system, which supplies nutrients to each and every cell of the body and the lymphatic system, removing waste products from the body through the flow of lymph.

Technique

On one hand, press the thumb onto the side of the middle fingernail.

Press the ring finger against the other side of the middle fingernail.

Then press the little finger against the side of the ring fingernail.

The index finger remains extended.

Place both hands in this mudra.

BHRAMARA MUDRA (bee gesture)

Bhramara means the bee and this mudra is so called because it looks like a bee. It strengthens the immune system and alleviates allergies.

Technique

Curl the index finger into the root of the thumb.

Bend the middle finger so that the tip of the thumb touches the side of the middle fingernail closest to the thumb.

Extend the ring and little fingers.

Do the same with both hands.

LINGA MUDRA (gesture of the primal symbol)

Linga mudra is similar in name and form as shivalinga mudra. In both mudras the placement of the thumb is the key feature. This mudra stimulates the immune system and increases the power of resistance against coughs, colds and chest infections, especially when practised at the onset of such illnesses. In addition, it loosens mucus that has collected in the lungs. Note that due to the increase in

216

body temperature created by this mudra, it should not be practised for a long time without necessity.

Technique

Place both palms together and interlace the fingers.
One thumb remains upright.
The thumb and index finger of the other hand encircles the upright thumb.
Rest the hands on the lap, or hold them at the level of the abdomen or sternum.
As an alternative, the elbows can be pointed outward and slightly forward. Make sure the palms remain together in this position.

MAKARA MUDRA (crocodile gesture)

According to kundalini yoga, swadhisthana chakra is related to *jala* or *apas tattwa*, the water element. The vehicle of this chakra is the crocodile or *makara*, which is considered to be the vehicle of Varuna, the water god. The *karmendriyas* or organs of action related to swadhisthana are the sexual organs, kidneys and urinary system. These are only a few of the attributes of swadhisthana, all of which are applicable to this mudra.

Therapeutically, this mudra activates the energy stored in the kidneys. It remedies ailments such as listlessness, depression and low energy.

217

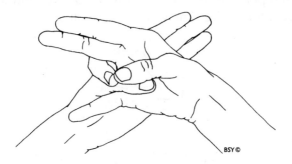

Technique
Place one hand on top of the other, palms facing upwards.

Extend the thumb of the lower hand through the little finger and ring finger of the upper hand, placing it in the middle of the palm of the upper hand.

Place the tip of the thumb and ring finger of the upper hand together.

REVITALIZING MUDRAS

UTTARABODHI MUDRA
(attitude of the highest enlightenment)

Uttar means 'highest' and *bodhi* means 'enlightenment'. The ancient yogis were fully aware of the importance of the breath; no breath, no life. Breath is life. It is written in *Hatha Yoga Pradipika* that a person who only half breathes, only half lives. One who breathes correctly acquires control of the whole being. On a physical level, shallow breathing leads to insufficient absorption of oxygen in the body. This causes functional disturbances and illnesses concerned with the circulatory, digestive and nervous systems. The efficiency of these systems is entirely dependent on healthy, well-nourished nerves and organs which depend entirely on oxygen for survival. This mudra encourages and strengthens inhalation which refreshes and revitalizes the body and mind. It also strengthens the energy of the lungs, large intestine and heart.

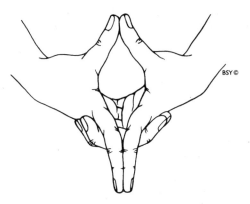

Technique

Interlace the fingers.

Straighten the index fingers so that the pads of the fingers touch.

Place the pads of the thumbs together.

Separate the thumbs and the index fingers making the shape of a yoni.

Place the hands in front of the stomach.

Point the index fingers up toward the ceiling and thumbs down towards the floor or the stomach.

If practising in shavasana, the tips of the thumbs may lie at the lower end of the sternum.

HAKINI MUDRA (attitude of Hakini)

Hakini is related to *ajna chakra*, which is essentially the chakra of the mind, symbolized by a two-petalled lotus, pale or light grey in colour. This symbol has many subtle aspects, one of which is Hakini. She has six faces which are said to be like many moons. Paramshiva is the presiding god of ajna chakra and he shines like a chain of lightning flashes.

On a physical level, Hakini mudra improves and deepens respiration, and builds up energy in the lungs

219

which refreshes and revitalizes the brain. It promotes cooperation between the right and left brain hemispheres, balancing, harmonizing and focusing the pranas and the mind. Hakini mudra is also said to open access to the right hemisphere of the brain where memory is stored, thus improving memory.

Technique

Spread the fingers.
Join the tips of the thumb and fingers of one hand with the other hand.
Keep the fingers relaxed.

BALANCING AND HARMONIZING MUDRAS

MATANGI MUDRA (attitude of Matangi)

Matangi is the ninth mahavidya and the goddess of inner harmony and royal rulership. According to acupuncture, the pericardium meridian runs through the middle finger. The pericardium protects the heart from physical and emotional stress and frees the flow of energy in the region of the chest. Furthermore, certain acupuncture points on this meridian especially harmonize the stomach function. Combined with breath awareness at manipura, this mudra balances the energy in the abdominal region.

Technique

Interlace the fingers and hold the hands in front of manipura chakra.

Straighten the middle fingers and rest them against each other.

Focus the awareness of the breath at manipura chakra or the abdominal area.

KALESHWARA MUDRA (attitude of Kaleshwara)

Kaleshwara is an epithet of Shiva, and the deity who rules over time. Kaleshwara mudra calms the flood of thoughts and agitated feelings.

Technique

Place the pads of the middle fingers together and keep them straight.

Bend the index fingers and connect the outer first two joints.

Bring the tip of the thumbs together.

Bend the ring and little fingers inwards.

Point the thumbs toward the chest and spread the elbows to the outside.

HRIDAYA MUDRA (heart gesture)

Hridaya mudra, or the heart gesture, stimulates the flow of energy to the heart and has a balancing effect both physically and psychologically. In relation to the physical heart, it is a very simple technique that may be used safely and easily, even in acute situations. Psychologically, the heart is the centre of emotion, and hridaya mudra helps to release pent-up emotions and unburden the heart. It may be practised during emotional conflict and crisis. For details of the technique, see Chapter 10.

16

Sadhana Mudras

Sadhana mudras refine the awareness and lead the senses inwards, from gross to subtle, preparing the mind for meditation. Awareness begins with the physical gesture and physical sensations within the hands. After some time, the quality of the mudra alters the consciousness and a shift in perception takes place, moving the experience into the pranic dimension. When the ability to retain the awareness has developed, transformation begins to occur in the subtle realms of the mind. It is the sustained focus of awareness on subtle internal sensations stimulated by the mudras that purifies and energizes the mind and pranas. Sadhana mudras include:

Pancha prana mudras
• Prana mudra (gesture of sthoola prana)
• Apana mudra (gesture of apana prana)
• Samana mudra (gesture of samana prana)
• Udana mudra (gesture of udana prana)
• Vyana mudra (gesture of vyana prana)

Hasta mudra pranayama (hand mudra pranayama)
• Combination of chinmudra pranayama (gesture of conscious breath), chinmaya mudra pranayama (gesture of pure wisdom breath), aadi mudra pranayama (primary gesture breath), brahma mudra pranayama (gesture of supreme spirit breath)

Symbolic mudras
* Kundalini mudra (gesture of the primal force)
* Padma mudra (lotus gesture)
* Shoonya mudra (gesture of the void)
* Naga mudra (snake gesture)
* Mahayoni mudra (gesture of the supreme source)
* Shankha mudra (conch gesture)
* Dhyani mudra (gesture of meditation and contemplation)

PANCHA PRANA MUDRAS

There are five primary forces, known as *pancha prana*, which operate in the physical body at all times. *Prana shakti*, the one sustaining force, assumes these five fields to enable the body to accomplish its various functions. Thus, prana is experienced differently in various parts of the body at the same time. These five forces also act on subtler levels, influencing and in turn being influenced by the mind and consciousness. The seers identified these five pranas as: prana, apana, samana, udana and vyana. They represent the inherent quality of motion which energizes every action from secretion of the digestive juices to the movement of the hands. They flow through all the elements, organs and the mind.

The five pranas are responsible for creation and existence at the individual level. They maintain the balance between the physical and mental levels. Their physical locations are relevant in regards to the functions of the body; however, they function more homogeneously in the subtler levels of the mind and consciousness, where their distinction is qualitative rather than physical. In this context, the yogic texts often differ in their description of the five pranas and their locations. This should not confuse the practitioner. One should remember that the energy body is comprehended in the realm of experience, where the boundaries are neither black nor white. The key is to continue honing one's own experience.

224

The five different kinds of prana are represented and invoked by hand mudras. The pancha prana mudras represent a subtle relationship between one's existence in gross matter and one's relationship to the more universal elements and forces, which interpenetrate all levels of creation. When performing these mudras, it does not mean that a particular prana is automatically felt surging through its normally specified location in the body, but on a subtle or pranic level that particular energy will be stimulated. While dealing with prana and its subtleties, one should have

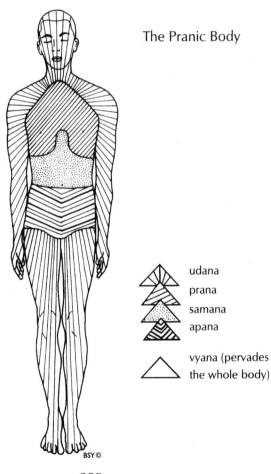

The Pranic Body

udana
prana
samana
apana

vyana (pervades the whole body)

BSY©

225

knowledge of these mudras, until finally a deeper awareness of the vital energies dawns, and of those same energies pervading the cosmos.

PRANA MUDRA (gesture of sthoola prana)

Prana is the first of the pancha pranas. It is also known as sthoola prana so that it is not confused with the all-pervasive prana. *Sthoola prana* refers to the energy currents located in the thoracic region between the diaphragm and the base of the neck.

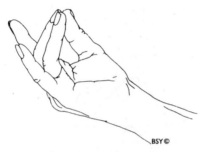

Technique

The tip of the thumb, middle finger and ring finger are placed together.

As the mudra is performed, the mantra *Om Pranaya Swaha* is chanted.

Effects: Prana mudra strengthens the flow of sthoola prana, which is in the form of light particles moving upwards in the chest region. Sthoola prana maintains the heart and lungs, and all the activities in the chest region such as breathing, swallowing and circulation of blood. When the pathways of sthoola prana are not clear, the heart and lungs malfunction and there is a poor intake of oxygen. At the mental level, one is not able to access positive impressions and it is difficult to concentrate or access intuitive knowledge. By strengthening and supporting the uninterrupted flow of sthoola prana, prana mudra allows the purer qualities of the heart, such as strength, courage and greatness to be expressed, and

226

one-pointedness of mind and intuitive knowledge to be experienced. At a subtle level, at the level of the mind, prana mudra also augments the intake of impressions and ideas.

Meridian effects: The end points of the lung and pericardium meridians, located on the tips of thumb and middle finger respectively, are linked with the starting point of the triple burner meridian, stimulating the flow of Qi in all three of them. The lung meridian governs the function of the lungs. The pericardium meridian, through its internal branch, contributes to the energy supply to the whole of the chest region. The triple burner meridian is responsible for the hypochondriac region, the area in the abdomen below the ribs and the space into which the diaphragm descends during deep inhalation. Therefore, the overall effect of prana mudra is the assistance of deep breathing and through this, the enhancement of the natural flow of vital force, the prana, in the lungs and chest.

APANA MUDRA (gesture of apana prana)

Apana prana is the second prana, which operates in the pelvic region between the navel and the perineum.

Technique

The tip of the thumb, index and middle fingers are placed together.

227

As the mudra is performed, the mantra *Om Apanaya Swaha* is chanted.

Effects: Apana mudra stimulates apana prana, which is experienced in the form of light particles moving downwards from the navel to the perineum. Apana mudra supports the many functions that apana sustains in relation to the kidneys, bladder, bowels, excretory and reproductive organs, such as the elimination of gas, wind, faeces and urine, and the flow of semen and ova. It helps alleviate conditions related to poor elimination. Apana also nourishes the foetus and expels it from the uterus at the time of childbirth.

Apana mudra strengthens the presence of the earth and water elements in the body associated with apana, and has a grounding effect. On a subtle level, apana mudra enhances the flow of energy down through the koshas, from subtle to gross. Swadhisthana and mooladhara chakras are activated with apana mudra, as well as the kundalini force that lies within the periphery of apana prana. Apana prana can be controlled through apana mudra, leading to control of the sexual instinct and the instilling of brahmacharya. At the mental level, apana mudra helps to alleviate depression and negativity, encouraging the release of negative thoughts and emotions.

Meridian effects: The end points of the lung and pericardium meridians, located on the tips of the thumb and middle finger respectively, and the first point on the large intestine channel, located on the tip of the index finger, are brought together. A pranic circuit is created between these three meridians, modifying the usual flow and exchange of vital energy. It is interesting to note that the pericardium meridian connects to and controls the tongue, which is the *jnanendriya* or sense organ of swadhisthana chakra that is governed by apana. This meridian also communicates with all three body cavities, including the pelvic region, which again is the domain

228

of apana. The large intestine meridian connects to and controls the nose, the jnanendriya of mooladhara chakra. It also supplies vital force to the organ of the large intestine, the colon, which in turn is one of the primary areas of responsibility of apana.

The lung meridian, for its part, actually originates in the abdomen where at its very beginning it connects with the colon. In apana mudra, it appears that the role of the thumb, and subsequent stimulation and redirection of vital energy flow along the course of the lung meridian, serves the purpose to actually augment the vibrancy of Qi in the large intestine meridian to which the lung meridian is closely interconnected.

SAMANA MUDRA (gesture of samana prana)

Samana is the third prana. It operates between the navel and the diaphragm. The word 'samana' is derived from the root *saman*, meaning 'equal' or 'balanced'. Thus it acts as a balancer or equalizer for the two opposite forces of prana and apana.

Technique
The tip of the thumb, little finger and ring finger are placed together.

The mantra used is *Om Samanaya Swaha*.

Effects: Samana mudra encourages the flow of samana prana, between the navel and the diaphragm. Samana is experienced as a sideways movement of light, like the swinging of a fast pendulum, from right to left and left

229

to right. It is associated with the digestive fire, *jatharagni*, activating and maintaining the digestive organs and their secretions, and governing metabolism. Samana mudra strengthens the flow of samana and the function of its related organs: liver, stomach, duodenum, spleen, and the small and large intestines. Samana is responsible for the manipura experience of vitality and dynamism. However, whenever there is turbulence in the body and the senses, samana becomes agitated and causes disorders. Poor assimilation of food is a result of samana imbalance, causing the build-up of toxins as well as psychological blockages. Samana mudra pacifies and calms the agitation of samana whenever one's mental peace and harmony are disturbed, and just as it helps digest food, samana mudra assists in the digestion of the mind-stuff.

Meridian effects: The end points of both the lung and heart meridians, located at the tip of the thumb and the tip of the little finger respectively, are joined together with the starting point of the triple burner meridian located at the tip of the ring finger. The triple burner meridian controls all internal organs, the majority of which are situated in the abdomen: stomach, small intestine, liver, spleen, pancreas, etc., in the area of samana. The heart meridian also has an internal connection with these organs. The energizing influence on these meridians provides a stimulating effect on the abdominal organs, which in turn are governed by samana, indicating that samana is actually stimulated when this mudra is adopted. In addition, the triple burner meridian and the heart meridian have offshoots that connect them to the eyes, thus they are used in clinical practice to treat eye disorders. The fact that the eyes are the jnanendriya of manipura chakra, which is responsible for the distribution of samana prana in the pranic body, supports the inference that this mudra enhances the flow of samana in the abdominal region.

UDANA MUDRA (gesture of udana prana)

Udana is the fourth manifestation and operates in the extremities: the arms, legs, neck and head.

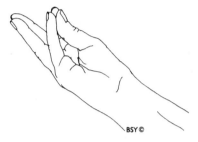

Technique

The tip of the thumb, index and little fingers are placed together.

The mantra is *Om Udanaya Swaha*.

Effects: Udana mudra stimulates and strengthens the flow of *udana prana*, which is experienced as spiralling flows of energy in the form of light down the arms and legs and up through the neck and head. Udana mudra accentuates the flow of udana, ensuring that proper functioning of its various activities: coordinating and controlling the movements of the legs, arms and neck; directing the activities of the brain and sensory organs, the eyes, tongue, nose, ears and skin; assisting prana in inhalation and exhalation, intake of food and drink, as well as vomiting, spitting and swallowing saliva; maintaining the pranic link between the heart and the brain, sustaining the functions of the throat and mouth; keeping the body upright and performing anti-gravitational activities of the body, particularly by the hands and the feet. Udana mudra alleviates problems resulting from an irregular flow of udana, such as: breathing troubles, inefficiency in physical and mental work, inability to think clearly or express oneself, uncoordinated speech, weakened will and lack of cheer. On a subtle level, udana mudra supports the performance of positive mental work and enhances the quality of speech. Udana facilitates the exchange of prana between the head and heart, thereby establishing contact between the subtle and causal bodies, and maintaining the relationship between the gross, subtle and causal bodies. This connection is enhanced by udana mudra. Udana pervades ajna, bindu and sahasrara chakras and udana mudra assists in bringing the energy through the koshas, from gross to subtle.

Meridian effects: The energy circuit is created connecting the lung, large intestine and heart meridians together in this mudra. The lung meridian, apart from connection to the chest and lung, also connects and supplies energy to the throat, the area through which udana prana flows upward. The large intestine meridian along its course connects tightly with the head, including the mouth, teeth, nose, throat and face, while the heart meridian, apart from being connected to the chest and heart, connects clearly with the brain also. All these areas of the body are the domain of udana prana. Thus, the flow of vital energy in the whole region of the neck and head with numerous organs situated in that area is enhanced and an energy circuit is created in the area through which udana prana shoots upward.

VYANA MUDRA (gesture of vyana prana)

Vyana, the fifth prana, pervades the whole body and acts as reserve energy.

Technique
The tip of the thumb, index, middle, ring and little fingers are placed together.
Its mantra is *Om Vyanaya Swaha*.

Effects: In vyana mudra, all five elements that determine the state of the matter and energy in man, represented by five fingers, are brought together in harmony. The whole

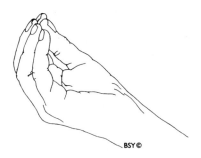

body is recharged and vyana prana is stimulated. As vyana permeates the whole body, it assists all the other pranas when they require an extra boost. When one overexerts and feels extremely tired, a rush of energy comes, which enables one to continue. This 'second wind' is the vyana experience. Vyana mudra assists vyana with: regulating and coordinating all the muscular movements, sending impulses to different parts of the body, and causes the flow of perspiration and gooseflesh; circulation through all the five koshas and establishing their differentiation; the functioning of all the pranas, major and minor as their accessory.

Vyana pervades the spatial element in the body, and is the vehicle of consciousness through the body. When vyana is an excited state, due to its swift motion, it excites the mind and creates delusion. At such times, the motion of consciousness becomes intense. Vyana mudra brings balance to vyana, restoring coordination and the ability to reach out to people, alleviating tremors, and focusing and calming the mind.

Meridian effects: All yin and yang meridians that run along the arm and hand are joined together, and a complex energy circuit between them is created that affects the meridians running along the trunk and legs also. A natural process of energy transfer from the lung meridian, point 'Lu 11' at the tip of the thumb, into the large intestine meridian, point 'LI 1' at the tip of index finger, is facilitated. The increase in energy flow in the large intestine meridian in turn has a stimulating effect on the stomach meridian, because these two meridians have a 'mother and son relationship'. This manifests in a natural transfer of peak energy flow from the large intestine meridian straight into the stomach meridian within every twenty-four-hour energy flow pattern in the body. Subsequently, this energy-boosting effect transfers further down this natural twenty-four-hour loop into the spleen meridian. The spleen energizes and nourishes all soft tissue spread throughout the body, the four limbs, thus governing and supplying energy to all the muscles in the body. Here the function of the spleen corresponds with the domain of vyana prana and its function. In acupuncture, general and debilitating weakness and a feeling of being 'totally out of energy', as if the reserve force of vyana is exhausted, is treated by activating and toning the spleen. The same happens in vyana mudra.

COMBINED PRACTICE OF THE
PANCHA PRANA MUDRAS

Technique
Sit comfortably in a meditation asana with the spine straight but relaxed.
Perform prana mudra, keeping your awareness on your natural breath and the region of the body where the sthoola prana manifests.
Continue for a few minutes, then begin to chant its mantra mentally.
Do the same with each of the pancha prana mudras in turn, spending up to 10 minutes on each one.
Slowly, the awareness of these subtle energies will begin to stir.
Practice note: These mudras may be used with any prana-yama or pre-pranayama practice.

HASTA MUDRA PRANAYAMA (hand mudra pranayama)

Hasta mudra pranayama is a practice that combines pranayama with four *hasta* or hand mudras: chinmudra, chinmaya mudra, aadi mudra and Brahma mudra, with pranayama. As a result, all five pranas are stimulated and an expansion of energy occurs throughout the whole pranic system. This subtle yet powerful practice internalizes the awareness, purifies and activates the pranas, and prepares the mind for meditation. These mudras are subtle techniques and their effects may not be immediately noticeable without awareness and sensitivity.

Technique
Mudra 1: Chinmudra Pranayama (gesture of conscious breath)
Sit in vajrasana or any other asana with the spine straight.
Place the hands on the thighs in chin mudra with the palms upwards.
Inhale and exhale through the nostrils, maintaining the same comfortable length of inhalation and exhalation. This is a ratio of 1:1.
Continue for up to 27 rounds.

Mudra 2: Chinmaya Mudra Pranayama (gesture of pure wisdom breath)
Place the hands in chinmaya mudra with the palms downwards on the thighs.
Inhale and exhale through the nostrils, maintaining the same comfortable length of inhalation and exhalation. This is a ratio of 1:1.
Continue for up to 27 rounds.

Mudra 3: Aadi Mudra Pranayama (primary gesture breath)
Place the hands on the thighs in aadi mudra with the backs of the hands upwards.
Do not clench the thumb tightly.
Inhale and exhale through the nostrils, maintaining the same comfortable length of inhalation and exhalation. This is a ratio of 1:1.
Continue for up to 27 rounds.

Mudra 4: Brahma Mudra Pranayama (gesture of Supreme Spirit breath)

Practise brahma mudra with the knuckles of the hand together and the thumbs away from the body.

Inhale and exhale through the nostrils, maintaining the same comfortable length of inhalation and exhalation.

This is a ratio of 1:1.

Continue for up to 27 rounds.

This completes the practice.

Complete practice: By practising each for 27 rounds, one will perform 108 rounds, which comprises the total practice.

Benefits: The physical position of the hand mudras used in this practice encourage ventilation of the lower, middle and upper lobes of the lungs and influence other vital organs indirectly. Chinmudra ventilates the lower lobes of the lungs and stimulates the region of apana below the navel. Chinmaya mudra ventilates the middle lobes of the lungs. Energy is directed to the area of samana and prana between the navel and the throat. Aadi mudra ventilates the upper lobes of the lungs, moving energy to the region of udana in the neck and head. Brahma mudra revitalizes the whole body through the stimulation of vyana. It helps to stimulate full yogic breathing, that is, using the abdomen, chest and clavicles for each respiration.

Advanced practice: The advanced variation of this practice includes breath retention or *kumbhaka*. After inhalation, retain the breath inside. Exhale, and then retain the breath outside. Throughout the practice try to maintain an even ratio of 1:1:1:1, which means using the same length and count for inhalation, retention, exhalation and retention. Avoid straining by using a comfortable count. The same precautions apply for breath retention; the practice is not recommended for those with heart problems, high blood pressure, emphysema or other major disorders.

SYMBOLIC MUDRAS

Each of the symbolic mudras depicts an object or idea representing a state of consciousness. By holding the hands in the mudra, the practitioner tries to attain that state.

KUNDALINI MUDRA (gesture of the primal force)

Kundalini mudra is associated with the primal force that is to be awakened or activated. It represents the unification of masculine and feminine, the opposites of polarity and the union of the individual soul with the cosmic soul. The four encircling fingers of the right hand symbolize the outer, perceptible world. The left index finger is the mind and soul, while the thumb represents the divine.

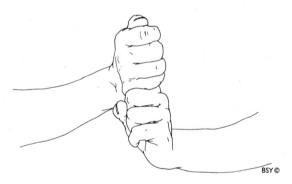

BSY©

Technique

Form loose fists with both hands.

Now extend the left index finger and stick it into the right fist from below.

Place the tip of the right thumb on to the left fingertip. Hold the mudra as low as possible in front of the abdomen.

237

PADMA MUDRA (lotus gesture)

This mudra affects anahata chakra, the centre situated in the spinal column directly behind the centre of the chest. This heart centre is also known as *hridayakasha*, which means 'the space within the heart where purity resides.' This chakra is a very delicate centre, for it is directly connected with that part of the brain which is responsible for all the creative sciences and fine arts such as painting, dance, music, poetry, and so on. The first preparation to awakening anahata is to change the entire way of thinking. One must become extremely optimistic and positive, always full of hope and never dwelling in the negativity of the mind. Even though the world is full of conflicts, contradictions and deep animosities, one must always cultivate deep peace throughout one's being. The classic example is the lotus flower. It grows in water, it is nourished by water, it is surrounded by water and it cannot exist without water, yet the leaves and the flower remain totally unaffected by water and are absolutely dry. That is how a yogi has to be. A yogi is like a magician who is able to manage the psychic, invisible and spiritual, the physical, material and sensorial, and find the balance.

Technique

Place both hands in front of the chest so that only the edges of the hands and tips of the fingers touch each other.

This is the bud of the lotus flower.

While keeping the tips of the little fingers, the outer edges of the thumbs and the edge of the hand together, open the hands and spread the other fingers as wide as possible.

This is the open lotus flower.

After four deep breaths, close both hands back into a bud.

Turn the palms outwards so that the backs of the hands and the fingernails touch each other.

In this position, rotate the hands downwards so the fingers are pointing towards the ground, and let the hands hang down for a few moments.

Then in the same way, bring the hands back into the bud and then the open flower.

Repeat a few times, flowing from the lotus bud to the lotus in full bloom.

SHOONYA MUDRA (gesture of the void)

The word *shoonya* means 'voidness' or 'emptiness'. It is often used by Buddhists to describe the indescribable state of *nirvana*, supreme enlightenment. In this context it does not mean, as often believed, a state of nothingness. It means exactly the opposite: a state of totality, of oneness, devoid of ego, devoid of even the slightest turmoil, craving or dissatisfaction. It also expresses openness and acceptance.

Technique

Rest the palms in the lap or thighs with the palms facing up.

The fingers are not spread apart, they are gently touching each other and the thumb rests against the index finger.

Meridian effects: Shoonya mudra has a deep and multi-layered balancing effect on the yin-yang relationship achieved. Out of these opposite and complementing cosmic qualities emerges Qi, vital force that permeates the whole of creation. By resting the back of the hands

239

and wrists in the lap, yang meridians in the hands and wrists are connected with yin meridians that run along the inner side of the legs and lower abdomen. The upper part of the body is yang in relation to the lower part of the body, which is yin. The consequent interchange that happens between these two basic qualities in the body keeps the interplay between the two in perfect balance. A state of pure harmony, tranquillity, stability (yin qualities) is complemented with alertness, mindfulness, stamina (yang qualities). In addition, the palms facing up expose yin meridians in the hands to the influence of yang from the outer space. The human being as an individual is yin in relation to the surrounding space and existence. They become one, the individual merges with universal. A state of oneness and completeness is the result.

NAGA MUDRA (snake gesture)

Mythologically, the serpent has always represented power, strength and wisdom. One example is in the Old Testament where the snake pointed out the tree of life to Adam and Eve and introduced them to the sweetness of the apple. According to the Old Testament, the fruit from the tree of life was the fruit which gave knowledge of good and bad, right and wrong. The snake indicated the way to such wisdom. From another perspective, the snake still represents power, yet it is a power that one does not possess, therefore it invokes fear. In relation to yoga, the force of kundalini and human evolution is represented in the form of a serpent. It is only after the rising of kundalini that new areas of perception open up and deeper insight is experienced.

Technique

Place the left hand on top of the right hand creating an 'X' shape with the hands.
Place the right hand thumb on to the palm of the left hand.

Place the left hand thumb on top of the right hand thumb so that the thumbs are also crossed.
Place the hands comfortably in front of the chest.

MAHAYONI MUDRA (gesture of the supreme source)

This is a mudra that is widely practised in tantra. The word *maha* means 'great' or 'supreme'. The word *yoni* means 'womb', 'source' or 'origin'. Therefore, this mudra can be called the 'supreme source mudra'. This is an important mudra for it symbolizes the unity between the individual consciousness and Supreme Consciousness. It symbolizes the return of the individual to the source, the origin. It is not only a symbol, for this mudra is used to help invoke this realization and experience. It possesses vast powers of invocation if done under the correct circumstances.

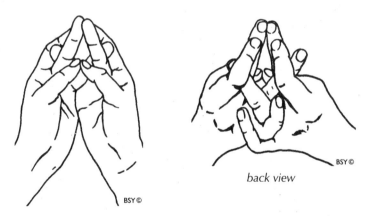

back view

Technique

Once the hands are in maha yoni mudra, hold the hands in front of the chest or rest them on the lap.

SHANKHA MUDRA (conch gesture)

The word *shankha* means 'shell' or 'conch', the type that can be easily found on a quiet beach. The conch is an integral part of the Indian tradition, as many deities, such as Vishnu, Lakshmi and Shiva are shown blowing or holding this symbolic object. The conch was also blown to indicate the commencement of battle, as depicted in the opening chapter of the *Bhagavad Gita*, where all the great warriors blow their conches. In ancient European tradition also the conch was often utilized; for example in Greek mythology, the attendants of the sea god Poseidon, the Tritons, used the conch as a trumpet.

The conch, or rather its sound, represents the inner cosmic sound of each and every individual. This is the sound that links the individual with the highest consciousness, like a puppet on a string. This is called *nada* or *shabda* in Sanskrit, and its Greek counterpart could be the word *logos*, meaning the 'word of God'. When the conch is blown it makes a penetrating sound like a long *Aum*. This is the reason it is sounded during religious ceremonies.

Technique

Place the left thumb on the palm of the right hand at the base of the fingers.

Encircle the thumb with the four fingers.

Bring the left hand fingers towards the right hand thumb.

242

Have the tip of the index finger touching the tip of the right thumb.

Together, the two hands make the shape of a conch shell. While sitting for meditation practice, the most comfortable method is to rest them on the lap.

However, for a short practice the hands can be held in front of the sternum.

Effects: Shankha mudra is said to alleviate many problems of the throat and the abdominal region. The stomach is referred to as shankha, as it is shaped like a conch. The thumb represents manipura chakra which governs the fire element and the abdominal region. In shankha mudra, the thumb is encircled and subdued by the four fingers of the other hand. The contact between the left index finger and the right thumb increases the air element. According to Ayurveda, shankha mudra decreases pitta qualities and may increase vata and kapha within the body. These qualities influence digestion and the digestive organs.

Variation: Note that some texts state that in the final position it is the middle finger that touches the tip of the right thumb rather than the index finger.

DHYANI MUDRA (gesture of meditation and contemplation)

Dhyani means 'one who meditates'. This mudra introverts the mind, increases concentration and enhances meditation. This mudra is a combination of jnana mudra, the variation which has the tips of the thumb and index finger touching, and bhairava mudra.

Technique
On each hand, join the tip of the thumb to the tip of the index finger.
Place one hand on top of the other.
Place the hands in the lap.

243

17

Other Mudras

In the Indian tradition, mudras are used in a multitude of practices. This includes worship, offered through a wide range of rituals, ranging from simple pouring of water, to elaborate fire ceremonies, to dance. There are many rules and guidelines that govern the acts of worship, and the use of mudras here is an intricate subject. Therefore, a qualified teacher or guide is necessary to provide an understanding and personal experience of these mudras in the context in which they have been discussed. Techniques included in this category include:

- Benediction mudras
- Nritya mudras
- Yajna, havan, homa mudras
- Nyasa mudras
- General pooja mudras
- Sandhya mudras
- Deva upasana mudras
- Upachara mudras
- Panchadeva mudras
- Mudras for the manifestations of shakti (cosmic energy)
- Shanti-rakshana mudras
- Other worship mudras

BENEDICTION MUDRAS

The hand mudras of deities or saints represent a divine quality that is being expressed. Performing the mudra or meditating on the form of the mudra held by the divine one leads to experience of that quality within. The two common mudras in which deities and saints are seen are *abhaya mudra*, the gesture of bestowing fearlessness, and *varad mudra*, the gesture of bestowing boons. They denote that blessings are being given in the form of freedom from fear, and boons.

In abhaya mudra, the upper left arm is parallel to the torso, the forearm parallel to the floor, palm held open and fingertips pointing upwards. In varad mudra, the upper right arm is parallel to the torso, the forearm raised, the right hand pointing downwards and the palm open.

Abhaya mudra is seen in many depictions of deities promising protection and freedom from fear. In this context, abhaya is that state of mind designated to those who have transcended even the most deep-rooted fear of death. Fear is one of the basic instincts to overcome and has infinite

245

forms of expression; however, it always causes weakness. Fear keeps one in a state of ignorance about one's real nature. People are weakened as a result of inner conflicts, due to a lack of unity within. Overcoming fear, and purifying and transforming the negative patterns of the mind occur through intense sadhana under the guidance of guru. When one concentrates on a deity or one's guru in this mudra, one is able to connect with this quality of freedom from fear.

NRITYA MUDRAS

Throughout the history of formal worship in India there have been dancers, known as *devadasis*, who perform worship in temples by dancing before the deity that resides there. The dances have varied from region to region. Nevertheless, they were all conceived as supplication to the gods and goddesses. Strict rules governed every aspect of the art, including the training of the dancer and the way in which it was presented and performed. *Natya Shastra* is the earliest known text on classical dance written by Bharata Muni, dating around the second century AD. These ancient dances continue today in essentially the same form, yet without the preliminary rites connected with the method used in temples.

In its purest form, Indian dance is performed to awaken a spontaneous inner vision of beauty and to create a vision of the divine truth in the mind of the one watching. The element of communication or expression is known as *abhinaya* and through the different aspects of abhinaya the dancer endeavours to arouse rasa in the audience. *Rasa* is the equivalent of beauty in the philosophical sense; it is a harmonious expression that reveals the inner nature of things, where the theme, expression, content and form are in balance. Rasa is said to result from *bhava*, a divine feeling or state of mind. Abhinaya is made up of *angika*, movements and gestures; *vachika*, voice and speech; *aharya*, dress, adornment and makeup; and *satvika*, the expression of emotions, moods and sentiments. In angika abhinaya, nearly every part of the body is called upon. It is written that in the face and head there are more than eighty localized actions for registering fleeting nuances of feeling, and the eyes alone have thirty-six kinds of glances.

The hands are an essential feature of angika abhinaya and are an important part of the language of dance. There are two types of hand gestures, ornamental and symbolic. *Nrita hastas* are the purely ornamental hand gestures, *asamyuta hasta* are symbolic gestures made with a single hand and *samuyuta* are symbolic combined hand gestures. They symbolize innumerable experiences, feelings and actions ranging from the mundane to the spiritual. One hand gesture can convey different meanings depending on the accompanying movements and the context in which it is used. For example, the hand gesture known as pataka mudra is used to denote the beginning of a dance, a cloud, a forest, night, a river, a horse, the act of cutting, taking an oath, silence, benediction, and so on.

There are many hand mudras used in Indian dance. Here are some examples:

Padmakosha mudra (lotus bud gesture)

Separate and bend the fingers a little and have the palm slightly hollowed.

Sola padma or ala padma mudra (gesture of lotus in full bloom)

All the fingers are separated, turned about the little finger.

Sarpa shirsha mudra (snakehead gesture)

Begin with an open palm with the fingers pointing upwards. Bend the fingers slightly forming the shape of a snakehead.

Mriga shirsha mudra (deer's head gesture)

In the sarpa shirsha hand, the thumb and little finger are extended.

Simha mukha mudra (lion's face gesture)

The tips of the middle and ring fingers are applied to the thumb, the rest extended.

Hamsaya mudra (swan's face gesture)

The middle, ring and little fingers are separated and extended, the index finger and thumb joined.

Hamsa paksha mudra (swan feather gesture)
The little finger of the sarpa shirsha hand is extended.

Samdamsa mudra (gesture of grasping)
The finger of the padmakosha hand are repeatedly opened and closed.

Trishula mudra (gesture of the trident)
The thumb and little finger are bent and touch each other. The other three fingers are extended.

Urna nabha mudra (spider gesture)
The fingers of the padmakosha hand are bent, rather than slightly curved.

Bana mudra (arrow gesture)
The index, middle and ring fingers touch the thumb, and the little finger is extended.

YAJNA, HAVAN AND HOMA MUDRAS

Yajnas are sacrificial rites which involve offering oblations into the fire. The word 'yajna' consists of three syllables, 'ya', 'ja' and 'na', which refer to the three processes involved in every act performed and which must be balanced: production, distribution and assimilation. Thus, yajna has three components: *pooja*, ritual or worship; *satsang*, association with the wise; and *daan*, unconditional giving. *Havans* are smaller fire rituals used to evoke the cosmic energies, for purposes such as healing and purification, or to evoke the grace of the divine, and *homa* is a fire ritual performed by an individual at home. During all three rituals of worship, various common hand mudras are used.

Mrigi, hamsi and sukari are examples of mudras used to make offerings during yajna, havan and homa. In *mrigi mudra* (female deer gesture), the ring and middle fingertips touch the tip of the thumb. This mudra is used for offering *samagri*, materials offered into the fire during the performance of havan. In *hamsi mudra* (female swan gesture), the little, ring and middle finger tips touch the tip of the thumb, and in *sukari mudra* (boar gesture), the fingertips touch the tip of the thumb so they all join to form the shape of a beak. Other mudras for homa include: *avagunthini mudra* (attitude of veiling), *saptajihva mudra* (gesture of worshipping the seven tongues of fire), *jvalini* (gesture for havan fire) and *prajvalini mudra* (gesture for havan fire).

In the performance of most homas and havans, the final oblation, or *poornahuti*, in the form of samagri, is offered at the end of the ceremony into the fire from a clean plate that is held in both hands. This is known as *avashishtika mudra*, gesture of the final oblation. This final oblation is also called *svishtakrit homa*.

250

NYASA MUDRAS

Nyasa is traditionally performed before every form of worship. It is the practice of rotating the awareness through different parts of the body, purifying them, energizing them, and creating an armour around them. This practice protects the sadhaka from the negative powers that may come to disturb, distract and hamper spiritual attainment. *Nyasa* means to place in trust, and in this context it means to place each body part in the trust of a particular deity with the use of mantra. Thus, the practice of nyasa is both the removal of impurities such as negativity and the placement of the positive and the divine. This is a process which is performed mentally, with the aid of mudras and mantra.

In the practice, one becomes aware of each and every part of the body: the tip of the thumb, the first joint, the second joint, the whole thumb, and so on throughout the whole body. While the awareness touches each part, a mantra is chanted, whether *Hreem, Hraum, Hrah, Kleem, Klaum*. There is a specific mantra for each part. Every organ is protected by a specific mantra so that no physical hindrance or obstacle can impede or obstruct the practice of concentration and *dhyana*, meditation. The practice uses each part of the body as a trigger to awaken the prana shakti within, which becomes the armour around the body.

Anga nyasa mudras (gestures purifying parts of the body)
Anga refers to a limb or part of the body. *Anga nyasa mudras* are used to purify and to energize certain parts of the body. Each part of the body has a corresponding mantra that is chanted in conjunction with the mudra and visualization.
* Touch the index finger, middle finger and ring finger to the heart or centre of the chest.
* Touch the head with the index and middle fingers.
* Touch the *shikha*, the top back of the head with the thumb.

251

- Cross the arms across the chest. Touch the right shoulder with the five fingers of the left hand and the fingers of the right hand touch the left shoulder like an armour or *kavacha*.
- Touch the index, middle and ring fingers to both eyes. See the practice note below.
- Clap the index and middle fingers of the right hand on the open left palm.

Practice note: In daily practice, both eyes are touched. However, when performing anga nyasa in the presence of a deity, instead of touching one's own eyes, the eyes of the deity are touched or meditated upon. The *netra nyasa*, or touching the eyes, is performed according to the specific number of eyes of the deity. For example, Shukra has one eye, Surya has two eyes, Shiva, Shakti, Ganesha and Narasimha have three eyes, Brahma has eight, the Panchamukhi Rudra has ten and Kartikeya has twelve.

Kara nyasa mudras (gestures purifying the hands)

Kara nyasa mudras are mudras used to purify and energize the hands. In sequence, one after the other, touch the tips of the thumbs together, then the index fingers, the middle fingers, the ring fingers and the little fingers. Lastly join all the fingers and both palms together.

Jiva nyasa mudras (gestures purifying the individual)

In jiva nyasa, the following mudras are used: *nada mudra* (attitude of primal sound), in which the right fist is raised with the thumb held upright; *bindu mudra* (gesture of the source), with the thumb and index finger joined together to form a circle; and *soubhagya dayini mudra* (gesture bestowing good fortune), where the left hand is made into a fist, the index finger is kept straight and used to draw a circle near the ear. Other jiva nyasa mudras include: *bija mudra* (seed gesture), *leliha mudra* (gesture of moving the tongue) and *trikhanda mudra* (gesture of three parts).

Matrika nyasa mudras (gestures of purification with sacred syllables)

In matrika nyasa, letters of the Sanskrit alphabet are placed on the limbs of the body. There are two types of matrika nyasa: the outer and the inner. In the outer type, letters are placed on the limbs of the physical body by touching that part of the body, while in the latter they are placed on the six chakras. Nyasa can also be performed simply by meditating on the parts, touching them with a flower or using only the thumb and ring finger. The following are examples of mudras used in outer matrika nyasa.

- Touch the middle and ring fingers of the right hand to the forehead.
- Place the thumb of the right hand on the right eye and the little finger on the left eye.
- Touch all the fingers of the right hand to the top of the head and the lips.
- Touch the middle finger of the right hand to the ribs below the armpits.
- Touch the thumb of the right hand to both ears.
- Touch the thumb of the right hand to the right nostril and the little finger to the left nostril.
- Touch the face and cheeks with the index, middle and ring fingers of the right hand.
- Touch the teeth and tongue with the ring finger of the right hand.
- Touch the back with the ring and little fingers of the right hand.
- Touch the navel with the thumb, middle, ring and little fingers of the right hand.
- Touch the groin area with the thumb, middle, ring and little fingers of the right hand.
- Touch the heart or centre of the chest with the palm of the right hand.

GENERAL POOJA MUDRAS

Pooja is an act of worship or ritual. One mudra that is used in all forms of worship throughout the world is *pranam mudra*, the gesture of paying obeisance. It has many other names, such as *namaskara mudra*, the gesture of greeting or prayer, and *prarthana mudra*, the gesture of prayer. The palms of the hands are simply placed together in front of the chest. This mudra is used in many situations to express reverence and gratitude. For example, in the first and last posture of *surya namaskara*, salutations to the sun, namaskara mudra is used to pay homage to the sun, the source of all life and the symbol of spiritual consciousness. The mudra supports harmony, balance, repose, silence and peace. Pranam mudra also activates and harmonizes coordination of the left and right brain hemispheres, establishing a state of concentration and calmness. It quietens the thoughts, stabilizes the mind, creates clarity and builds strength.

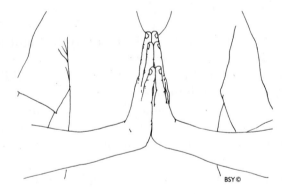

According to acupuncture, three important yin meridians of the lung, pericardium and heart run along each palm. By joining the palms together in pranam mudra, exchange of energy between these six meridians is enhanced. The concept of yin corresponds to that of ida, and this mudra helps to induce the state of introversion that enables the

254

awareness to be directed to prayer, to recognition of or salutation to the higher forces of nature. These yin meridians have connections with the region of the chest, and internal connecting channels that supply energy to the heart, the area of anahata chakra, that in yogic scriptures has been said to be stimulated by this mudra.

In other traditions, such as Christianity, this mudra is adopted in prayer and the concentration directed into the heart space. Joining of the tips of the thumbs together establishes a direct connection between the lung meridians on both sides of the body, each one of them controlling the flow of air in the nostril on the opposite side. The overall effect is one of equalizing the flow of breath in both nostrils and inducing the balance in the flow of ida and pingala and in the activity of the left and the right brain hemispheres.

Other pooja mudras include:

Ankusha mudra (goad gesture)
Make a fist with the right hand. The index finger is bent in the shape of a hook or goad. This is the mudra which bestows the ability to attract the three worlds, triloka.

Kunta mudra (spear gesture)
Make an upright fist with the right hand, with the index finger held up. Touch the tip of the index finger with the thumb. This is the all-protective kunta or bhala mudra.

255

Kumbha mudra (pot gesture)

Join the thumbs of both hands and interlace the other fingers together like a concave fist held upright. This mudra is performed while taking a ritual bath.

Tattwa mudra (gesture of the elements)

Join the tips of the ring finger and thumb. This mudra is traditionally performed while immersing oneself in water in a river or lake, or in front of the water vessel at home before having a bath.

SANDHYA MUDRAS

A daily worship ritual that has been practised since the vedic times is *sandhya*. Every individual was supposed to perform the sandhya during dawn, noon and dusk, the day's conjunction moments or *sandhi*. This included chanting of the Gayatri mantra, pranayama, purification rituals, and performance of twenty-four mudras:

- Sammukhi mudra (gesture of holding the deity before oneself)
- Samputi mudra (gesture of accessing the depth of a mantra)
- Vitata mudra (gesture of expansiveness)
- Vistrita mudra (gesture of expansiveness)
- Dwimukhi mudra (two-face gesture)
- Trimukhi mudra (three-face gesture)
- Chaturmukhi mudra (four-face gesture)
- Panchamukhi mudra (five-face gesture)
- Shanmukhi mudra (six-face gesture)
- Adhomukhi mudra (downward facing gesture)
- Vyapaka mudra (gesture of pervasiveness)
- Anjalika mudra (gesture of offering)
- Shakata mudra (gesture of a bullock cart)
- Yama-pasha mudra (gesture of the noose of Yama)
- Grathita mudra (gesture of tying up)

- Sammukhonmukha mudra (gesture of being face to face and raising the face)
- Pralaya mudra (attitude of dissolution)
- Mushtika mudra (fist gesture)
- Matsya mudra (attitude of Matsya)
- Kurma mudra (attitude of Kurma)
- Varaha mudra (attitude of Varaha)
- Simhakranta mudra (attitude of a lion)
- Mahakranta mudra (attitude of greatness)
- Mudgara mudra (hammer gesture)

Of these, the first seventeen are specific to this practice, while the other seven are *moola*, or principle mudras used in various practices. There are a further eight mudras performed on the completion of the sandhya ritual:

- Surabhi or dhenu mudra (gesture of the divine cow)
- Jnana mudra (attitude of knowing)
- Vairagya mudra (attitude of non-attachment)   .
- Yoni mudra (gesture of the source)
- Shankha mudra (conch gesture)
- Padma or pankaja mudra (lotus gesture)
- Linga mudra (gesture of the primal symbol)
- Nirvana mudra (attitude of final liberation)

DEVA UPASANA MUDRAS

These mudras are used while offering worship to the gods. Some are common with the sandhya mudras:

Anjali mudra (gesture of offering)
Place the tips of the thumbs at the base of the little fingers of both hands and make a hollow by joining the hands together. Offerings are made in this mudra, often of flowers.

Sthapani mudra (gesture of establishing a deity)
Point the anjali mudra downwards. It is used to establish the deity in the place of worship.

257

Sannidhapani mudra (gesture of establishing nearness with the deity)

Make a fist with both hands and point the thumbs upwards. It is used to establish nearness with the deity.

Sannirodhini mudra (gesture of obstruction)

Tuck the thumbs into the fists. It is used to obstruct negative forces during worship.

Sammukhikarani mudra (gesture of holding the deity before oneself)

Raise both fists upwards. It is used to assume that the deity is before the worshipper.

Avagunthini mudra (gesture of veiling)

Place the index finger of the left hand downwards and flat upon the index finger of the right hand which faces upwards and turn them in a clockwise direction.

Dhenu mudra (cow gesture)

Join both palms, touch the tips of the right ring finger to the left little finger and the left ring finger to the right little finger. Touch the right middle finger to the left index finger and the left middle finger to the right index finger. Another name for this mudra is *amritikarani*. This mudra is performed while offering *naivedya*, food, to the gods.

Paramikarana mudra (attitude of the supreme instrument)

Join both hands together to form a triangle.

UPACHARA MUDRAS

These mudras are used when performing *upachara*, the offering of certain materials during worship:

Gandha mudra (gesture of offering perfume)

When offering gandha, or perfume, join the tips of the thumb, middle and ring fingers of the right hand. The moola mantra is to be chanted at this time.

Pushpa mudra (gesture of offering flowers)

When flowers, tulsi and other leaves are offered, they are held with the thumb and index finger of the right hand.

Dhoopa mudra (gesture of offering incense)

When dhoopa is offered it is held with the middle and ring fingers, and the tip of the thumb.

Deepa mudra (gesture of offering a lamp)

Place the tip of the thumb at the base of the middle finger of the right hand while offering the lamp.

Naivedya mudra (gesture of offering food)

This mudra uses *tattwa mudra*, where the tips of the ring finger and thumb of the right hand are joined. With the hands in tattwa mudra, prasad is offered while chanting both the Gayatri and the moola mantra of the deity being worshipped.

Achamana mudra (gesture of sipping water)

Cupping the right hand, water is sipped along with the moola mantra.

Tambula mudra (gesture of offering betel nut)

With the hands in tattwa mudra, betel nut is offered.
During upachara the pancha prana mudras: prana, apana, samana, udana and vyana, are performed as a gesture to offer oneself, one's vital energy to the divine.

PANCHADEVA MUDRAS

Within tantra, there are five main deities who represent the five aspects of the supreme transcendental force: Shiva, Shakti, Narayana, Surya and Ganesha. They are known collectively as the *panchadevas*. There are two schools of thought regarding the panchadevas. The second school of thought replaces Surya with Brahma. These groups of deities were created by the ancients, and the philosophy and the sadhana which developed around them became aids to realize their power. The following mudras are gestures which invoke different aspects relating to the panchadevas. For example, shankha mudra is the gesture of the conch which is used by Lord Vishnu, or Narayana. Similarly, Matsya, Kurma, Varaha, Hayagriva, Narasimha, Rama and Krishna are avataras of Lord Vishnu. Thus, by worshipping these different aspects one is worshipping the panchadevas. The mudras for the panchadevas include:

MUDRAS FOR VISHNU

Shankha mudra (conch gesture)

As described in Chapter 16, place the thumb of the left hand in the palm of the right hand. Bend the fingers of the right hand over the left hand thumb. Bring the fingers of the left hand towards the thumb of the right hand. Join the tip of the right hand thumb to the tip of the index finger of the left hand, making the shape of a conch.

Dhanusha mudra (bow gesture)

Dhanusha means a bow, which Lord Vishnu wields. Join the tips of the left hand middle and index fingers press the little and ring fingers with the thumb and place them near the left hand shoulder.

Vana or bana mudra (arrow gesture)

Bana means an arrow, which Lord Vishnu wields. Hold out the right hand straight from the shoulder and point the index finger ahead.

Garuda mudra (gesture of Garuda)

This is different from the mudra described in Chapter 15. Place both palms upright and back to back, link the little fingers of both hands as well as join the index fingers of both hands. Flutter the middle and ring fingers like wings. Garuda mudra is used to worship Lord Vishnu, Garuda being the vehicle of Lord Vishnu.

Matsya mudra (fish gesture)

Place the right palm on the back of the left hand and wiggle the thumbs. This mudra is used in the worship of Vishnu as Matsya avatara, the form of a fish.

Kurma mudra (tortoise gesture)

Place the middle and ring fingers of the right hand facing downwards on the portion between the thumb and index finger of the left hand. This mudra is used in the worship of Vishnu as Kurma avatara, the form of a tortoise.

Varaha mudra (attitude of Varaha)

Place the right hand upon the left hand and bring them up and down together. This mudra is used in the worship of Vishnu as Varaha avatara.

Hayagriva mudra (attitude of Hayagriva)

Place the inverted fingers of the right hand upon the palm of the left hand. This mudra is used in the worship of Vishnu as Hayagriva avatara, the form of a man-horse.

Narasimhi mudra (gesture of Narasimha)

Squat with the hands between both feet and place the palms flat on the ground, put on a frightening expression on the face and bring the tongue out like a lion. This mudra is used in the worship of Vishnu as Narasimha avatara, the form of a man-lion.

Parashu mudra (axe gesture)

Parashu means an axe, wielded by Parashurama, an avatara of Vishnu. Join both hands from the tips of the fingers to the base of the palms and spread the fingers in the shape of an axe. This mudra is used in the worship of Vishnu as Parashuram avatara, the sage-warrior called Parashuram.

Jnana mudra (attitude of knowing)

This is different from the mudra described in Chapter 10. Place the tips of the index finger and thumb of the right hand near the centre of the chest or heart, and the left hand rests on the left side of the waist. Jnana mudra is used in the worship of Lord Rama.

Vasudeva mudra (attitude of Vasudeva)

Vasudeva is an epithet of Sri Krishna. Join both hands together in the position of making an offering. When this mudra is performed during dhyana, it is said to confer perfection in all actions.

Jaganmohana mudra (attitude of one who has charmed the whole world)

Jaganmohana means one who has charmed the whole world, and is an epithet of Vishnu or Krishna. Place the thumbs on top of the fists of both hands.

Vanshi mudra (flute gesture)

Vanshi means the flute, which Sri Krishna is always playing. In the manner a flute is played, place the thumb of the left hand near the lips and wiggle the ring, middle and index fingers while holding the little finger out.

Vanamala mudra (gesture of garland of wild flowers)

A garland of wild flowers is called *vanamala*, worn by Sri Krishna. Joining the thumb and index finger of both hands and run the hands from the throat down towards the feet.

MUDRAS FOR SHIVA

Bilva mudra (gesture of the bael leaf)

Encircle the raised left hand thumb with the right hand thumb and tightly interlock the fingers of both hands. Place the hands near the centre of the chest or heart. This mudra is performed while chanting the bija mantra *Kleem*. *Bilva* means bael leaf, and it is the bael leaf that is offered during worship to Shiva. Similarly, this mudra is used in the worship of Shiva.

Linga mudra (gesture of the primal symbol)

The linga and yoni represent the Shivalingam, the symbol of Shiva. Join the upright thumbs of both hands together and clasp the fingers of the left hand with those of the right hand. This is slightly different from the linga mudra depicted in Chapter 15.

Yoni mudra (gesture of the source)

This is different from the yoni mudras described in Chapters 10 and 11. Link the little fingers of both hands, touch the raised ring fingers to the index fingers and spreading the middle fingers outwards, bring the thumbs close to the little fingers.

Trishula mudra (gesture of the trident)

Trishula means the trident, wielded by Shiva. Fold the little finger towards the palm with the thumb and raise the ring, middle and index fingers.

Aksha mudra (rudraksha gesture)

Aksha is another term for rudraksha; Shiva wears a garland made up of these sacred seeds. Join the tips of the thumb and index finger to make a circle. The middle, ring and little fingers are held upright and a little apart.

Mriga mudra (deer gesture)

Mriga means a deer; Shiva holds a deer in one hand indicating that he has removed the tossing or wandering nature of the mind. Join the tips of the middle and index fingers with the tip of the thumb to make a circle and holding the ring and little fingers upright and a little apart.

Khatvanga mudra (gesture of the stick mounted with a skull)

Khatvanga is the stick mounted with a skull which Shiva wields. Join all the fingers of the right hand together and hold them upwards.

Damaru mudra (hand drum gesture):

Damaru is the small hourglass-shaped drum that Shiva holds, representing the primordial sound. Form a loose fist with the right hand and bend the middle finger to touch the centre of the palm while shaking the fist near the right ear.

MUDRAS FOR DEVI

Danta mudra (bared teeth gesture)

Danta means teeth; Devi in her fierce form is seen with bared teeth. Form a loose fist with the right hand and hold the middle finger upright.

Pasha mudra (noose gesture)

Pasha means a noose; it is the weapon of the Devi to ensnare the individual soul. Make a fist with both hands. Raise and hold the index fingers upright and touch the tips of the thumbs to them.

Kapala mudra (skull gesture)

Kapala is a skull. Devi in the form of Kali wears a garland of skulls. Form the left hand like a cup and hold it up with the elbow bent.

Ankusha mudra (goad gesture)

Ankusha is a goad, with which Devi controls the individual. Hold the middle finger upright and bend the index finger like a hook or a goad.

Avahani mudra (gesture of invocation)

Avahana means invocation. Place the tips of the thumbs at the base of the little fingers of both hands. The hands rest next to each other. This mudra, while seated in vajrasana, is performed during chanting the *Saundarya Lahari* to invoke Devi.

BSY©

MUDRAS FOR GANESHA

Vighna mudra (attitude of removing obstacles)

Vighna means an obstacle, and Ganesha is *vighnavinayaka*, the remover of obstacles. Tilt the danta mudra sideways.

Modaka mudra (gesture of Ganesha's favourite sweet)

Modaka is the favourite ball-shaped sweet of Ganesha. Hold all the fingers of the right hand up and join their tips together to make a rounded form with a pointed top.

Bijapura mudra (guava gesture)

Bijapura is a guava, the favourite fruit of Ganesha. Join both the hands together in the shape of a seed pod.

MUDRAS FOR SURYA

Arghya mudra (gesture of offering water)

Arghya is an offering of water usually made to Surya. Cup both hands together in the posture of making an offering and place flowers, leaves etc., before Surya deva.

Other panchadeva mudras include: *kama mudra* (attitude of Kama), *ghanta mudra* (gesture of offering the bell), *chakra mudra* (wheel gesture), *gada mudra* (mace gesture), *padma mudra* (lotus gesture), *srivatsa mudra* (attitude of Vishnu) and *kaustubha mudra* (kaustubha jewel gesture).

MUDRAS FOR MANIFESTATIONS OF SHAKTI (COSMIC ENERGY)

In addition to the mudras mentioned above, individual mudras are attributed to the different manifestations of Devi.

MUDRA FOR DURGA

Durga mudra (attitude of Durga)
Place the left fist on top of the right fist and bring them close to the forehead.

MUDRAS FOR KALI

Mahayoni mudra (gesture of the supreme source)
Mahayoni means the Supreme Source or womb. Kali, the goddess who rules over time, dissolves everything into this supreme womb at the time of dissolution. Place the index finger on the middle finger, the middle finger on the ring finger and the ring finger on the little finger and join the thumbs to all of them.

MUDRAS FOR LAKSHMI

Pankaja mudra (lotus flower gesture)
Join both palms and flare out the fingers while keeping the thumbs and little fingers joined together to look like a *pankaja*, or lotus flower, the abode of Lakshmi.

MUDRAS FOR SARASWATI

Veena mudra (lute gesture)
Veena is the lute that Saraswati is seen playing. Hold both hands as if playing the veena. The left arm is bent at the elbow with the left hand held up, palm facing backwards as if holding the frets and the right hand below as if strumming the strings. Shake the head gently from side to side.

Vyakhyana mudra (gesture of speech)

Join the tips of the thumb and index finger of the right hand and then bring them apart. *Vyakhyana* means a lecture or recital. This mudra represents Saraswati as the goddess of speech.

Pustaka mudra (gesture of reading)

Pustaka means a book; Saraswati is the goddess of learning. Hold the slightly cupped left palm facing upwards and towards the body.

MUDRAS FOR TARA

Dhumini mudra (attitude of the veil of smoke)

Dhuma means smoke. Tara is the goddess who shows the way when one's vision is hazy. Place the little finger upon the back of the ring finger, link the thumb and the middle fingers, touch the tip of the ring finger to the base of the thumb and hold the index finger upright.

Leliha mudra (gesture of moving the tongue)

The word *leliha* relates to the movement of the tongue. Join the tips of the ring, middle and index fingers and the thumb and then straighten the fingers out. A variation is to extend the tongue out of the mouth and move it about while the hands are in this mudra.

Other mudras for Tara include: yoni mudra (gesture of the source), bhutini mudra (attitude of a female spirit) and bija mudra (gesture of the seed).

MUDRAS FOR TRIPURA

Sarva vikshobhakarini mudra (attitude of one who causes agitations of the mind)

Tripura is *sarva vikshobhakarini*, the cause of all the agitations of the mind as she is the ruler of the three worlds. This mudra is performed by touching the index fingers of both hands, pressing the little finger down with the thumb, keeping the index finger straight and placing the ring finger on top of the middle finger.

Sarvakarshani mudra (attitude of one who attracts all)
Tripura is *sarvakarshani*, one who attracts all that exists. Place the thumb over the little and ring fingers.

Other mudras for the worship of Tripura are: *sarva vidravini mudra* (attitude of one who defeats all), *sarva vashvakari mudra* (attitude of one who has all under her power), *unmadini mudra* (attitude of one who is intoxicated with bliss), *mahankusha mudra* (gesture of the great goad), *khechari mudra* (gesture of the tongue lock), *bija mudra* (seed gesture) and *yoni mudra* (gesture of the source).

MUDRA FOR BHUVANESHWARI

Mudras include: *pasha mudra* (noose gesture), *ankusha mudra* (goad gesture), *varada mudra* (gesture of bestowing boons), *abhaya mudra* (gesture of bestowing fearlessness), *pustaka mudra* (gesture of reading), *jnana mudra* (attitude of knowing), *bija mudra* (seed gesture) and *yoni mudra* (gesture of the source).

OTHER SHAKTI MUDRAS

Khadga mudra (sword gesture)
Khadga is a sword wielded by Devi. Hold the little and ring fingers together with the thumb of the right hand and raise the middle and index finger.

Charma (dhala) mudra (shield gesture)
Charma is the shield held by Devi. Hold the left arm across the body and form a fist with the left hand.

Mushala mudra (mace gesture)
Mushala is the mace held by Devi. Hold the arms in front of the body and place the left fist on top of the right fist. This mudra destroys obstacles.

SHANTI – RAKSHANA MUDRAS

These mudras are performed for the protection of peace, and include the following:

Sphota (chhotika) mudra (gesture of snapping the fingers)
Sphota or *chhotika* relates to snapping of the fingers. Join the tips of the thumb and index finger.

Shubhankari mudra (gesture of auspiciousness)
Shubhankari means causing auspiciousness. Join the tips of the thumb and middle finger.

Mushti mudra (fist gesture)
Mushti means the fist. Raise the right fist above the head. This mudra breaks all obstacles.

Shakti mudra (attitude of cosmic energy)
Hold both the fists near the forehead with the left hand above the right one.

Panchamukhi mudra (five-face gesture)
Shiva is *panchamukhi*, one who has five faces. Join both hands together with the palms facing each other, touch the tips of the fingers together and spread each pair of fingers a little apart. This mudra confers the protection of Shiva.

Samhara mudra (attitude of destruction)
Samhara is destruction, a task assigned to Shiva. In this context, it means destruction of all that is negative. Interlock the fingers of both hands with the right hand held above the left hand and switch the position of the hands.

Shanti-rakshana mudras also include some mudras that have been described earlier: padma mudra, prarthana mudra, pasha mudra, gada mudra, khadga mudra, mushala mudra and *ashani mudra* (gesture of lightning, performed in the same way as trishula mudra). Within this category are also four *balidan*, or sacrifice mudras. For sacrifice to Ganesha, the middle finger of the right hand is bent a little. For sacrifice to Batuka-Bhairava, the thumb and index finger of the right hand is joined together. For sacrifice to Kshetrapala, the thumb and ring finger of the left hand are joined together, and for sacrifice to the six yoginis, the left hand ring and middle fingers are joined together with the thumb.

MISCELLANEOUS MUDRAS

Japa mudra (gesture of holding a mala)
This mudra is used for *japa dhyana*, meditation with the repetition of mantra. Rotate the beads of a mala over the tips of the thumb and ring finger by using the tip of the middle finger.

BSY©

Tarjani mudra (forbidding gesture)
Tarjani is the index finger. Make a fist with the left hand and raise the index finger. This mudra is made while expressing 'no' or forbidding something.

Krodha mudra (attitude of anger)

Krodha means anger. Raise the closed fist with the index finger pointing out and upwards. This is similar to tarjani mudra.

Ripu jihva graha mudra (gesture of capturing the enemy's tongue)

The phrase *ripu jihva graha* literally translates to 'catching the tongue of the enemy'. Make a fist with the right hand with the thumb held inside the fingers, then bring the thumb past the index finger and extend the thumb out from the fist.

Mukula mudra (bud gesture)

Join both palms and the tips of the fingers together bending the fingers slightly outwards. This makes a *mukula*, or bud.

Vyakroshi mudra (gesture of blossoming)

Vyakrosha means to blossom. This mudra is performed by making the mukula mudra and holding the index fingers of both hands extended outwards.

Appendix

Practices Relevant to Mudra

The following techniques can be used in conjunction with the mudra practices outlined within the text. Many are advanced techniques and should be attempted only under the guidance of a competent teacher so that they are learnt and practised in a systematic way. Read the general guidelines in each chapter before attempting any of the practices. For more information on these practices as individual techniques, see *Asana Pranayama Mudra Bandha* (Yoga Publications Trust, Munger). Techniques included are:

- Advasana (reversed corpse pose)
- Bhadrasana (gracious pose)
- Bhujangasana (cobra pose)
- Gorakshasana (Yogi Gorakhnath's pose)
- Halasana (plough pose)
- Jalandhara Bandha (throat lock)
- Matsyasana (fish pose)
- Mayurasana (peacock pose)
- Moola Bandha (perineum contraction)
- Namaskarasana (salutation pose)
- Naukasana (boat pose)
- Padmasana (lotus pose)
- Pranamasana (prayer pose)
- Sarvangasana (shoulder stand pose)
- Shashankasana (pose of the moon or hare pose)
- Shavasana (corpse pose)

275

- Siddhasana (accomplished pose for men)
- Siddha Yoni Asana (accomplished pose for women)
- Uddiyana Bandha (abdominal contraction)
- Ushtrasana (camel pose)
- Utthanpadasana (stretched leg pose)
- Vajrasana (thunderbolt pose)
- Vipareeta Karani Asana (inverted pose)
- Yogamudrasana (psychic union pose)

ADVASANA (reversed corpse pose)

Technique
Lie on the stomach.
Stretch both arms above the head with the palms facing downward.
The forehead should be resting on the floor.
Relax the whole body in the same way as described for shavasana.
If there is difficulty breathing or a sense of suffocation is experienced, a pillow may be placed under the chest.
After some time, again become aware of the body and surroundings, and gently and smoothly release the posture.

Breathing: Natural and rhythmic. The number of breaths may be counted as in shavasana while gently pushing the abdomen against the floor.

Awareness: Physical – on relaxing the whole body, and on the breath. Spiritual – on ajna or manipura chakra.

Practice note: Mantra may also be synchronized with the breath as in shavasana.

276

BHADRASANA (gracious pose)

Technique

Sit in vajrasana.

Separate the knees as far as possible, while keeping the toes in contact with the floor.

Separate the feet just enough to allow the buttocks and perineum to rest flat on the floor between the feet.

Try to separate the knees further, but do not strain.

Place the hands on the knees, palms downward.

When the body is comfortable, practise nasikagra drishti, concentration on the nose tip.

As the eyes become tired, close them for a short time and then resume nose tip gazing.

Breathing: Slow and rhythmic with awareness of the breath at the nose tip.

Awareness: Physical – sensations of opening and relaxing the perineum, and on the natural breath or the nose tip. Spiritual – on mooladhara chakra.

Practice note: If any strain is experienced, stop the asana. If necessary, a folded blanket may be placed under the buttocks. Whether a blanket is used or not, it is important that the buttocks rest firmly on the ground in order to stimulate mooladhara chakra.

BHUJANGASANA (cobra pose)

Technique

Lie flat on the stomach with the legs straight, feet together and the soles of the feet uppermost.

Place the palms of the hands flat on the floor, below and slightly to the side of the shoulders, with the fingers together and pointing forward.

Position the arms so that the elbows point backward and are close to the sides of the body. Rest the forehead on the floor and close the eyes.

Relax the whole body, especially the lower back.

Slowly raise the head.

Gently tilt the head backward, so that the chin points forward and the back of the neck is compressed, then raise the neck and then the shoulders.

Straighten the elbows, using the back muscles first, followed by the arm muscles to raise the trunk further and arch the back.

In the final position, the pubic bone remains in contact with the floor and the navel is raised a maximum of 3 cm.

If the navel is raised too high, the bend tends to be in the knees and not in the back.

The arms may or may not be straight; this will depend on the flexibility of the back.

Hold the final position.

To return to the starting position, slowly release the upper back by bending the arms, lower the navel, chest, shoulders and finally the forehead to the floor.

Relax the lower back muscles.
This is one round.

Breathing: Inhale while raising the torso. Breathe normally in the final position or retain the breath if the pose is held for a short time. Exhale while lowering the torso.

Duration: Practise up to 5 rounds, gradually increasing the length of time in the final position.

Awareness: Physical – on the smooth, systematic arching movement of the back, the stretching of the abdomen, and on synchronizing the breath with the movement. Spiritual – on swadhisthana chakra.

Contra-indications: People suffering from peptic ulcer, hernia, intestinal tuberculosis or hyperthyroidism should not practise this asana without the guidance of a competent teacher.

GORAKSHASANA (Yogi Gorakhnath's pose)

Technique

Sit with the legs stretched out in front of the body.
Bend the knees, take hold of the feet and place the soles together.
Draw the heels up to the perineum.
Raise the heels, keeping the balls of the feet on the floor.
Place the hands behind the buttocks, fingers pointing backward, and lever the body forward until the feet become vertical.

The knees should remain on the floor.
Do not strain.
Cross the wrists in front of the navel.
Hold the left heel with the right hand and the right heel with the left hand.
Straighten the spine and face forward.
Perform nasikagra drishti.
This is the final position.
Hold for as long as is comfortable.

Breathing: Breathe normally throughout the practice.

Awareness: Physical – on maintaining balance, or on the feet and knees. Spiritual – on mooladhara chakra.

Contra-indications: This pose should not be attempted until the knees and ankles have become very flexible.

Practice note: To perform this asana, the muscles of the legs and feet need to be slowly stretched over a period of time.

HALASANA (plough pose)

BSY©

Technique

Lie flat on the back with the legs and feet together.
Place the arms beside the body with the palms facing down.
Relax the whole body.
Raise both legs to the vertical position, keeping them straight and together, using only the abdominal muscles.
Press down on the arms and lift the buttocks, rolling the back away from the floor.

280

Lower the legs over the head.

Bring the toes towards the floor behind the head without straining, but do not force the toes to touch the floor.

Turn the palms up, bend the elbows and place the hands behind the ribcage to support the back, as in sarvangasana.

Relax and hold the final pose for as long as is comfortable. Return to the starting position by lowering the arms with the palms facing down, then gradually lower each vertebrae of the spine to the floor, followed by the buttocks, so that the legs resume their initial vertical position.

Using the abdominal muscles, lower the legs to the starting position, keeping the knees straight.

Breathing: Inhale while in the lying position. Retain the breath inside while assuming the final pose. Breathe slowly and deeply in the final pose. Retain the breath inside while returning to the starting position.

Duration: Beginners should hold the pose for 15 seconds, gradually adding a few seconds per week until it can be held for one minute. Adepts may hold the final pose up to 10 minutes or longer.

Awareness: Physical – on the abdomen, relaxation of the back muscles and neck, the respiration, or the thyroid. Spiritual – on manipura or vishuddhi chakra.

Sequence: To move from sarvangasana to halasana, bring the feet slightly over the head for balance, slowly remove the arms from their position behind the back and place them on the floor in the starting position, palms facing down. Relax the body and slowly lower the legs over the head, keeping them straight and together, until the toes touch the floor. Release as described above. Follow halasana with either matsyasana, ushtrasana or supta vajrasana as a counterpose, practised for half the combined duration of sarvangasana and halasana. Halasana is a good preparatory practice for paschimottanasana.

Contra-indications: This asana should not be practised by those who suffer from hernia, slipped disc, sciatica, high blood pressure or any serious back problem, especially arthritis of the neck.

JALANDHARA BANDHA (throat lock)

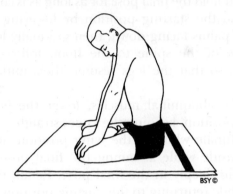

Technique
Sit in padmasana or siddha/siddha yoni asana with the head and spine straight.
The knees should be in firm contact with the floor.
Place the palms of the hands on the knees.
Close the eyes and relax the whole body.
Inhale slowly and deeply, and retain the breath inside.
While retaining the breath, bend the head forward and press the chin tightly against the chest.
Straighten the arms and lock them firmly into position, pressing the knees down with the hands.
Simultaneously, hunch the shoulders upward and forward.
This will ensure that the arms stay locked, thus intensifying the pressure applied to the neck.
Stay in the final position for a few seconds to begin with. Do not strain.
Relax the shoulders, bend the arms and slowly release the lock.

282

Raise the head and then exhale.

Repeat when the respiration has returned to normal.

Breathing: The practice is performed during internal retention. It may also be performed with external breath retention.

Duration: Jalandhara bandha can be held for as long as the practitioner is able to comfortably retain the breath. Maintain a count while retaining the breath and gradually increase the count. This practice may be repeated up to 5 times.

Awareness: Physical – on the throat pit and sensations connected with breath retention. Spiritual – on vishuddhi chakra.

Contra-indications: People suffering from cervical spondylosis, high intracranial pressure, vertigo, high blood pressure or heart disease should not practise jalandhara bandha. Although the neck lock reduces blood pressure, long retention of the breath strains the heart. Jalandhara is the first bandha to be taught, as the effects are light and soothing. Refrain from the practice if any vertigo or dizziness arises.

Practice note: Do not exhale or inhale until the chin lock and arm lock have been released and the head is fully upright. If suffocation is felt, end the practice and rest. Once the sensation has passed, resume the practice.

MATSYASANA (fish pose)

Technique

Sit in padmasana and relax the whole body.

Carefully bend backward, supporting the body with the arms and elbows.

Lift the chest slightly, take the head back and lower the crown of the head to the floor.

Hold the big toes and rest the elbows on the floor.

Adjust the position of the head so that the maximum arch of the back is attained.

Relax the arms and the whole body, allowing the head, buttocks and legs to support the weight of the body.

Close the eyes and breathe slowly and deeply.

Return to the starting position, reversing the order of movements.

Repeat the asana, with the legs crossed the other way.

Breathing: Breathe deeply and slowly in the final position.

Duration: The final position may be held for up to 5 minutes, although 1 to 3 minutes is sufficient for general health.

Awareness: Physical – on the abdomen, chest, neck and head or breath. Spiritual – on manipura or anahata chakra.

Contra-indications: People who suffer from heart disease, peptic ulcers, hernia, back conditions or any serious illness should not practise this asana. Pregnant women should also not attempt it.

Practice note: It is important that the body is slowly lowered into and raised from the final position by using the elbows as a support. The movement should be performed with control and care as it is very easy to injure the spine.

MAYURASANA (peacock pose)

Technique

Kneel on the floor.

Place the feet together and separate the knees.

Lean forward and place both palms between the knees on the floor with the fingers pointing towards the feet.

The hand position will have to be adjusted according to comfort and flexibility.

Bring the elbows and forearms together.

Lean further forward and rest the abdomen on the elbows and the chest on the upper arms.

Stretch the legs backward so they are straight and together.

Tense the muscles of the body and slowly elevate the trunk and legs so that they are horizontal to the floor.

Hold the head upward.

The whole body should now be balanced only on the palms of the hands.

Try to elevate the legs and feet higher, keeping them straight by applying more muscular effort and by adjusting the balance of the body.

Do not strain.

In the final position, the weight of the body should be supported by the muscles of the abdomen and not the chest.

285

Maintain the pose for a short period of time, then slowly return to the base position.
This is one round.
The asana may be repeated when the breathing rate has returned to normal.

Breathing: Exhale while raising the body from the floor. Inhale while lowering the body back to the floor. To begin with, hold the breath out in the final position. Advanced practitioners may breathe slowly and deeply in the pose. Allow the breathing to return to normal before attempting a second round.

Duration: Up to 3 rounds. In the beginning, this asana should be held for a few seconds, slowly increasing the duration with practice. Adepts may hold the final position for a few minutes.

Awareness: Physical – on the pressure on the abdomen and on maintaining balance. Spiritual – on manipura chakra.

Sequence: Perform at the end of an asana session. Mayurasana speeds up the circulation quite vigorously and tends to increase the amount of toxins in the blood as part of the process of purification. Therefore, it should never be practised before any inverted asana as it may direct excess toxins to the brain.

Contra-indications: Mayurasana should not be practised by people with high blood pressure or any heart ailment, hernia, peptic or duodenal ulcer. This pose should not be attempted if there is any sign of illness or physical weakness. Pregnant women are strongly advised not to practise this asana. Cautions for inverted postures apply.

Practice note: As women have a different muscular system to men in the abdomen and chest areas, they may find mayurasana difficult to perform. It is very easy to fall forward from the final position and crush the nose on the floor. So be careful and, if necessary, place a small cushion on the floor under the face.

MOOLA BANDHA (perineum contraction)

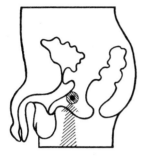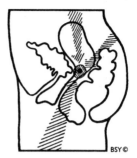

Technique 1: Moola Bandha (perineum contraction)

Stage 1: Sit in a comfortable meditative asana, preferably
siddha/siddha yoni asana, so that pressure is applied to
the perineal/vaginal region.

Close the eyes and relax the whole body.

Be aware of the natural breath.

Focus the awareness on the perineal/vaginal region.

Contract this region by pulling up on the muscles of the
pelvic floor and then relaxing them.

Continue to briefly contract and relax the perineal/
vaginal region as rhythmically and evenly as possible.

Breathe normally throughout the practice.

Stage 2: Continue to breathe normally; do not hold the
breath.

Slowly contract the perineal/vaginal region and hold the
contraction.

Be totally aware of the physical sensation.

Contract a little tighter, but keep the rest of the body
relaxed.

Contract only those muscles related to the mooladhara
region.

In the beginning, the anal and urinary sphincters will
also contract, but as greater awareness and control is
developed, this will minimize and eventually cease.

Ultimately, only one point of contraction will be felt.

Relax the muscles slowly and evenly.

287

Adjust the tension in the spine to help focus on the point of contraction.

Repeat 10 times with maximum contraction and total relaxation.

Technique 2: with internal breath retention and jalandhara bandha

Close the eyes and relax the whole body for a few minutes.

Inhale deeply, retain the breath inside and perform jalandhara bandha.

Perform moola bandha and hold the contraction as tightly as possible.

Do not strain.

This is the final lock.

Hold the contraction for as long as the breath can comfortably be retained.

Slowly release moola bandha, then jalandhara, raising the head to the upright position, and exhale.

Practise up to 10 times.

Breathing: The above practice may also be performed with external breath retention.

Awareness: Physical – at the point of perineal contraction. Spiritual – on mooladhara chakra.

Contra-indications: This practice should only be performed under the guidance of a competent teacher. Moola bandha raises the energy, and may precipitate hyper-activity. Do not practise during menstruation.

Practice note: Moola bandha is the contraction of specific muscles in the pelvic floor, not the whole perineum. In the male body, the area of contraction is between the anus and the testes. In the female body, the point of contraction is behind the cervix, where the uterus projects into the vagina. On the subtle level, it is the energizing of mooladhara chakra. The perineal body, which is the convergence of many muscles in the groin, acts as a trigger point for the location of mooladhara chakra. Initially, this area is difficult to isolate, so it

288

is recommended that ashwini and vajroli mudras be performed in preparation for moola bandha.

NAMASKARASANA (salutation pose)

Technique

Squat with the feet flat on the floor about 60 cm apart.
The knees should be wide apart and the elbows pressing against the inside of the knees.
Bring the hands together in front of the chest in a gesture of prayer.
This is the starting position.
The eyes may be open or closed.
Inhale and bend the head backwards.
Feel the pressure at the back of the neck.
Simultaneously, use the elbows to push the knees as wide apart as comfortable.
Hold this position for 3 seconds while retaining the breath.
Exhale and straighten the arms directly in front of the body.
At the same time, push in with the knees, pressing the upper arms inward.
The head should be bent forward with the chin pressed against the chest.
Hold this position, retaining the breath, for 3 seconds.
Return to the starting position.

This is one round.
Practise 5 to 10 rounds.

Breathing: Inhale while bringing the palms together in front of the chest. Exhale while extending the arms forward.

Awareness: On the stretch on the groin and compression at the back of the neck, then changing to relaxation of the upper back and shoulder muscles in the forward position, and the breath.

Contra-indications: Not for people with knee problems or sciatica.

NAUKASANA (boat pose)

BSY©

Technique

Lie in the starting position.
Keep the eyes open throughout.
Breathe in deeply.
Hold the breath and then raise the legs, arms, shoulders, head and trunk off the ground.
The shoulders and feet should be no more than 15 cm off the floor.
Balance the body on the buttocks and keep the spine straight.
The arms should be held at the same level and in line with the toes.
The hands should be open with the palms down.
Look towards the toes.
Remain in the final position and hold the breath.
Mentally count to 5 (or for longer if possible).
Breathe out and return to the supine position.
Be careful not to injure the back of the head while

returning to the floor.
Relax the whole body.
This is one round.
Practise 3 to 5 rounds.
Relax in shavasana after each round, gently pushing out the abdomen with inhalation to relax the stomach muscles.

Variation: Repeat the same process as above, but clench the fists and tense the whole body as much as possible in the raised position.

Breathing: Inhale before raising the body. Retain the breath while raising, tensing and lowering the body. Exhale as you return to the starting position.

Awareness: On the movement, mental counting and tensing of the body (especially the abdominal muscles) in the final position, and the breath.

PADMASANA (lotus pose)

Technique

Sit with the legs straight in front of the body.

Slowly and carefully bend one leg and place the foot on top of the opposite thigh.

The sole should face upward and the heel should be close to the pubic bone.

When this feels comfortable, bend the other leg and place the foot on top of the opposite thigh.

Both knees should, ideally, touch the ground in the final position.

The head and spine should be held upright and the shoulders relaxed.

Place the hands on the knees in chin or jnana mudra.

Relax the arms with the elbows slightly bent and check that the shoulders are not raised or hunched.

Close the eyes and relax the whole body.

Observe the total posture of the body.

Make the necessary adjustments by moving forward or backward until balance and alignment are experienced. Perfect alignment indicates the correct posture of padmasana.

Contra-indications: Those who suffer from sciatica or weak or injured knees should not perform this asana. This asana should not be attempted until flexibility of the knees has been developed through practice of the pre-meditation asanas. It is not advisable during pregnancy as the circulation in the legs is reduced.

PRANAMASANA (prayer pose)

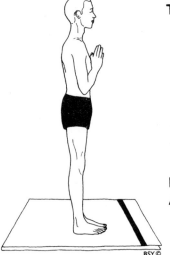

Technique

Keep the eyes closed.

Remain standing upright with the feet together.

Slowly bend the elbows and place the palms together in front of the chest in namaskara mudra, mentally offering homage to the sun, the source of all life.

Relax the whole body.

Breathing: Breathe normally.

Awareness: Physical – on the chest area. Spiritual – on anahata chakra.

SARVANGASANA (shoulder stand pose)

Technique

Lie on the back on a folded blanket.

Check that the head and spine are aligned and that the legs are straight with the feet together.

Place the hands beside the body with the palms facing down.

Relax the entire body and mind.

Contract the abdominal muscles and, with the support of the arms, slowly raise the legs to the vertical position, keeping them straight.

When the legs are vertical, press the arms and hands down on the floor.

Slowly and smoothly roll the buttocks and spine off the floor, raising the trunk to a vertical position.

Turn the palms of the hands upward, bend the elbows and place the hands behind the ribcage, slightly away from the spine, to support the back.

The elbows should be approximately shoulder width apart.
Gently push the chest forward so that it presses firmly against the chin.

In the final position, the legs are vertical, together and in a straight line with the trunk.

The body is supported by the shoulders, nape of the neck and back of the head.

The arms provide stability, the chest rests against the chin and the feet are relaxed.

Close the eyes.

293

Relax the whole body in the final pose for as long as is comfortable.

To return to the starting position, bring the legs forward until the feet are above and behind the back of the head. Keep the legs straight.

Slowly release the position of the hands and place the arms on the floor beside the body with the palms down.

Gradually lower each vertebra to the floor, followed by the buttocks, so that the legs resume their initial vertical position.

Lower the legs to the floor slowly, keeping the knees straight.

Perform this action without using the arms for support.

The whole movement should combine balance with control so that the body contacts the floor slowly and gently.

Relax in shavasana until the respiration and heartbeat return to normal.

Breathing: Inhale in the starting position. Retain the breath inside while assuming the final pose. Practise slow, deep abdominal breathing in the final pose. Retain the breath inside while lowering the body to the floor.

Duration: When first practising, hold the final position for a few seconds only, gradually increasing the time over a period of weeks to an optimum of 3 to 5 minutes for general health. This practice should be performed only once during the asana program.

Awareness: Physical – on the various sensations of the body adjusting to its inversion, on control of the movement, on the neck or thyroid gland, and on the breath. Spiritual – on vishuddhi chakra.

Contra-indications: This asana should not be practised by people suffering from enlarged thyroid, liver or spleen, cervical spondylitis, slipped disc, high blood pressure or other heart ailments, weak blood vessels in the eyes, thrombosis or impure blood. It should be avoided during menstruation and advanced stages of pregnancy.

SHASHANKASANA (pose of the moon or hare pose)

Technique

Sit in vajrasana, placing the palms on the thighs just above the knees.

Close the eyes and relax, keeping the spine and head straight.

While inhaling, raise the arms above the head, keeping them straight and shoulder width apart.

Exhale while bending the trunk forward from the hips, keeping the arms and head straight and in line with the trunk.

At the end of the movement, the hands and forehead should rest on the floor in front of the knees.

If possible, the arms and forehead should touch the floor at the same time.

Bend the arms slightly so that they are fully relaxed and let the elbows rest on the floor. Retain the breath for up to 5 seconds in the final position.

Then simultaneously inhale and slowly raise the arms and trunk to the vertical position.

Keep the arms and head in line with the trunk.

Breathe out while lowering the hands to the knees.

295

This is one round.

Practise 3 to 5 rounds.

Duration: Beginners should slowly increase the length of time in the final position until they are able to hold it comfortably for at least 3 minutes with normal breathing.

Awareness: Physical – in the final position, on the pressure of the abdomen against the thighs; on the alignment of arms, neck and head moving into and out of the asana; on the breath synchronized with the physical movement. Spiritual – on manipura or swadhisthana chakra in the final position.

Contra-indications: Not to be performed by people with very high blood pressure, slipped disc or those who suffer from vertigo.

SHAVASANA (corpse pose)

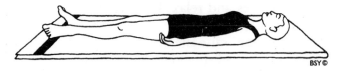

Technique

Lie flat on the back with the arms about 15 cm away from the body, palms facing upward.

A thin pillow or folded cloth may be placed behind the head to prevent discomfort.

Let the fingers curl up slightly.

Move the feet slightly apart to a comfortable position and close the eyes.

The head and spine should be in a straight line.

Make sure the head does not fall to one side or the other.

Relax the whole body and stop all physical movement.

Become aware of the natural breath and allow it to become rhythmic and relaxed.

After some time, again become aware of the body and surroundings, and gently and smoothly release the posture.

Breathing: Natural and relaxed, or begin to count the breaths from number 27 backwards to zero. Mentally repeat, "I am breathing in 27, I am breathing out 27, I am breathing in 26, I am breathing out 26", and so on, back to zero. If the mind wanders and the next number is forgotten, bring it back to the counting and start again at 27. If the mind can be kept on the breath for a few minutes, the body will relax.

Duration: According to time available. In general, the longer the better, although a minute or two is sufficient between asana practices.

Awareness: Physical – first on relaxing the whole body, then on the breath. Spiritual – on ajna chakra.

Practice note: Do not move the body at all during the practice, as even the slightest movement disturbs the practice. A personal mantra may be repeated with every inhalation and exhalation. For maximum benefit, this technique should be performed after a hard day's work, before evening activities, or to refresh the body and mind before sitting for meditation, or just before sleep.

SIDDHASANA (accomplished pose for men)

Technique

Sit with the legs straight in front of the body.

Bend the right leg and place the sole of the foot flat

against the inner left thigh with the heel pressing the perineum (the area midway between the genitals and anus).

Bend the left leg.

Push the toes and the outer edge of the left foot into the space between the right calf and thigh muscles.

If necessary, this space may be enlarged slightly by using the hands or temporarily adjusting the position of the right leg.

Place the left ankle directly over the right ankle so that the ankle bones are touching and the heels are one above the other.

Press the pubis with the left heel directly above the genitals.

The genitals will therefore lie between the two heels.

If this last position is too difficult, simply place the left heel as near as possible to the pubis.

Grasp the right toes and pull them up into the space between the left calf and thigh.

Again adjust the body so that it is comfortable.

Sit on top of the right heel.

This is an important aspect of siddhasana.

Adjust the body until it is comfortable and the pressure of the heel is firmly applied.

The legs should now be locked, with the knees touching the ground and the left heel directly above the right heel.

Make the spine erect and feel as though the body is fixed on the floor.

Place the hands on the knees in jnana, chin or chinmaya mudra.

Close the eyes and relax the whole body.

Contra-indications: Siddhasana should not be practised by those with sciatica or sacral infections.

Practice note: Siddhasana may be performed with either leg uppermost. Many people experience discomfort due to the pressure applied where the ankles cross each other. If necessary, place a folded cloth or piece of sponge between the legs at this point. At first the pressure at the perineum may be uncomfortable to maintain, but with practice this will be eased.

SIDDHA YONI ASANA (accomplished pose for women)

Technique

Sit with the legs straight in front of the body.

Bend the right leg, placing the sole of the foot flat against the inner left thigh and the heel firmly against the groin.

Adjust the body position so that there is comfortable pressure of the right heel.

Bend the left leg and wedge the left toes down into the space between the right calf and thigh.

Grasp the toes of the right foot and pull them up into the space between the left calf and thigh.

The left heel is above the right heel and may exert a light pressure against the public bone.

Again adjust the position so that it is comfortable.

Ensure that the knees are firmly on the ground.

Make the spine fully erect and straight as though it were planted solidly in the earth.

Place the hands on the knees in chin, jnana or chinmaya mudra.

Close the eyes and relax the whole body.

Contra-indications: As for siddhasana.

UDDIYANA BANDHA (abdominal contraction)

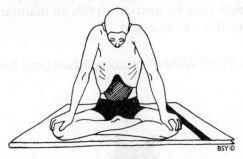

Technique

Sit in siddha/siddha yoni asana or padmasana with the spine erect and the knees in contact with the floor.

Place the palms of the hands flat on the knees.

Close the eyes and relax the whole body.

Inhale deeply through the nostrils.

Exhale fully.

Hold the breath outside.

Lean forward and press down on the knees with the palms of the hands.

Straighten the elbows and raise the shoulders, allowing further extension of the spinal cord.

Practise jalandhara bandha, pressing the chin against the chest.

Contract the abdominal muscles inward and upward.

Hold the abdominal lock and the breath outside for as long as possible without straining.

Then release the abdominal lock, bend the elbows and lower the shoulders.

Raise the head and then slowly inhale.

Remain in this position until the respiration returns to normal, then begin the next round.

Breathing: Uddiyana bandha is performed with external breath retention only.

Duration: Practise 3 rounds in the beginning and gradually increase to 10 rounds over a few months as the system becomes accustomed to the practice.

300

Awareness: Physical – on the abdomen and breath. Spiritual
– on manipura chakra.

Precaution: Uddiyana bandha is an advanced technique
and should be attempted only under the guidance of a
competent teacher. It should be practised after attaining
proficiency in external breath retention, and jalandhara
and moola bandhas.

Contra-indications: Persons suffering from colitis, stomach or
intestinal ulcer, diaphragmatic hernia, major abdominal
problems, high blood pressure, heart disease, glaucoma
and raised intracranial pressure should not perform this
practice. It should also be avoided during pregnancy.

Practice note: Uddiyana bandha must be practised on an
empty stomach. The bowels should also be empty.

USHTRASANA (camel pose)

BSY©

Technique

Sit in vajrasana.

Stand on the knees with the arms at the sides.

The knees and feet should be together, but may be
separated if this is more comfortable.

Lean backward, slowly reaching for the right heel with
the right hand and then the left heel with the left hand.
Do not strain.

Push the hips forward, keeping the thighs vertical, and
bend the head and spine backward as far as is comfortable.

301

Relax the whole body, especially the back muscles, into the stretch.

The weight of the body should be evenly supported by the legs and arms.

The arms should anchor the shoulders to maintain the arch of the back.

Remain in the final position for as long as is comfortable. Return to the starting position by slowly releasing the hands from the heels one at a time.

Breathing: Normal. Do not try to breathe deeply because the chest is already stretched.

Duration: Practise up to 3 times as a dynamic asana. Hold the final position up to 3 minutes as a static pose.

Awareness: Physical – on the abdomen, throat, spine or natural breathing. Spiritual – on swadhisthana or vishuddhi chakra.

Contra-indications: People with severe back ailments such as lumbago should not attempt this asana without the guidance of a competent teacher.

UTTHANPADASANA (stretched leg pose)

Technique

Sit with the legs outstretched.

Bend the left knee and press the left heel firmly into the perineum at the location point of mooladhara chakra.

The right leg remains outstretched.

Place both hands on the right knee.

302

Adjust the position so that it is comfortable.

Bend forward just enough to be able to clasp the right big toe with both hands.

Hold the position for a comfortable duration.

Return to the upright position with both hands resting on the right knee.

Repeat on the other side, and then with both legs outstretched.

This is one round.

Practise 3 rounds.

VAJRASANA (thunderbolt pose)

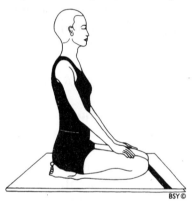

Technique

Kneel on the floor with the knees close together.

Bring the big toes together and separate the heels.

Lower the buttocks onto the inside surface of the feet with the heels touching the sides of the hips.

Place the hands on the knees, palms down.

The back and head should be straight but not tense.

Avoid excessive backward arching of the spine.

Close the eyes, relax the arms and the whole body.

Breathe normally and fix the attention on the flow of air passing in and out of the nostrils.

Duration: Beginners should slowly increase the length of time in the final position until they are able to hold it comfortably for at least 3 minutes with normal breathing.

Awareness: Physical – on the sensations in the legs, buttocks and spine. When comfortable in the asana become aware of the normal breathing process. This will bring tranquillity to the mind if practised with the eyes closed. Spiritual – on manipura chakra.

Practice note: If any strain is experienced, stop the asana. If there is pain in the thighs, the knees may be separated slightly while maintaining the posture. Beginners may find that their ankles ache after a short time in vajrasana. To remedy this, release the posture, sit with the legs stretched forward and shake the feet vigorously one after the other until the stiffness disappears. Then resume the posture.

VIPAREETA KARANI ASANA (inverted pose)

Technique

Lie flat on the back with the legs and feet together in a straight line.

Place the hands and arms close to the body with the palms facing down.

Relax the whole body.

Raise both legs, keeping them straight and together.

Move the legs over the body towards the head.

Push down on the arms and hands, raising the buttocks.

Roll the spine from the floor, taking the legs further over the head.

Turn the palms up, bend the elbows and let the top of the hips rest on the base of the palms near the wrist.

The hands cup the hips and support the weight of the body.

Raise the legs to the vertical position and relax the feet.

In the final position, the weight of the body rests on the shoulders, neck and elbows, the trunk is at a 45-degree angle to the floor and the legs are vertical.

Note that the chin does not press firmly against the chest.

Close the eyes and relax in the final pose for as long as is comfortable.

To return to the starting position, lower the legs over the head, then place the arms and hands close to the body, palms facing down.

Slowly lower the spine, vertebra by vertebra, along the floor.

Do not lift the head.

When the buttocks reach the floor, lower the legs, keeping them straight.

Relax the body in shavasana.

Breathing: Inhale while in the lying position. Retain the breath inside while assuming the final pose. Once the body is steady in the final pose, practise normal or ujjayi breathing. Retain the breath inside while lowering the body to the floor.

Duration: When first practising, hold for a few seconds only, gradually increasing the time over a period of months to an optimum of 3 to 5 minutes for general health purposes. This practice should be performed only once during the asana program.

Other details: As for sarvangasana.

Practice note: To begin with, it may be necessary to bend the knees when raising and lowering the legs.

YOGAMUDRASANA (psychic union pose)

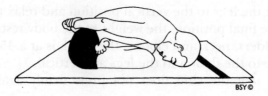

Technique
Sit in padmasana and close the eyes.
Relax the body for some time, breathing normally.
Hold one wrist behind the back with the other hand.
Inhale deeply.
While exhaling, bend forward, keeping the spine straight.
Bring the forehead to the floor or as close as is comfortable.
Relax the whole body in the final position, breathing slowly and deeply.
Be aware of the pressure of the heels on the abdomen.
Stay in the final position for as long as is comfortable.
Do not strain the back, ankles, knees or thighs by forcing the body into the posture or staying in it for too long.
Slowly return to the starting position.
Repeat the pose with the legs crossed the other way around.
Breathing: Inhale slowly and deeply in the starting position. Exhale while bending forward. Breathe deeply and slowly in the final position. Inhale while returning to the starting pose.
Duration: Remain in the final position for one or two minutes if comfortable.
Awareness: Physical – on the back, abdomen or breathing. Spiritual – on manipura chakra.
Contra-indications: People with serious eye, back or heart conditions, or with high blood pressure, and those in the early post-operative or post-delivery period should not attempt this asana.

306

Glossary

Abhaya – freedom from fear; fearlessness

Adhara – basis, that which supports, foundation

Agocharam – beyond sensory perception; unknown; invisible

Ajna chakra – the third eye, the command or monitoring psychic/pranic centre, also known as guru chakra; represents intuition or the pure inner awareness engendered by the confluence of ida, pingala and sushumna nadis

Amrita – literally 'deathless' (God); immortal, immortality; life; the nectar of immortality which descends from bindu; also called soma

Anahata chakra – psychic centre in the region of the heart, the vibration or 'beat' of which regulates life from birth to death; corresponds to the cardiac plexus in the physical body; corresponds to hridayakasha in meditative practice; centre of emotions which, when developed, gives the psychic force to materialize desire

Anandamaya kosha – the level of bliss and beatitude; the state of bliss attained in samadhi; subtlest sphere of existence, consciousness; the innermost sheath (kosha) of the embodied spirit

Anga – a limb or branch; part of the body

Anima – subtlety; the power of making the body subtle; reducing the physical mass and density at will; one of the eight siddhis

307

Annamaya kosha – sheath or body of matter; the sphere of existence created by food, maintained by food and which ultimately becomes food; the physical body

Antar kumbhaka – internal breath retention; suspension of breath after full inhalation

Apana – one of the five energies or pancha pranas; the energy moving downwards from the navel to the perineum, governing the lower abdominal region and responsible for elimination and reproduction

Arohan – ascending; ascending energy flow in the subtle body; counterpart of avarohan

Ashabda – not expressed in words; without any sound

Ashta siddhi – eight siddhis

Atman – the self beyond mind and body; also called the principle of life, supreme consciousness, spirit, soul, etc.

Balidan – sacrifice

Bharat Natyam – a classical Indian dance

Bhava – feeling or mood; condition; state, inclination or disposition of mind

Bheda – pass through, pierce; differentiate; purify

Bhoga – experience and craving for pleasure; enjoyment, delight; object of pleasure

Bindu – point, seed, source, drop; centre or source of individual creation from where psychic vibrations first emanate

Bodhi – spiritual wisdom, knowledge, intelligence; awakening; enlightenment

Brahma granthi – the psychic knot of creation, situated in mooladhara chakra, symbolizing material and sensual attachment. It is the knot of ignorance (avidya), desire (kama) and action (karma)

Chandra – the moon; shining, bright; representing mental energy

Chidakasha – the space or sphere within, where the capacity of sense perception is internalized to observe the process and reactions of individual awareness; the inner space visualized in meditation behind the closed eyes or in the region of ajna chakra; the state of pure, unbounded consciousness; Brahman in its aspect of limitless knowledge or unbounded intelligence; the pure consciousness (chit) is, like space (akasha), an all-pervading continuum; mind conceived as all-pervading space

Chidghana – that which has its roots in the limitless consciousness

Chinmaya – manifested consciousness; supreme consciousness

Chitta – individual consciousness, including the subconscious and unconscious layers of mind; thinking, concentration, attention, enquiry; the stuff of the mind; storehouse of memory or samskaras; one of the four parts of the antahkarana or inner instrument; seat of consciousness which includes the conscious, subconscious, unconscious and superconscious

Chitta vritti – pattern of the mind; in yoga philosophy the inward working of the mind, its mental vision or inward purpose; in raja yoga Sage Patanjali lists five main categories of chitta vritti in the *Yoga Sutras*: 1. right knowledge (pramana) 2. wrong knowledge (viparyaya) 3. imagination (vikalpa) 4. sleep (nidra) and 5. memory (smriti)

Daan – unconditional giving

Deva – luminous being; a god or divine being

Devata – form of divine dignity or power; divine being representing the higher state of evolution; illumined form; divinity, deity

Devi – great goddess

Dharana – concentration or complete attention

Dhyana – spontaneous state after deep concentration or meditation; the intermediate internal process where the power of attention becomes so steadily fixed upon the object of meditation that other thoughts do not enter the mind

Garima – heaviness; the power of increasing the weight of the body at will, one of the eight major siddhis

Gheranda Samhita – classical text written by Sage Gheranda on the seven limbs of yoga (saptanga): shatkarma, asana, mudra, pratyahara, pranayama, dhyana and samadhi

Gupta – hidden; secret

Guru – one who dispels the darkness caused by ignorance (avidya); teacher; preceptor; teacher of the science of ultimate reality who, because of extended practice and previous attainment of the highest states of meditation, is fit to guide others in their practice towards enlightenment

Hasta – hand

Havan – fire ritual performed by a group of people to invoke the cosmic energies for purposes such as healing and purification, or to invoke the grace of the divine

Homa – fire ritual performed by a smaller group of people for the same purposes as havan

Hridayakasha – psychic space of the heart centre where the creative hues of emotion are observed, experienced between manipura and vishuddhi chakras, associated with anahata chakra

Ishitva – superiority, greatness, lordship; one of the eight siddhis which gives the power to wilfully create and destroy

Ishta devata – personal deity, one's favourite god, one's tutelary deity, the aspect of God which is dear to you

Ishwara – higher reality; unmanifest existence; non-changing principle or quality; principle of higher consciousness defined by Patanjali in the *Yoga Sutras* as a special purusha (soul) beyond the effect of karma (actions) and klesha (affliction); a state of consciousness beyond the physical and mental realms governing the entire physical universe; supreme being, lord, master; one who rules; powerful, able, capable

Jala – water

Japa – repetition of mantra

Jatharagni – digestive fire

Jivatma – individual consciousness; individual or personal soul

Jnana – knowing, understanding; hearing; consciousness, cognizance; higher knowledge derived from meditation or from inner experience; wisdom; the organ of intelligence, sense, intellect

Jnanendriya – sensory organ; five subtle organs of perception, viz. ears (karna or shrotra), skin (twacha), eyes (chakshu), tongue (jihva) and nose (nasika or ghrana)

Jyoti – light, brightness, fire

Kaka – crow

Kapala – forehead; kapala refers to the skull, cranium and forehead from the eyebrows to bindu

Kara – hands

Karmendriya – motor organs, five physical organs of action, viz. vocal cords (vach), hands (hasta), feet (pada), genital organ (upastha) and anus (payu)

Kavacha – protection, armour

Kayakalpa – intensive purificatory practice; rejuvenation; changing the total content of the body

Kshetram – chakra trigger points located in the frontal psychic passage

Kuhar – hole; pit in the earth

Laghima – lightness; the power of making the body light; reducing the weight of the body at will; one of the eight major siddhis of yoga practice

Lalana chakra – minor chakra at the back of the throat above the palate where nectar (amrit) can be collected as it falls from bindu; closely associated with vishuddhi chakra

Linga – mark, sign, characteristic; sign of gender, male organ; idol of Shiva; a naturally-formed oval stone; often means the Shivalingam, an archetypal symbol

Maha – great, noble or supreme

Mahima – greatness; glory, majesty, dignity; might, power; high or exalted rank or position; one of the eight major siddhis, the power of increasing size at will

Maithuna – physical union; fusion of male and female energies; copulation

Makara – crocodile, the symbolic animal associated with swadhisthana chakra

Mala – wreath, garland, necklace; rosary; in yoga, a mala is made of beads of various substances such as tulsi,

311

rudraksha, sandalwood, sphatik (crystal). One function is
to aid mantra repetition

Mana – mind

Manduka – frog

Manipura chakra – psychic/pranic centre situated behind
the navel in the spinal column, corresponding to the solar
plexus and associated with vitality and energy; centre of
willpower; literally 'city of jewels'

Manomaya kosha – mental sheath or body; mental sphere
of life and awareness

Matrika – little mother; Sanskrit syllable with intense creative
potential; letters of the Sanskrit alphabet; creative energy
concealed in mantra

Moksha – liberation

Mooladhara chakra – the basic psychic and pranic centre
in the human body situated in the perineum in men and
the cervix in women and also connected to the coccygeal
plexus; it is the seat of kundalini (the primal evolutionary
energy in human beings)

Nada – subtle sound vibration created by the union of Shiva
and Shakti tattwas; subtle sound vibration heard in the
meditative state; the primal sound or first vibration from
which all creation has emanated; the first manifestation
of the unmanifest absolute; the inner sound on which the
yogi concentrates in meditation; the cosmic, inner sound
of each and every individual that links the individual with
the highest consciousness

Nadi – a river or channel of energy, corresponding, though not
identical, to the modern idea of nerves or the meridians of
acupuncture; psychic current; flow of energy

Nirvana – cessation of suffering, final liberation or emancipation in Buddhist thought (whereas Vedantins claim that not
only absence of suffering, but also the positive experience
of bliss characterizes the ultimate state); higher state of
existence or awareness; supreme enlightenment

Nyasa – renunciation; laying down; to place in trust;
committing; the ritual performed before every form of

worship wherein the awareness is rotated through different parts of the body, purifying them, energizing them and creating an armour around them

Ojas – vitality, subliminal sexual energy, bodily strength, vigour, energy; virility, the generative faculty; kundalini shakti; splendour, light

Panchadeva – five aspects of the supreme transcendental force: Shiva, Shakti, Narayana, Surya and Ganesha

Pancha dharana – five types of concentration practices

Pancha tattwa – the five elements: earth, water, fire, air and ether

Parangmukhi – inverted order, backwards; having the face turned away or inverted; turning the back upon

Pooja – act of ritual or worship

Poornahuti – final oblations

Prajna – intuition; knowledge with awareness; awareness of the one without a second; individual consciousness, intelligence, understanding, intellect, wisdom; discernment, discrimination, judgement; intention

Prakamya – psychic power by which yogis touch the higher sphere of existence; freedom of will; one of unobstructed fulfilment of desire; one of the eight major siddhis

Prakasha – brightness, shining, brilliance; spiritual brilliance, clarity, light; light of consciousness

Prakriti – individual nature; manifest and unmanifest nature; cosmic energy; the active principle of manifest energy; nature or primordial matter (source of the universe)

Prana – vital energy force, essence of life permeating both the macrocosmos and microcosmos; the sum total of all energy residing within the universe, both in the unmanifest states and in manifest nuclear states; breath, respiration; principle of life; vital energy that functions in various ways for the preservation of the body and is closely associated with the mind; one of the five vital airs (pancha pranas), which operates in the region of the heart and lungs

Pranamaya kosha – energy sheath, or vital or pranic body; the sheath (kosha) covering the self that is composed of

313

pranic vibration and the rhythm of pranic forces; the energy field of an individual

Prapti – attainment; a power by which the yogi acquires everything; one of the eight major siddhis

Pratyahara – drawing back, retreat; restraining the sensory and motor organs; withdrawal and emancipation of the mind from the domination of the senses and sensual objects; training the senses to follow the mind within

Purusha – literally 'who dwells in the city', the body being the dormant receptacle of consciousness, the soul; the totality of consciousness; the Supreme Being, God; in Samkhya philosophy purusha designates pure consciousness, undefiled and unlimited by contact with prakriti or matter

Saundarya Lahari – an ode to Shakti believed to have been written by Adi Shankaracharya

Sadhaka – a spiritual practitioner; one who practises spiritual sadhana

Sadhana – spiritual practice or discipline performed regularly for the attainment of inner experience and self-realization; worship, adoration

Sahasrara – the thousand-petalled lotus; abode of Shiva or superconsciousness; highest chakra or psychic centre which symbolizes the threshold between the psychic and spiritual realms and is located at the crown of the head

Sakshi bhava – attitude of remaining the witness; seer

Samagri – material; materials offered into the fire during the performance of havan

Samana – one of the five pranas, it is essential for digestion; a sideways-moving flow of energy situated between the navel and diaphragm which augments the pranic force of manipura chakra; the balancing prana or vital air with the function of uniting prana and apana, an essential step in the awakening of kundalini

Samskara – mental impression stored in the subtle body as an archetype; impression on the memory of all patterns and mental impressions of the past, which remains unnoticed in the mind, yet sets up impulses and trains of thought

Satsang – association with the wise

Shabda – sound; object of the sense of hearing and property of space (akasha); note (of birds, human voice, etc.); sound of a musical instrument

Shakti – primal energy; manifest consciousness; power, ability, capacity, strength, energy; in Samkhya, the power inherent in a cause to produce its necessary effects; the female aspect of creation and divinity worshipped by the Shakta sect; power that is eternal and supreme and of the nature of consciousness; counterpart of Shiva; the moving power of nature and consciousness; in Hindu mythology Shakti is often symbolized as a female deity

Shambhavi – name for Parvati, consort of Shambhu (Shiva)

Shankha – the conch shell, which was traditionally blown in battle and worship. It is said to purify the physical and mental atmosphere; the bone of the forehead; the stomach in yogic terminology

Shanmukha – literally 'with six mouths', another name for Kartikeya, the six-headed god of war and the son of Shiva and Parvati

Shanti – pacification, allayment, removal; peace, calmness, tranquillity; absence of passion, complete indifference to all worldly enjoyment

Shikha – the tuft of hair kept at the upper portion of the back of the head; peak; flame

Shiva – auspicious one or good; name of the god of the sacred Hindu trinity who is entrusted with the work of destruction; destroyer of ego and duality; the first or original yogi; cosmic consciousness, counterpart of Shakti

Shivalingam – oval-shaped stone, usually black in colour; symbol of Lord Shiva; symbol of consciousness

Shoonya – zero, voidness, emptiness

Siddha – perfect and knowledgeable; perfected being; sage, seer; semi-divine being of great purity and holiness; accomplished soul particularly characterized by eight supernatural faculties called siddhis

Siddhi – paranormal or supernatural accomplishment; control of mind and prana; psychic abilities; eight supernatural powers obtained by yogis as a result of long practice. They are associated with opening of the chakras and the resultant power over the elements, viz. 1. anima, 2. laghima, 3. prapti, 4. prakamya, 5. mahima, 6. ishitvam, 7. vashitva, 8. garima. Other siddhis include the power of entering other bodies, the ability to read another person's thoughts, clairvoyance, clairaudience, omniscience, effulgence, vanishing from sight, etc. However, they are considered to be obstacles on the path to realization because they maintain interest in samsara

Surya – the sun; vital pranic energy; the sun god; symbol of the atma

Surya namaskara – literally 'salute to the sun', the sun being a symbol of the atma or soul; a series of twelve asanas for revitalizing prana

Swadhisthana chakra – literally 'one's own abode'; psychic/pranic centre situated at the base of the spinal column in the lumbar region (level of the generative organs), associated with the sacral plexus, and the storehouse of subconscious impressions

Trataka – to gaze steadily; a concentration practice of gazing with unblinking eyes at one point to focus the mind; an important yogic practice for developing concentration and extrasensory perception, which consists of gazing at any external object with open eyes or at an internal object with the inner (third) eye for a relatively long period; a cleansing practice of hatha yoga

Udana – one of the five pranas (energies), which is located in the extremities of the body: arms, legs and head

Unmani – literally 'no mind'; thoughtlessness or meditation; the centre beyond mind and thought where the mind is turned completely inwards

Unmani avastha – the state of no thought; the state beyond mind

Upachara – the materials or services offered during worship

Uttara – upper, higher; superior, chief, excellent

Vachaka – speaking, declaring, expressing; voice and speech

Vashitva – one of the eight siddhis by which the yogi gains control over everything

Vajra – thunderbolt, lightning; the mighty one; the weapon of Indra; diamond

Veena – a stringed instrument with a fretted fingerboard over two gourds; the instrument of the goddess Saraswati

Veerya – semen, virility; heroism, prowess, valour; vigour, strength, energy, firmness, courage; power, potency; efficacy (of medicines); splendour, lustre; the result of mastering brahmacharya according to Sage Patanjali's *Yoga Sutras*

Vijnanamaya kosha – astral or psychic (higher mental) sheath or body (kosha); one of the sheaths of the soul, consisting of the principle of intellect or buddhi, the subtler level of existence with its vision, intuition, wisdom and power of understanding; the covering of the self that is made of knowledge

Vimarsha – term for the counterpart of prakasha or light, the aspect of prakasha by which it knows itself; the inner nature of Shiva, the self-consciousness of the supreme; another name for the Shakti aspect; vibration

Vishuddhi chakra – literally 'centre of purification', the psychic/pranic centre located at the level of the throat pit or the thyroid gland and associated with the cervical and laryngeal plexus at the base of the throat. The psychic centre particularly connected with purification and communication

Vyana – one of the five energy fields (prana), the reserve of pranic energy pervading the whole body and which circulates the energy from food and air

Yajna – a sacred fire ritual performed on a large scale in which the three processes involved in every act must be balanced: ya or production, ja or distribution and na or assimilation; yajna has three components: worship, satsang and unconditional giving

Yoganga – limbs, parts or aspects of yoga

Yogavit – literally 'knower of yoga', which is equated to knowledge of Brahman in *Gheranda Samhita*; yoga specialist

Yoni – womb, source or origin

Bibliography

Boskovic, Milan, *Yogic Mudras and Acupuncture*, M.Sc. Applied Yogic Science Dissertation, 2000 (Bihar Yoga Bharati, Munger).

Dev, Keshav, *Mudra Vigyan – A Way of Life*, Acharaya Shri Enterprises, Delhi, India, 1996.

Fumagalli, Luigi, *Mudras and States of Awareness*, M.A. Yoga Psychology Dissertation, 1999 (Bihar Yoga Bharati, Munger).

Hirschi, Gertrud, *Mudras – Yoga in Your Hands*, Sri Satguru Publications, Delhi, India, 2000.

Khokar, Mohan, *Traditions of Indian Classical Dance*, India Library.

Sharma, Bhadrasheel, *Mudrayen evam Upachara*, Kalyan Mandir Prakashan, Prayag, India.

Sahai, Krishna, *The Story of Dance: Bharata Natyam*, Indialog Publications Pvt. Ltd., New Delhi, India, 2003.

Tai, David, *Acupuncture and Moxibustion*, Harper and Row Publishers, Sydney, Australia, 1987.

Alphabetical List of Mudras

319